teach yourself...

Access 2.0

Charles Siegel

MIS:
PRESS

A Subsidiary of
Henry Holt and Co., Inc.

First Edition—1994

ISBN 1-55828-351-X

Printed in the United States of America.

10 9 8 7 6 5 4 3 2 1

MIS:Press books are available at special discounts for bulk purchases for sales promotions, premiums, fund-raising, or educational use. Special editions or book excerpts can also be created to specification.

For details contact: Special Sales Director
MIS:Press
a subsidiary of Henry Holt and Company, Inc.
115 West 18th Street
New York, New York 10011

Publisher: ***Steven Berkowitz***
Development Editor: ***Judy Brief***
Production Editor: ***Patricia Wallenburg***
Assistant Production Editor: ***Cari Littman***
Copy Editor: ***Gaby Cacioppo***
Technical Editor: ***Eric Barnes***

Dedication

To my son, Beni.

Acknowledgments

Thanks to all the people at MIS:Press who helped on this book, particularly to my developmental editor, Judy Brief, my lay-out editor, Patty Wallenburg, the technical reviewer, Eric Barnes, and to Steve Berkowitz.

Table of Contents

CHAPTER 2

CHAPTER 3

CHAPTER 4

Querying and Sorting Your Data 91

CHAPTER 8

Working with Expressions ....

CHAPTER 11

CHAPTER 12

Introduction

Is This Book for You?

Access is such a rich and powerful application that most people do now know where to begin when they start using it.

Access makes it easy for users to work with databases. You can create tables, edit data, and use queries to find the data you want with very little effort, and the Form and Report "wizards" can do the work of designing data entry forms, reports, and mailing labels for you.

Access also makes it easy for developers to create applications. Though it includes an entire programming language called *Access BASIC*, its interface is so powerful that developers can create many custom applications without programming. Access' queries, forms, reports, and macros are powerful enough to do most of the tasks that used to require programming. You should note that this book does not cover designing or programming applications. Access BASIC and the theory of computer programming require a book of their own.

When users learn Access, they often find they have to wade through long discussions of power features to learn about the simple features they need to work with on their own data. The Help system and cue cards are so extensive and complex that it is hard to use them just to get started. Most other books make you read complex discussions of properties, expressions, and other advanced features along with instructions on the basics of creating tables, queries, simple forms, reports, and mailing labels that the average user actually needs. *teach yourself...Access 2.0* is for people who want to get started with Access quickly, and it is also for people who want to learn the power features of Access.

The book is divided into two parts, and it is unique because it begins with a section called *Access The Easy Way*, which introduces all the basic features of Access. It teaches how to create databases and tables, to add and edit data, and to do basic queries to find the data you want. It covers for FormWizards and ReportWizards, which you can use to produce all your forms and reports.

Part I concludes with a chapter on relational databases which teaches you to use these basic features of Access to deal with more complex data. Even when a database program is very simple, the data being used is often complex. This is when knowing how to manipulate relational databases come in handy. By using Access' basic features and the introduction to relational databases in this book you can deal with almost any complex practical application.

After you have learned the necessary basics of Access, you can go on to the second part of this book, Power Features. Part II teaches you how to use action queries to update your data with less effort, how to use Access expressions to calculate values, how to create custom forms and reports, and how to use simple but powerful macros to automate tasks that you do repeatedly. These are all features that can increase your power and save you time.

The features of Access covered in this book take you to the edge of being a developer, because Access makes it easy even for non-programmers to create turn-key applications that *anyone* can use.

Part I

Access the Easy Way

ACCESS

Chapter 1

A Quick Tour of Access

*A*ccess has become the best-selling database management program because of its combination of power and ease of use. It is powerful enough that developers can use it to create entire applications with little or no programming, and it contains an entire programming language, Access BASIC, used to develop more advanced applications. Yet it is also easy enough to use that in a short time beginners can learn to manage their own data with Access.

It is easy for you to get started with Access by taking a quick look at how it is organized. This chapter gives you a quick tour of Access. It covers:

❏   starting Access
❏   opening a database file
❏   using the Database Window to view different types of Access objects
❏   opening a table in Datasheet View and Design View
❏   opening a query in Datasheet View and Design View

1

❏   opening a form in Form View, Datasheet View, and Design View

❏   opening a report in the Print Preview window

❏   the need for multitable databases

❏   using special forms of help available with Access

❏   quitting Access

Before You Begin

This chapter includes a few exercises to give you a feel for the basic features of Access. To do them, you must already have Access installed on your computer and you must know the basic ways of using Windows applications.

If you are working on a computer where Access is not yet installed, see Appendix A for instructions on installing Access on a stand-alone personal computer. If you are working on a network, see your network administrator for help on installing Access.

If you have never used a Windows application before and know nothing about how to work with them, read the tutorial in Appendix B before you go on with the rest of this book. This book assumes that you know only the most basic Windows techniques, such as how to use the mouse, how to make selections from drop-down menus, and how to scroll through a window.

The Access Database and its Objects

If you have used other database management programs, you know that they generally use the term *database* to refer to tables that hold data. Access uses the term more broadly. An Access database consists of the tables that hold the data and also of all the related objects such as queries, forms, and reports used to manage the data.

In this chapter, you take a quick tour of a sample database distributed with Access so you can see the types of objects it includes. You learn how to create and use these objects in the rest of Part I of this book.

This chapter is meant to give you a quick overview of a database. You should not try to memorize what is covered here. You need not worry about understanding the details of the objects you look at. Everything mentioned here is covered thoroughly in later chapters. For now, you should simply open an Access database and look through it quickly to see how it is organized.

Starting Access

To start Access, you must double-click its icon in one of the groups of the Windows Program Manager.

Windows runs automatically when you start most computers. If it is not already running on your computer, start it by entering **WIN** at your DOS prompt. If Windows does not start, try again by entering **CD \WINDOWS** and then entering **WIN**.

By default, Access is installed in the Microsoft Office Group, but it may have been installed in or moved to another group in the computer you are working on. For example, it may be in the Applications, StartUp, or a special Microsoft Access group.

SHORTCUT

If there are many groups in the Program Manager, it is easiest to look though them by using the Window menu, shown in Figure 1.1. To do so, click **Window**, and then click any of the numbered group names on the drop-down menu to open that group and bring it to the front of the Program Manager.

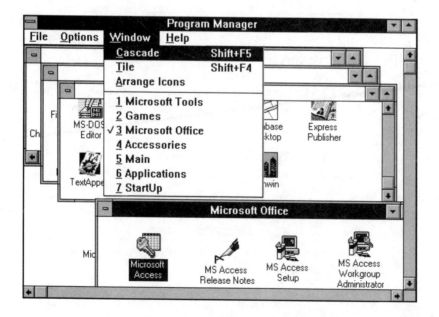

FIGURE 1.1   THE WINDOW MENU AND ACCESS ICON.

Start Access now, so you can do the rest of the exercises in this chapter:

1. If necessary, start Windows and find the group with the Microsoft Access icon.

2. Double-click this icon to start Access.

3. If this is the first time this copy of Access is being used, it will display a welcome screen. Click **Close** to continue.

The Access startup screen is now displayed. The options available on the Access menu and tool bar change depending on which window you are using within Access. The startup screen gives you the fewest options, as shown in Figure 1.2.

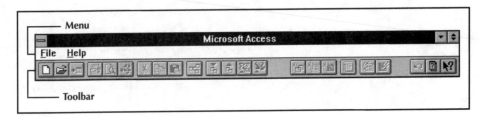

FIGURE 1.2   THE ACCESS STARTUP SCREEN MENU AND TOOLBAR.

Opening a Database

Now, try opening a sample database distributed with Access. You open a database in the same way you open files in other Windows applications:

1. Click **File** on the menu bar to display the drop-down File Menu. Then click **Open Database**. Access displays the Open Database dialog box, with the Access folder open. These folders represent directories and subdirectories.

2. Double-click the **sampapps** folder below the Access folder to display the databases in this subdirectory, as shown in Figure 1.3.

3. Click **nwind.mdb** to select it, and then click **OK** to open it—or simply double-click **nwind.mdb** to open it.

Instead of choosing **Open** from the File menu, you can click the **Open Database** tool, the second tool on the toolbar, which looks like an open folder.

FIGURE 1.3   OPENING A SAMPLE DATABASE FILES IN ACCESS.

The Database Window

When you open a database, Access displays the Database window, shown in Figure 1.4, which lets you work with all of the objects in the database. This window is sometimes called the *database container*, because it contains all these objects.

FIGURE 1.4   THE DATABASE WINDOW.

As you can see, this window has *object buttons* down its left side. Click one of these to display a list of all objects of that type in the list box in this window. In the illustration, the **Table** button is selected, and all the tables in the database are displayed in the list box. These types of objects are described later in this chapter.

You can use the buttons at the top of the Database window to work with these objects in different ways:

❏ Select the **New** button to create a new object of the type that is displayed.

❏ Click an object in the list to select (highlight) it, and select the **Open** button to view and enter data. You can also double-click an object in the list instead of using its Open button.

❏ Click an object in the list to select it, and select the **Design** button to change the object's design.

When you work with Access, you will probably find that you use the menu system less than you do with other applications, because you can do so many things simply by using the Database window.

Reports, Macros, and Modules have different buttons instead of the Open button, but all objects have New and Design buttons, like Tables.

Once you have opened a window to display an object, you can switch between views to display its data or change its design, either by using the View menu or the toolbar.

Using a Table

Tables are the most fundamental object in Access, the first object that you must design. Display one of the tables in the sample application:

1. If necessary, click the **Table** button to display the Tables list. Click the **Categories** table, the first table in the list, to select (highlight) it.

2. Once the Categories table is selected, click the **Open** button to display the table, shown in Figure 1.5.

SHORTCUT

You can also open the table simply by double-clicking its name in the list or by selecting its name and pressing **Enter**.

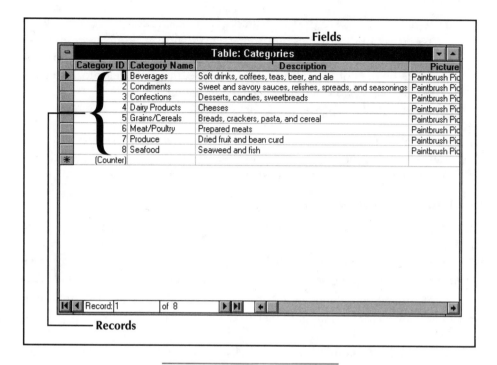

FIGURE 1.5   THE CATEGORIES TABLE.

HOW A TABLE IS ORGANIZED

You can see that an Access table holds a list of repetitive data. In the rest of this book, you will create a table to hold a list of names and addresses, which is the most common use of a database management program. This sample table holds a list of product categories. This sort of repetitive data was kept in a file cabinet, a rolodex, or a box of index cards before record keeping was computerized.

There are two terms which you should know, as they are almost always used when computerized databases are discussed. They are simply new names for familiar things.

❑ A *record* is all the data on a single entity. For example, if you have a list of names and addresses, each record includes the name and address of one person. In the sample table, where you have a list of product categories, each record includes the name and other details for one category.

❏ A *field* is one piece of data that appears in each record. For example, if you have a list of names and addresses, the first name might be the first field, the last name might be the second field, and the street address might be the third field. In the sample table, there are fields for Category Name, Description, and for a Picture illustrating the category. The picture is not actually displayed in the table, but it can be included in forms.

A table is made up of all the similar records that you want to work on together. For example, you might want to keep the names and addresses of all your clients in one table and the names and addresses of all your friends in a second table.

SWITCHING TO DESIGN VIEW

Before you can use a table, you must design it by specifying what fields it will include. You can use the two tools at the left of the toolbar to switch between the *Design View* of a table, which lets you define its fields, and *Datasheet View*, which lets you see the data in those fields.

You are looking at the table in Datasheet View, and you should glance at it in Design View before going on to look at other objects:

1. Click the **Design View** tool to display this table in Design View, as shown in Figure 1.6.

2. When you are done looking at it, click the box at the upper left corner of the Table window to display its Control menu drop-down, and choose **Close** from the Control menu to close the window.

SHORTCUT

You can also close a Window simply by double-clicking the Control Menu box.

You can see that the design of the table includes a name and a definition of each field in the table. You learn to design a table in Chapter 2, and to work with data in it in Chapter 3.

Using a Query

The simplest and most important sort of query is a *select query*, which lets you select which data from a table is displayed. You can specify which fields are displayed, enter criteria to specify which records are displayed, and specify the sort order of these records.

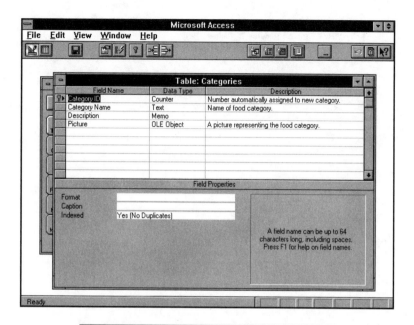

FIGURE 1.6 **THE CATEGORIES TABLE IN DESIGN VIEW.**

Like the Table window, the Query window can be displayed in Datasheet View or Design View. The toolbar for a Query window also includes an *SQL View button*, which displays the underlying programming code that is used to create this query, but this advanced feature of Access is not covered in this book.

Try displaying a very simple query that is based on the Category table in Figure 1.6, which you just looked at, in both of these views:

1. Click the **Query** button of the Database window to display the Queries list. Double-click the query named **Category List** (or click this query and click the **Open** button) to open it in Datasheet View, as shown in Figure 1.7. You can see that this query includes just two fields from the Category table—the Category Name and the Category ID.

2. Now, click the **Design View** tool to display the design of this query, as shown in Figure 1.8. You can easily see that the Design View lets you specify which fields are included and the Sort order. You can also see that it has cells where you can enter criteria to specify which records are displayed, though there are none in this simple query.

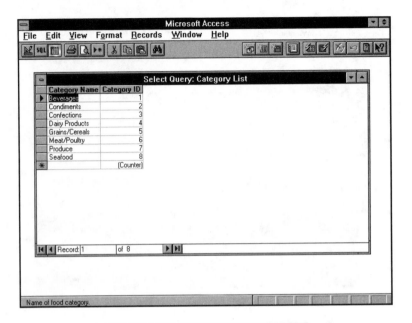

FIGURE 1.7   A QUERY IN DATASHEET VIEW.

FIGURE 1.8   A QUERY IN DESIGN VIEW.

Select queries are fundamental to Access because you can use them instead of tables as the basis of forms or reports in order to specify which records the forms or reports include. In fact, you can use a select query instead of a table as the basis of another query.

You learn more about select queries in Chapter 4. Select queries that include more than one table are covered in Chapter 6. There are also other types of queries, such as *action queries*, which let you change the data in a table. These are covered in Chapter 10.

Using a Form

Forms let you display data on the screen, usually one record at a time. When you design a form, you can arrange the fields on the screen and add many graphic enhancements.

As you learned earlier, a table displays each record on a single line, and each field in a column. This format lets you look at a number of records at the same time, but it generally does not let you see all of the information on each record, because there is usually too much to fit across the screen.

A form usually displays one record at a time. You can select which fields to include in the form, and you can usually arrange the fields on the screen in a way that lets you see them all at once. You can also make a form much more interesting visually than a table, and you can display pictures in it.

When you open the Form window, there are three buttons at the left of its toolbar, as shown in Figure 1.9.

These buttons let you do the following:

❏ Design View lets you change the design of the form.
❏ Form View lets you view the data in the form.
❏ Datasheet View lets you view the fields included in the form as a table.

When you are using a form, it often is convenient to switch back and forth between Form View and Datasheet View, in order to look at one record or many.

Try looking at a sample form based on the Categories table in all of these views:

1. Click the **Form** button of the Database window to display the Forms list. Double-click **Categories** in the list to display the Categories form

shown in Figure 1.9. You can see that the form includes all the fields of the Categories table and actually displays the picture that was not shown in the table. There is also a subform in the lower half, which lists fields from another table. Subforms are covered in Chapter 5.

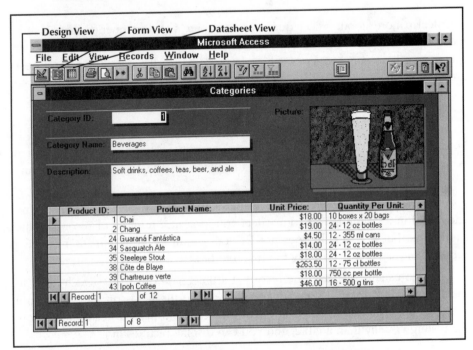

FIGURE 1.9   THE CATEGORIES FORM IN FORM VIEW.

2. Now, click the **Datasheet View** tool to display this form as a table, as shown in Figure 1.10. This datasheet contains only the fields included in the form, not necessarily all the fields in the table it is based on.

3. Finally, click the **Design View** tool to display this form in Design View, as shown in Figure 1.11. When you are done looking at it, close the Form window by choosing **Close** from its Control menu.

Access also includes easy-to-use FormWizards that let you answer simple questions so it can automatically design forms for you. These Wizards are powerful enough that many users find they do not need to use Design View to create custom forms. Chapter 5 covers forms and FormWizards. Chapter 7 discusses how to design custom forms.

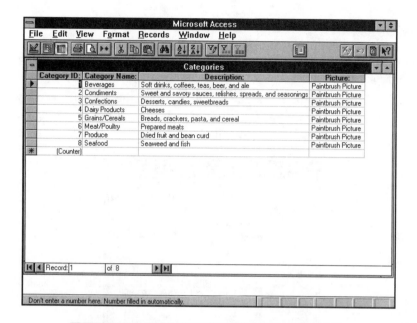

FIGURE 1.10   THE CATEGORIES FORM IN DATASHEET VIEW.

FIGURE 1.11   THE CATEGORIES FORM IN DESIGN VIEW.

Using a Report

Though they can be printed, the objects you have looked at so far are usually used to display data on the screen. Reports are meant specifically for printing data.

For this reason, when you display the Reports list, the Database window button has a Preview button instead of the Open button, as shown in Figure 1.12. You can display reports in either the Print Preview window or in Design View.

FIGURE 1.12   THE DATABASE WINDOW FOR REPORTS.

SHORTCUT

You can simply double-click a report in the Reports list or select it and press **Enter** to display it in the Print Preview window, as you can do to open other types of objects.

You cannot edit data displayed in reports as you can in tables, queries, and forms. Instead, the Print Preview window displays them in a way that makes it easy for you to see how they will appear when they are printed. You just have to click the window to switch between viewing the report in full size and viewing an entire page.

The Print Preview window is a separate Access window. It is not a view of the Report window. When you close it, Access will display the window under it, which is either the Database window or the Report Design window, depending on which you opened the Print Preview window from.

The Report window in Design View is very similar to the Form window, though it is a bit more complex. Access includes a number of ReportWizards, which are like the FormWizards and which design reports for you. Many users can get by without designing custom reports.

For now, you should just look at a report in the Print Preview window. You will see that this report includes categories from the Categories table that you looked at earlier, as well as a list of the products in each category:

1. Click the **Report** button of the Database window to display the Reports list. Double-click **List of Products by Category** to display it in the Print Preview window, as shown in Figure 1.13.

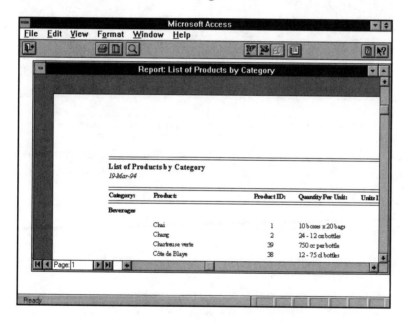

FIGURE 1.13   PREVIEWING A REPORT.

2. Now move the mouse pointer to the Print Preview window. The pointer is displayed as a magnifying glass. Move the magnifying glass pointer to the Report view and click to view a full page of the report, as shown in Figure 1.14. Click again to display the report in full size. When you are done looking at it, press **Esc** to close the Print Preview window.

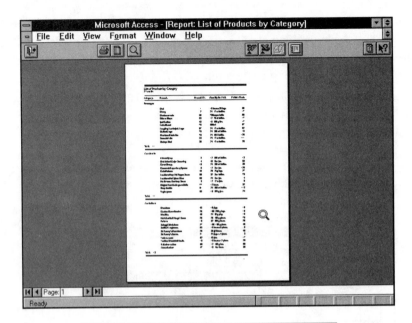

FIGURE 1.14   ZOOMING THE PRINT PREVIEW WINDOW.

Chapter 5 teaches you how to use the ReportWizards to generate reports and mailing labels. Chapter 9, in Part II of this book, covers how to use the Report window in Design View to create custom reports.

Macros and Modules

The next two objects in the Database window are power features of Access:

❑ *Macros* let you automate and speed up your work, and are also used when you develop applications. A macro is a list of actions. Access performs all the actions in the list when you run the macro. Macros can save time for Access users. They are covered in Chapter 11 of this book.

❑ *Modules* let you write programs in the Access BASIC language to develop advanced applications. This book does not cover programming.

Why You Need Multitable Databases

Some of the objects you looked at in this chapter were based on more than one Access table. The Categories form included all the fields from the Category table, but also had a subform with data on all the products in each category. Likewise, the report listed products for each category. Yet you have looked at the Categories table and you know that the products themselves are not listed in it.

This is an example of a multitable or *relational database*. Most business applications require relational databases because there are many types of data that you cannot store effectively in a single table.

When businesses first began to use computers, they discovered they could eliminate repetitious data by breaking up some databases into multiple tables. When businesses kept records on paper, for example, the Payroll Department had a file with each employee's name, address, social security number, and data on how much each was paid. Likewise, the Benefits Department had a file with each employee's name, address, social security number, and data on the benefits each was entitled to. The Training Department also had a file with each employee's name, address, social security number, and data on the training courses each one had taken.

You can see that a large company with many departments could easily have had many copies of the same basic information on each employee, such as name, address and social security number, stored in many different files. All this data would have to be entered several times, and then, if an employee moved, the address would have to be changed several times.

This repetition was impossible to avoid when records were kept on paper. When you computerize, however, you can break up this data into several tables. One table may have basic information, such as name, address, and social security number. Another may contain data on payroll, and still others may have data on benefits training, and so on.

The computer can look up the name and address that goes with each payroll record. It can retrieve data so quickly that it can display the name and address from one table and the payroll data from another table just as quickly as if they were in a single table.

You only have to enter the basic data once, though. When someone moves, you only have to change the address in one table, and it will automatically be changed in all the forms used by all the departments.

Relational databases are not needed for very simple data, such a mailing list, but they are needed for most business applications. Chapter 6 covers relational databases in more detail, and Chapter 2 includes more details on the type of data you can store in a single table.

WARNING

For now, you should simply realize that you cannot deal with complex data without breaking it up into multiple tables. The most common error people make when using database programs is to try to create a single table to hold data that should be kept in multiple tables. If you try to do this, it causes problems later on. It is best to design the tables properly from the beginning.

Getting Help

Access has the same sort of help system used by other Windows applications. Further information is provided in Appendix B. If you are not familiar with other Windows help systems, you should read "The Help System" in Appendix B. This appendix also covers the use of cue cards.

There are also a couple of special forms of help provided with Access which are easier to use than conventional Windows help and they are described in this chapter.

Quick Help For Menus and Toolbars

It is easy to get quick help on the Access menu and toolbar:

❑   *Help on menu drop-downs* is available when you click one of the options on the menu bar and hold down the mouse button. The status bar displays a help line describing the function of that entire drop-down menu.

❑   *Help on menu commands* is available after you have released the mouse button to display the drop-down menu. You can get help on each command by scrolling through the commands with the mouse button held down or with the Up and Down arrow keys. Access displays a help line in the status bar describing the function of the highlighted menu option.

❑   *Help on Toolbar tools* is available if you move the mouse pointer to any of the toolbar tools. Access displays a help line in the status bar describing the function of that tool. After you keep the pointer on it for a moment, Access also displays the name of the tool in a box next to it.

Interface Help

Interface Help is a special feature of the Access Help System that lets you get more extensive context-sensitive help on menus, tool bars, Windows, and other features of the Access interface.

To use it, press **Shift+F1** or click the **Help on Interface** tool at the far right of the toolbar. The mouse pointer is displayed with a question mark next to it, as shown in Figure 1.15. You can then click any feature of the Access interface or choose any menu item to display the Access Help System with help on that feature.

FIGURE 1.15   USING INTERFACE HELP.

To restore the pointer to its normal appearance without using interface help, press **Shift+F1** or click the **Help on Interface** tool a second time.

Quitting Access

When you are finished working with Access, choose **Exit** from the File menu or choose **Close** from the Application Control menu to close Access and return to the Windows Program Manager.

You can also close Access simply by double-clicking its Application Control-menu box.

The Application Control menu is at the left of the application's title bar, which has the name Microsoft Access on it. Do not confuse it with control menus of the windows within Access.

To Sum Up

In this chapter, you learned to start Access and to open a database. You also used the buttons of the Database window to display the most important Access objects—tables, queries, forms, and reports. You learned how to look at different views of these objects, including Datasheet View, Design View, Form View, and Print Preview, either by using the toolbar or the Database window buttons.

Now that you have gotten a general idea of how Access is organized, you can go on to learn how to use each of its objects. In Chapter 2 you begin by designing a sample table.

Designing and Using a Table

A simple database holds repetitive data, and when you store this data in a computer, the first step is to design the table. This is a bit like deciding what blank spaces you should include on a paper form—one line for a name, two lines for an address, and so on—except that you must be more precise when you design the fields of a computerized database table.

You must specify a name for each field, the type of data it will hold, and the length for some types of field. You must decide in advance, for example, whether a field will hold text or numbers and the maximum size of the text or numbers the field can hold.

When you design a table in Access, you can also define properties of fields. For example, you can create an *input mask* which includes characters that are in the field in every record, such as the hyphens in a social security number, so you do not have to enter them by hand.

In this chapter, you learn to create a table and get hands-on experience by creating a sample table. You learn how to:

❏ create a database
❏ create a table using the TableWizard
❏ create a table using the Table window in Design View
❏ name and save a table
❏ define field names and data types
❏ define field properties for the different data types
❏ create a *primary key* field
❏ use a table in Design View and Datasheet View
❏ modify the design of an existing table

Some of the tables you create in these exercises will be used again in later chapters.

Creating a Database

As you learned in Chapter 1, an Access database is a collection of all the related objects you use to manage data including tables, queries, forms, reports, macros, and modules. Every object must be part of a database.

Most of this chapter discusses how to design tables. Before you create a table, however, you must create a database to hold it.

How to Create a Database

You create a new database in Access in the same way that you create new files in other Windows applications.

To create a new database, choose **New Database** from the File menu or select the **New Database** tool displayed on the far left of the toolbar. Access displays the New Database dialog box, shown in Figure 2.1. This dialog box is similar to the dialog box used to create new files in many Windows applications. Use the controls on this dialog box to specify the name and directory of this database.

FIGURE 2.1   THE NEW DATABASE DIALOG BOX.

In the File Name text box, type the name of the new file. This file name may have up to eight letters followed by a dot, and an extension of up to three letters. Names do not take account of capitalization and cannot contain blank spaces.

You should give the file extension **.MDB** (Microsoft Database). Access adds this extension automatically if you type a name without any extension. You can create database files with other extensions, but it is more convenient to open files that have the MDB extension because they are displayed by default when you open a database.

Access suggests names such as DB1.MDB or DB2.MDB, but you should use a meaningful name to make it easier to keep track of the file. Notice that the suggested file name is highlighted when the dialog box is first displayed, so you can type a new name over it and Access will add the MDB extension.

If you want a name similar to the name of an existing file, you can click that file in the File Name list to display its name in the text box, and then edit its name. You can also create a new file with the same name as an existing file, but this will overwrite the existing file and destroy all the data in it. Access asks for confirmation before overwriting a file.

As in other Windows applications, the Drives list box and the Directories list box let you specify the directory for the new file. Use the Drives list box to select the drive. The directories on that drive are displayed in the Directories list box. Double-click a directory in this list to make it the current directory and to display its parent and child directories.

N O T E

In other Windows database applications, however, it is usually best to create a new directory for every database you work with. In Access, though, because all the objects of the database are kept in a single file, it is not necessary to create a directory to keep them organized. The .MDB file in Access does the work that the directory does in other database management programs. You may want to keep the databases in the same directory as the sample files distributed with Access or in some other directory that you use to hold your work.

A Sample Database

Now, let's create a sample database to use in the exercises in this book. You can name the sample database after the book:

1. Choose **New Database** from the File menu. Access displays the New Database dialog box.

2. The File Name text box is highlighted, so you can simply type **teachslf** to replace its contents. The Access directory should be the current directory by default. Double-click the *sampapps* folder below it to make it the current directory.

3. Select **OK** (or press **Enter**) to create the file. Access displays the new Database window, shown in Figure 2.2.

FIGURE 2.2   THE NEW DATABASE WINDOW.

All the work you do in this book will be held in this single database file, and you can archive it or simply delete it when you are done with the exercises in this book.

N O T E

The Database Window and Toolbar

The options available on Access menus and toolbars change depending on the type of window displayed. It will help you get a general overview of Access if you look at the toolbar displayed with the database you just created.

You learned in Chapter 1 that the Database window (or database container) itself has buttons on its left that you use to view lists of different types of Access objects—tables, queries, forms, reports, macros, and programming modules. It also has buttons above the list that let you create a new object, display an existing one, or change the design of an existing object.

Now let's take a quick look at the toolbar, which is illustrated in Figure 2.3.

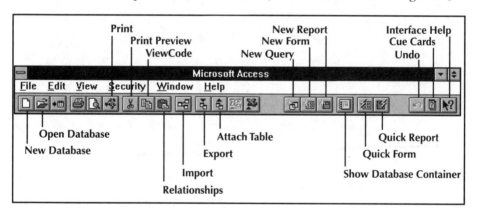

FIGURE 2.3 THE DATABASE TOOLBAR.

The following are descriptions of the most important icons in the toolbar:

❏ *New Database* creates a new database.

❏ *Open Database* opens an existing database.

❏ *Print* prints the object currently selected in the Database window. You do not have to open the object before printing it. Printing is discussed later in this chapter.

❏ *Print Preview* opens the Print Preview window, which lets you see how the object will look if it is printed. Print Preview is discussed in Chapter 5.

❏ *View Code* lets you view programming modules. Programming is not discussed in this book.

❏ *Relationships* is used to work with relational databases, which are covered in Chapter 6.

❏ *Import, Export,* and *Attach Table* are used to share data with other database programs. They are covered in Chapter 12.

❏ *New Query, New Form,* and *New Report* are used to design a new query, report, or form based on the table or query selected in the Database window. This is an alternative to using the New button of the Database window. Queries are covered in Chapter 4, and Reports and Forms are covered in Chapter 5.

❏ *Show Database Container* is used to bring the Database window to the front of any other windows that are open, which is useful if you are working simultaneously with many windows.

❏ *Quick Form* and *Quick Report* are used to create quick forms and reports, and are covered in Chapter 5.

❏ *Undo* is used to undo the last change you made.

❏ *Cue Cards* and *Interface Help* are used to work with two special forms of help available in Access, and were discussed in Chapter 1.

As you display different Access windows, you should look at the toolbars associated with them in this way, to get an overview of the features of Access.

Creating a Table

The Database window you have created is ready for you to create a table (see Figure 2.2). Notice that it has the **Table** button selected by default (it appears higher than the other buttons).

If you click the **New** button, Access displays the New Table dialog box shown in Figure 2.4. As you can see, it gives you the choice of using *TableWizards* to create a table or of creating a new table from scratch.

FIGURE 2.4 THE NEW TABLE DIALOG BOX.

The TableWizard

Access has a feature called *Wizards*, which let you create objects more quickly than you can by working from scratch. If you click the TableWizards button on the New Table dialog box, Access displays the TableWizard window shown in Figure 2.5.

FIGURE 2.5 THE TABLEWIZARD.

The TableWizard window contains a Sample Tables list box on its left. You can select the **Business** or **Personal** button to choose which list of tables is displayed here. The Personal sample tables are lists of friends, household inventory, recipes, and the like. The Business sample tables consist of mailing lists, contacts, products, and the like.

When you select a table from the Sample Tables list, all its fields are displayed in the Sample Fields list box. To add or remove fields from your table, click these buttons to the right of the Sample Fields list box:

❏ The > button moves the currently selected field to the Fields in My New Table list.

❏ The >> button moves all the fields to the Fields in My New Table list.

❏ The < button removes the currently selected field from the Fields in My New Table list.

❏ The << button removes all fields from the Fields in My New Table list.

When you are done adding fields to the new table, select the **Next** button, and the wizard prompts you to name the table and specify a primary key. Table names and keys are described below.

In general, it is better to use the Table design window to create a table with fields that have the exact specifications you want rather than to use the TableWizard.

The Table Window in Design View

If you select the **New Table** button in the New Table dialog box, Access displays the Table window, shown in Figure 2.6. If you look at the upper left of the tool bar, you will see that the Design View tool seems to be pressed down, showing that Access has displayed the Table window in Design View.

When you design a table, you specify the names of its fields and the type of data each field holds. Some fields hold only numbers, some only text, and some other types of data. All the available data types are discussed below. This is called *defining the structure* of a table or simply *designing a table*.

DESIGNING THE TABLE

As you can see, the Table window contains columns named Field Name, Data Type, and Description.

Move among columns by clicking them with the mouse or using the cursor keys. You can also press the **Tab** key to move a column right and **Shift+Tab** to move a column left. When you design a table, you use the same editing keys that you use to enter and edit data. These are described in detail in Chapter 3, which discusses editing data.

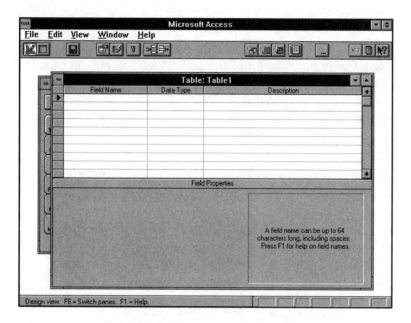

FIGURE 2.6   THE TABLE WINDOW IN DESIGN VIEW.

To enter the name of each field, type in the field name in the Field Name column.

When you move the cursor to the Data Type column, Access displays a list from which you can select options for data type.

Alternatively, you can just type the first letter of an Access data type here, and Access will enter that data type when you move the cursor out of the field. Once you get used to Access, you will find that this is the most convenient way of specifying data types.

Entering data in the Description column is optional. If you enter a description, it is displayed as a help line in the status bar when that field is selected in the table or in a form. If you do enter information in this column, you should use descriptions that would be helpful during data entry.

To insert a new field between fields that you have already defined, move the cursor into any row and choose **Insert Row** from the Edit menu, or click the **Insert Row** tool to add a new blank row above the one where the cursor is. To delete a field, move the cursor anywhere in the row and choose **Delete Row** from the Edit menu, or click the **Delete Row** tool.

When you specify a data type, Access displays the field properties available for that data type in the Field Properties panel, in the lower half of the window. You can select properties such as the maximum size of the data that can be entered in the field, the format of the field, and validation rules that check the data. You can move the focus to this panel by pressing F6 or by clicking it with the mouse. Properties are discussed later in this chapter.

The Table window also includes a help panel on its lower right, with brief context-sensitive help. Press **F1** to display the help system with more extensive context-sensitive help.

THE TOOLBAR

When you begin working with a new Access window or view, it is a good idea to look at the toolbar associated with it to get an overview of how it is used. The toolbar of the Table window in Design View is shown in Figure 2.7.

FIGURE 2.7   TABLE WINDOW TOOLBAR IN DESIGN VIEW.

The Table window toolbar contains the following icons:

❏ *Design View* and *Datasheet View* are used to switch between views of the Table window.

❏ *Save* may be used at any time to save changes to the table design. Other objects have a similar feature.

❏ *Properties* opens or closes a property sheet for the object. Many types of objects have property sheets, which let you define their properties.

❏ *Index* creates indexes for the table to speed up searches and sorts. Indexes are discussed in Chapter 4.

❏ *Set Primary Key* designates a field as the primary key and is discussed later in this chapter.

❏ *Insert Row* inserts a new field between ones you already defined by inserting a new blank row in the Table window.

❏ *Delete Row* deletes a field you already added to the definition.

❏ *New Query, New Form, New Report, Show Database Container, Undo,* and the two *Help* tools are the same as the icons associated with the Database window, and they were discussed earlier in this chapter.

Naming and Saving the Table

You can save changes at any time when you are defining the table by choosing **Save** from the File menu, or clicking the **Save** tool.

The first time you save the table, Access displays the Save As dialog box, shown in Figure 2.8, to let you name the table. This dialog box is not like the Save As dialog box that you are familiar with from other Windows applications, because it does not let you select drive and directory. You specified the drive and directory of the database file, when you first created it. This table is part of a database, so it does not have its own drive and directory: you just need to enter a name for it.

FIGURE 2.8   THE SAVE AS DIALOG BOX.

Access suggests the name *Table1, Table2,* or the like, but of course, you should give the table a meaningful name, in order to make it easier to identify and use it in the future.

ACCESS NAMING CONVENTIONS

Because the table is part of a database file rather than a seprate file, you also have much greater freedom in naming it.

The database file, as you learned earlier in this chapter, is restricted to an eight character name and a three character extension, the usual naming conventions. However, all Access objects, including tables, follow these Access naming conventions:

❏ Names can be up to 64 characters long.

❏ Names can include any characters except the square brackets ([and]), the period (.), and the exclamation point (!).

❏ Names can include spaces but cannot begin with a space.

These conventions let you give Access tables and other objects complete and meaningful names.

RENAMING A TABLE

As in other Windows applications, you can rename a table or other Access object by choosing **Save As** from the File menu. Again, Access displays the Save As dialog box with only a text box for the object name.

CLOSING THE TABLE WINDOW

When you are done defining the table, close the Table window by selecting **Close** from the File menu, by selecting **Close** from the window's Control menu, or by double-clicking the Control-menu box. If you have not done so already, Access prompts you to name the Table and save changes.

Defining Fields

To define the structure of the table, you must enter at least the name and data type of all fields.

For fields of certain data types, such as Text and Number fields, you should also specify the field size in the Field Properties list.

FIELD NAMES

Use the same naming conventions for fields as for other Access objects. Names can include up to 64 characters, as described in the previous section, "Access Naming Conventions."

DATA TYPES

Access, like other database management systems, requires you to specify the type of data that each field holds, as shown in Figure 2.9.

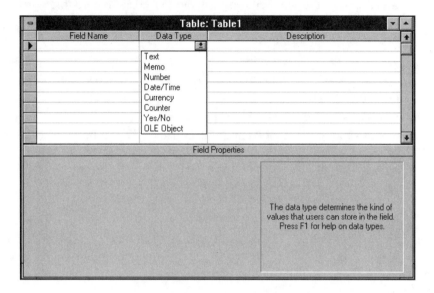

FIGURE 2.9   SELECTING A DATA TYPE.

You can choose among the following data types:

❏ *Text* holds up to 255 characters, including letters, numbers, and special characters.

❏ *Memo* holds text of up to 32,000 characters. Unlike text fields, memo fields are variable length. To store them, Access uses only the disk space that is needed to hold the text you entered.

❏ *Number* holds numbers actually used in calculations. The type of number it can hold and accuracy of calculations depends on the size you give to the number field. Number field properties are covered later in this chapter. Some number fields hold only integers and others can hold numbers with many decimal places.

❏ *Date/Time* holds dates and times. Whether you can enter a date or a time depends on the format you give to the field, described later in this chapter.

❏ *Currency* holds numbers used as amounts of money, or any numbers used in calculations with up to four decimal places of accuracy.

❏ *Counter* holds sequential numbers that Access automatically enters. Access places the number 1 in this field in the first record, the number 2 in the second record, and so on. You cannot change the numbers that Access enters in this field.

❏ *Yes/No* holds only two values, displayed as Yes and No, True and False, or On and Off depending on the format you give it in the Field Properties panel.

❏ *OLE Object* holds data from other Window applications that support Object Linking and Embedding (OLE). This field can be used to display pictures, sound, or any other type of data available in other Windows applications that support OLE. OLE objects are an advanced feature of Access, and are covered in Chapter 12 of this book.

Access validates data entry based on field type. For example, you can enter only numbers in number fields, and you can enter only valid dates in date fields. For example, you cannot enter **02/30/94** as a date, because February does not have thirty days. You can validate entries more precisely using the Validation Rule and Validation Text Field properties below.

FIELD PROPERTIES

As you know, when you specify the data type of a field, Access displays a panel with field properties that you can specify for that type of data. You can move between this panel and the main panel by pressing F6 or clicking a panel with the mouse.

It is important to set some field properties. Others such as Caption, which lets you specify the label used for the field in a form, are optional but can be convenient, even for beginners. Some properties are meant for more advanced users; some are covered later in this book. For example, validation rules require you to use Access Expressions, which are covered in Chapter 8.

Most properties work similarly when they are used with different data types, but there are a few very important exceptions:

❏ *Field Size* applies only to text and number fields, and works differently for the two.

❏ *Decimal Places* applies only to number and currency fields.

❏ *Format* also works differently for different types of fields since the formats you use to display text, numbers, and dates (for example) are obviously very different.

After looking at Field Size, Decimal Places, Format, and other properties for each data type, you will look at the properties that are common to many data types.

Text Properties

The Field Size property should always be set for text fields. You may also want to use the Format property.

Field Size

The size of a text field is the maximum number of characters it can hold. Text fields can contain from 1 to 255 characters. You should use the smallest number that will hold all the data in a given field, in order to save disk space.

By default, Access makes a text field large enough to hold 50 characters, but this is more space than you need for most fields. If you have a field that holds just one character, such as a middle initial or a code letter, and you leave the Field Size at the default 50 characters, you are wasting disk space. You should generally make text fields no larger than the length they need to hold the data you will be entering in them.

Format

You can specify the Format property of text fields by using the symbols shown in Table 2.1.

TABLE 2.1   SYMBOLS FOR FORMATTING TEXT FIELDS.

SYMBOL	MEANING
@	Character is required
&	Character is not required
<	Convert letters to lower case
>	Convert letters to upper case
Other characters	Used literally

For example, you might want to enter > as the format of a State field, so the characters are displayed in capital letters.

Apart from these four symbols, other characters are used literally and inserted in the data. For example, if you have a social security number entered in a text field with only numbers, you can display it with hyphens in the appropriate places by using the format **@@@-@@-@@@@**. The **@** symbol represents any character, and the hyphens are inserted literally.

The Format property determines only how fields are displayed. To control how data is entered, use a input mask, which is described later in this chapter.

N O T E

Memo Properties

Memo fields do not have a Field Size property. They can hold up to 32,000 characters, and Access uses only as much disk space to store them as it needs to hold what is entered.

Memo fields can be formatted in the same way as text fields, using the symbols listed in Table 2.1. It is less common to format memo fields than text fields, however.

Number Properties

You should always specify the size of number fields, because the size of a number field determines what sort of number it can hold. You may also find it convenient to use Format and Decimal Places properties for number fields.

Field Size for Number Fields

The size of a number field is based on the amount of computer memory needed to work with different types of numbers. You can select any of these sizes from the Field Size list:

- ❑ *Byte* holds numbers between 0 and 255 with no fractions or decimals.
- ❑ *Integer* holds numbers between approximately –32,000 and 32,000 with no fractions or decimals.
- ❑ *Long Integer* holds numbers between approximately –2 billion and 2 billion with no fractions or decimals.
- ❑ *Single* holds numbers between approximately -3.4×10^{38} and 3.4×10^{38}. Calculations are accurate to 6 decimal places.
- ❑ *Double* holds numbers between approximately -1.7×10^{308} and 1.7×10^{308}. Calculations are accurate to ten decimal places. Double is the

default size for number fields, but calculations with it can be slow because of the additional precision of their results.

N O T E

If you are doing calculations that must be accurate to up to four decimal places, it is best to use the Currency data type rather than the Number data type, even if the numbers do not represent amounts of money. Calculations with currency data use fixed point calculations that avoid rounding errors, rather than the floating point calculations used with single and double number data, and so they can be performed more quickly. Of course, integer calculations are faster than any calculations involving decimals.

Format

By default, number fields are displayed as you enter them. You can also give both number and currency fields these standard formats, which you select from their Format property lists:

- ❏ *General Number* is the default selection. The number is displayed as entered.

- ❏ *Currency* displays negative numbers in parentheses and in red. Two decimal places are displayed, and a comma (or other separator) is used to separate every three digits.

- ❏ *Fixed* displays at least one digit. Two decimal places are displayed if the Decimal Places property is not changed.

- ❏ *Standard* uses a comma (or other separator) to separate every three digits, and two decimal places are displayed if the Decimal Places property is not changed.

- ❏ *Percentage* displays the value as a percentage. This involves multiplying it by 100 and adding a percent sign. For example, 1 is displayed as 100% and .5 is displayed as 50%.

- ❏ *Scientific* displays the value in scientific notation, as a number between zero and ten multiplied by some power of 10.

Some of these formats include a comma or some other separator between every three digits. The comma is used as separator in the United States, but other characters are used in other countries. Access uses the separator specified in the International section of the Windows Control Panel, which you can display by double-clicking the **Control Panel** icon in the Main group in Windows.

You can also create custom number formats, but most users do not need them. For more information, see the Access Help topic on *Format Property—Number and Currency Data Types*.

Decimal Places

The Decimal Places Property list includes the option Auto, which displays the number of decimal places defined by the Format property. It also allows you to select the number of decimal places to display—from 1 to 15. If you select a number, it overrides the number of decimal places defined by the Format property.

Date/Time Properties

Format is the only property of Date/Time fields that we discuss. You can use the following standard formats for Date/Time fields by selecting them from the Format properties list box:

❏ *General Date* displays the date or time depending on your entry. If you entered only a date, the time is not displayed. If you entered only a time, the date is not displayed.

❏ *Long Date* displays the date with the day of the week and the month written out—for example, Tuesday, September 6, 1994.

❏ *Medium Date* displays the date with the month abbreviated and placed before the day and the year—for example, 06-Sept-94.

❏ *Short Date* displays the date as numbers separated by slashes, for example, 9/6/94.

❏ *Long Time* displays the time as hours, minutes, and seconds separated by colons and followed by AM or PM—for example, 2:45:26 PM.

❏ *Medium Time* displays the time in hour and minutes, separated by a colon and followed by AM or PM—for example, 02:45 PM.

❏ *Short Time* displays hours and minutes as a twenty-four hour clock—for example, 14:45.

You can also create custom Date and Time formats, but most users do not need them. For more information, see the Access Help topic on *Format Property—Date/Time Data Types*.

Currency Properties

The Currency data type can be thought of as a special case of the Number data type, which has a fixed size. You can format currency fields in the same ways you do number fields, to display any of the numeric format listed previously, such as currency, fixed, and percentage.

The difference between the two data types is that currency fields perform decimal calculations more quickly than number fields because they use fixed point rather than floating point arithmetic. They should be used for extensive calculations that do not require more than four decimal places of accuracy.

Size

You do not specify the size of a currency field. It can hold up to fifteen digits to the left of the decimal point and is accurate to four digits to the right of the decimal point.

Format and Decimal Places

A currency field can have the same Format and Decimal Place properties as a number field.

Counter Properties

Counters are integers that are automatically entered when you add records, and so they do not have a Field Size or a Decimal Places property. You can give counter fields the same formats as number fields.

Yes/No Properties

Yes/No fields can have three formats:

- ❑ Yes and No
- ❑ True and False
- ❑ On and Off

Simply select one of these three from the Format drop-down: the first option will be displayed for Yes and the second for No.

OLE Object Properties

OLE objects can have captions, validation rules, and validation text. They are created in other Windows applications and can be many different types of objects, such as pictures or sounds. OLE Objects are discussed in Chapter 12.

Common Properties

Now that you have looked at the special features of individual data types, you can look at properties that apply to different data types in similar ways.

Input Mask

Text, number, date/time, and currency fields can have a field *Input Mask*, property that specifies the format in which data is *entered*. Do not confuse an input mask with a format. A format specifies the format in which data is *displayed*, not how it is entered.

To use one of the built-in input masks, click on the Input Mask property box with the right mouse button. The shortcut menu is displayed. Choose the **Build** option from the menu, and Access displays the Input Mask Wizard. Answer its questions, and select a mask from the list. Choose the **Go** button to create the mask.

You can also create your own input masks by typing the input mask characters, shown in Table 2.2, in the Input Mask property box.

TABLE 2.2   INPUT MASK CHARACTERS.

CHARACTER	MEANING
0	Number required
9	Number or space can be entered but is not required
#	Number, plus or minus sign, or space can be entered but not required
L	Letter required
?	Letter can be entered but not required
A	Letter or number required
a	Letter or number can be entered but not required
&	Any character or a space required
C	Any character or a space can be entered but not required
<	Characters that follow converted to lowercase
>	Characters that follow converted to uppercase
!	Characters fill from right to left rather than from left to right. Can be used when characters on the left are optional, and can be included anywhere in the mask.
\	Following character is displayed literally rather than read as a code.

Other characters can be used literally in an input mask and will be inserted in the data that is entered. In addition, separators such as the decimal point (.), the thousands (,), the date (/) and the time (:) can be entered and will be used literally.

An input mask can be useful for a social security number, for example. Use the mask **000-00-0000** to require the numbers be entered and to display the hyphens literally in the appropriate places between the numbers. When you enter data in the table, the hyphens are displayed in the places you indicated, and there are spaces for the entry of the numbers.

Storing Inserted Characters

You can also add a comma followed by a **0** after the input mask to specify that the inserted characters from the input mask should be stored in the table. If you leave out this part or enter a comma followed by a **1**, Access stores only the characters that are entered, not those that are part of the input mask. For example, if you use the mask **000-00-0000,0**, Access stores the hyphens as well as the numbers in the table. If you use the mask **000-00-0000** or **000-00-0000,1**, Access stores only the numbers without the hyphens.

When you define the length of the field, you must take into account whether you are going to store these inserted characters. If you do not store them, you have to use the Format property to display them.

Displaying Spaces

You can also enter a third part to the input mask that specifies how blank spaces are displayed. After the second part of the mask, add any character following a comma. For financial uses, for example, it is common to display spaces as asterisks for security, like this:

```
$ 00.00,0,*.
```

Caption

All fields have a Caption property. The caption is used as the heading of that field's column in the Datasheet View. The caption can be any text up to 255 characters.

Default Value

Fields of all data types, except Counter and OLE Object, have a Default Value property. The value you enter is displayed as the default value of this field in every record. For example, if most of your customers live in California, you can enter **CA** as the Default Value property of the State field. CA is automatically displayed as the field's default value in each record. Access allows you to edit this field if you need to enter a different value: simply type over the highlighted default value.

Advanced users can also use an *expression* as a field's default value. Chapter 8 discusses expressions in detail.

Validation Rule and Validation Text Properties

All fields have Validation Rule and Validation Text properties, which let you test the data entered.

The Validation Rule is an expression that is evaluated whenever data is entered or edited in the field. The Validation Text is displayed if the entry does not conform to the Validation Rule. Validation Rule and Validation Text properties are discussed in detail in Chapter 8.

Required Property

The Required property lets you specify that data is required in a field.

Allow Zero Length

The Allow Zero Length property lets you specify that a zero-length string can be entered in the field. To enter a zero-length string in a field, type "" (two quotation marks with nothing between them).

You can enter a zero length string to specify that there is not a value for the field to distinguish it from blank fields, which have a value that is unknown or not entered yet. For example, if you have a field where you list the special interests of people in your mailing list, you can enter a zero length string for those who have said that they have no special interests. By contrast, a blank entry might indicate that you do not know whether a person has a special interest.

Indexed Property

The Index property lets you create an index based on a field of any data type except Memo, Yes/No, and OLE Object. Indexes can speed up access to data, and they are covered in Chapter 4.

Primary Key Fields

Access can retrieve data more quickly if you designate one of its fields as a *primary key*. This key field must always be used when you work with relational databases. It is discussed in more detail in Chapter 6 of this book.

When you use most database programs, there is no reason to create a primary key unless you are working with relational databases, but Access is designed so that it always works more effectively if a table has a primary key.

WHAT IS A PRIMARY KEY?

A *primary key* is a field or a combination of fields that uniquely identifies each record. The most common primary key is a field such as Employee Number or Customer Number, which is given an arbitrary value that is different for each record in the table. This field has no purpose except to be the primary key.

Though it is possible, it is not advisable to use meaningful fields as the primary key. If you use the Last Name field (or even a combination of Last Name and First Name fields) as a primary key, for example, then you cannot add a new person to the Table who has the same name as someone who has already been entered. If someone changes his or her name, you can also lose data—or create massive data entry problems—in a relational database.

A social security number is the only meaningful field that can sometimes be used as a primary key. It was designed to be a primary key for Social Security files, and it is actually an arbitrary number assigned to each American worker.

It is best to create primary key by using a field that is the Counter data type. For example, is an Employee Number field as a primary key, and make it the Counter data type, so its values are entered automatically.

CREATING THE PRIMARY KEY

It is very easy to create the primary key field in an Access table. Define the field in Design View as you would any other field. Select the field and either choose the **Set Primary Key** option of the Edit menu, or click on the **Primary Key** tool. Access displays a key graphic to the left of the primary key field. For example, the employee number is the primary key field in Figure 2.10.

AUTOMATICALLY CREATING A PRIMARY KEY FIELD

Access creates a primary key field for you if you do not create one yourself. When you close the Table window, Access displays the dialog box, shown in Figure 2.11, and asks you if you want a primary key field defined. Click on **Yes** if you want Access to create the field.

If one of the fields in the table is the Counter data type, Access designates it as the primary key. Otherwise, Access adds a new counter field to the table and gives it the name **ID**.

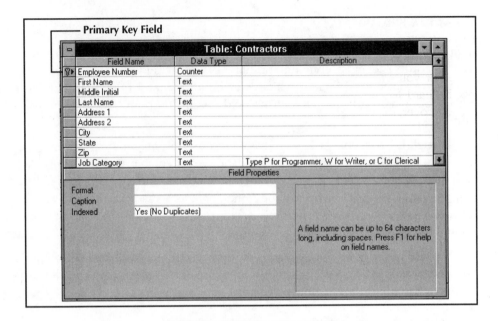

FIGURE 2.10   PRIMARY KEY FIELD.

FIGURE 2.11   ACCESS CAN CREATE A PRIMARY KEY FOR YOU.

Creating a Sample Table

Now that you have learned how to design a table, you should get some hands-on experience designing and creating a sample table. The table you create in this chapter will be used again in later chapters, so you should save your work.

Our sample database will be used to record hours worked and wages paid to contractors. We will record names, addresses, hourly rate of pay, hours worked, and other basic information about contractors.

After you have learned to work with this simple database in Access, it will not be hard for you to work with a more complex, relational database (which will be covered in Chapter 6).

Planning the Table

Let's assume our company is a small software development company named the Soft Tech Development Group. Our company has periods of heavy workloads, when we need to hire contractors in addition to our regular employees. We hire three types of contractors: programmers, technical writers, and clerical help.

For each person, we must record basic data such as name and address. We will also record whether each person is a programmer, a writer, or clerical help. Since contractors are not always free when you call them, we will include a field to record the date when a contractor becomes available. This field can generally be left blank, but we'll fill it in when a contractor will not be available until after a certain date. We will have a field to specify whether a contractor is willing to work overtime on short notice, and finally, we'll include fields that record the hourly wage and hours worked by each contractor.

NOTE

To save data entry time as you do the exercises in this book, the sample data does not include fields for telephone number, social security number, or fax number.

Our company is in New York City, and most of the employees live in the New York area, but some of the contract programmers and writers live elsewhere and communicate by modem and Federal Express.

BREAKING DOWN THE DATA

It is easier to search and sort a value if it is in a field by itself. When you have the option, it is generally a good idea to break down the data into more fields rather than fewer.

For example, if you create a single City/State/Zip field, you cannot produce mailing labels that are sorted by Zip Code, and it is difficult to search for all the records from a single state or city. It is always best to have three separate fields for city, state, and zip code.

Likewise, if you create a single field to hold first and last names, then you cannot produce a report that is sorted by last name.

Sometimes you can create a single field for first name and middle initial, though this depends on how you want to use the data. If you want to send form letters that address the people by first name, for example, you should have a separate field for middle initial. This allows you to produce letters with the salutation Dear John instead of Dear John Q. You may also want to consider whether you need a title field for titles such as Mr., Ms., or Dr. You need this field, for example, if you want to do a mailing with a salutation like Dear Mr. Smith.

In the sample application, let's assume our mailings will use the first name only. Therefore, we need to put the middle initial in a separate field, and we will not use a title field.

It takes extra time to work with your table if it has an extra field, but it can cause you hours of trouble later if you do not include a field you need from the start. In general, if you are in doubt, you should break up data into more fields rather than fewer.

ONE-TO-ONE RELATIONSHIPS

You should look for one-to-one relationships of each field to each record when designing a table.

In our sample database, for example, you must consider whether there is only one of each of the fields that you plan to use in the table for each contractor. You know that each person has one first name, one last name, one address, one wage rate, and so on. All of these have a one-to-one relationship with the record.

Let's assume, also, that everyone works as either a programmer, a writer, or clerical help, but not as more than one of these. Thus, this information is in a one-to-one relationship with the record and can be kept in a single field. The easiest way to store the information is in a one-character text field, where you enter the code letter **P** for programmer, **W** for writer, or **C** for clerical.

If some contractors did more than one of these jobs, you would have to design the table differently. You could create three Yes/No fields—one for Programmer, one for Writer, and one for Clerical—and enter yes in each that applies to a given person. This would make data entry a bit harder than keeping this information in one field because you would have to move through two extra fields as you typed each record. It is best not to use this method unless it is necessary.

There is some information you must store in this database, however, that does not have a one-to-one relationship with the records in the Contractor table. You must enter the time worked more than once for each person. For example, each contractor may send in a bill and timesheet every month. You have to enter the billing date, the number of hours worked, and the amount billed each time you get a bill. All this billing data is in a *many-to-one* relationship with the records in your contractor file.

Think about trying to enter this data in the same table that contains fields for the contractor's name and address. You could include a billing date, hours worked, and amount billed field in each record. You would have no problem entering this data when you got your first bill, but what would you do when you got your second bill?

Would you add a new record for the contractor, so that you had to reenter all the basic data for a contractor each time you got a bill? That would create a large table, filled with repetitive data.

Would you add new fields called **Billing Date 2**, **Hours Worked 2**, and **Amount Billed 2**? Soon, you would have so many fields that your table would be unwieldy. Keeping similar data in fields with different names also makes it difficult to produce a report that sums the total amount billed by each contractor.

In fact, the only viable way to record this data is by creating a separate table for it, which you could call the Billing table. This Billing table would have fields for the billing date, the number of hours worked, and the amount billed, and it would also have a key field—the Employee Number. Each record in the Contractor table also has an Employee Number field, and you would use these key fields to relate the two tables so you know which contractor each billing record applies to.

In Chapter 6 you will learn about relational databases and create a second table to store billing data. At this point, however, you cannot store this billing data in the single-table database you are working with.

Exercise: Creating a Table

Now that we have done the analysis needed to design your table, let's do the following exercise to create it. To save data entry time, we won't include the fields you would normally have in a table like ours such as Social Security Number and Telephone Number.

To create the table, follow these steps:

1. If necessary, start Access and use the File menu to open the sample database, **TEACHSLF.MDB**, which you created in the exercise at the beginning of this chapter.

2. Make sure the Tables list is displayed, and select the **New** button. Access displays the New Table dialog box. Select **New Table** to display the Table window in Design View.

3. The first field is the primary key. As the field name, type **Employee Number**. As the Data Type, select **Counter**. Then, to make it the primary key, choose **Set Primary Key** from the **Edit** menu (or click the **Primary Key** tool). Notice that a key graphic appears to the left of the field.

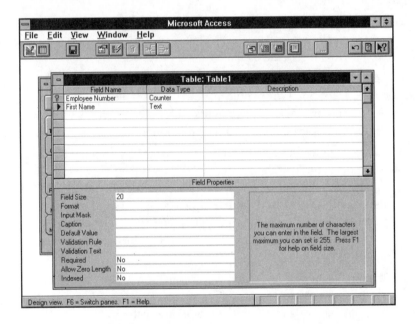

FIGURE 2.12 ADDING FIELDS TO A NEW TABLE.

4. Begin adding fields for name and address. As the next field name, type **First Name**. Press **Tab** to move to the Data Type column. It displays the default data type, Text, and Properties panel. Leave **Text** as the Data Type. Double-click the **Field Size** property to select its default value of **50**, and type **20** to replace it, as shown in Figure 2.12. You can leave the other properties as they are.

5. For the next field, enter the field name **Middle Initial**, the data type **Text**, and a field size of **1**. For the next field, enter the field name **Last Name**, the data type **Text**, and a field size of **25**.

6. For the next field, enter the field name **Address 1**, the data type **Text**, and a field size of **30**. For the next field, enter the field name **Address 2**, the data type **Text**, and a field size of **30**. For the next field, enter the field name **City**, the data type **Text,** and a field size of **25**. For the next field, enter the field name **State**, the data type **Text**, and a field size of **2**. For the next field, enter the field name **Zip**, the data type **Text**, and the field size of **5**.

Figure 2.13 show how your table looks so far now that you have added fields for all the basic name and address data.

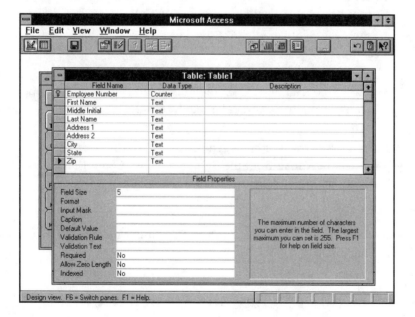

FIGURE 2.13   FIELDS FOR BASIC DATA.

Before going on, you should save your work. Choose **Save** from the File menu, In the Save As dialog box, enter the name **Contractors** and press **Enter** (or select **OK**).

Now you must add fields for the other types of data: job category (programmer, writer, or clerical), hourly wage, date available (entered only if the contractor is not currently available when you call), and whether the contractor is available for emergencies. You should also add a memo field to hold notes.

1. As the next field name, type **Job Category**. As the field type, select **Text**. Since users may need help when they are entering data in this field, enter the description **Type P for Programmer, W for Writer, or C for Clerical**. This description is displayed in the Status Bar as a help line when you enter data in this field. As the field size, enter **1**.

2. As the next field name, type **Hourly Pay**, and as the data type, select **Currency**.

3. As the next field name, type **Date Available**. As the data type, select **Date/Time**. As the description, type **Enter a Date Only if the Contractor is Not Available when You Call**.

4. As the next field name, type **Emergencies**, and as the data type, select **Yes/No**.

5. As the final field name, type **Notes** and as the field type, and select **Memo** as the data type. Click the **Maximize** button on the upper left of the Table window so you can see all the fields. The final table design is shown in Figure 2.14.

6. Click the **Restore** button to return the Table window to its normal size. Then choose **Close** from the Table window's Control menu (or choose **Close** from the File menu). When Access prompts you to save changes, select **Yes**.

The new table's name is displayed in the Database window, ready for you to work on in the future.

Using Datasheet View and Design View

After you have created a table, its name is added to the Database window, and you can open it at any time in either Datasheet View or Design View. You can easily switch between these two views. Datasheet View lets you add, view, or modify data. Design View lets you create or modify the design of a table.

You can open the table from the Database window in either view:

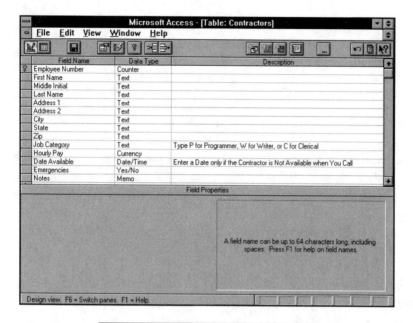

FIGURE 2.14   THE DESIGN OF THE NEW TABLE.

❑   Select the table and click on the **Open** button to open it in Datasheet View. You can also open the table in Datasheet View simply by double-clicking on the table name.

❑   Select the table and select the **New** button to open it in Design View. Access displays the Table Design window that you have learned about in this chapter.

When a table is open in either of these views, the Design View and Datasheet View tools are displayed on the far left of the toolbar. You can use them (or choose **Table Design** or **Datasheet** from the view menu) to switch between the two views.

WARNING

If you modify the design of a table that has already had data entered in it, you can lose data. This is discussed in more detail later in this chapter.

Sharing Data with Other Programs

There are two ways that Access shares data with other database applications:

1. *Importing and Exporting Data*—You can choose the **Import** option from the File menu to convert tables from other applications to Access tables. If you want to use this data in another application once again, you must choose the **Export** option from the File menu to convert the table from Access format to the format used by the other application.

2. *Attaching Tables*—You can choose the **Attach** option from the File menu to attach the table to an Access database. When you do this, data can be shared with other applications seamlessly, without importing and exporting.

Both of these options are available on the File menu when a database window is open.

These methods of sharing data are discussed in detail in Chapter 12.

Modifying the Design of a Table

When you use Design View, you can change the specifications you entered when you created the table in order to modify its design.

You can make selections from list boxes, just as you do when you create tables. You can use the usual Access editing methods to change specifications entered as text. You can also select, delete, insert, or move rows in Design View just as you do when you are editing the data in a table in Datasheet View.

Because these techniques are most important in editing data, they are discussed in detail in Chapter 3. Once you have become accustomed to editing data in Access, you will find it very easy to use the same techniques to modify the table design.

WARNING

When you modify the design of a table that you have already added data to, there is a danger of data loss. If you have changed the design in a way that might destroy data, Access warns you when you save the change. The following sections describe the changes are the most likely to cause data loss.

Data Loss When Changing Field Size

If you make a field size smaller, you lose existing data that cannot fit into the new size of the field. For example, text data is truncated if you reduce the size of a text field to 20 characters from 30 characters. Fields with data longer than 20 characters retain only the first 20 characters, and discard the rest.

Number data is rounded to fit into the new size, with a loss of some decimal places. Fields that do not fit in the range of values that can be held by the new size lose their data entirely and are displayed as blank fields. For example, if you change the size of a number field to Byte, all values are rounded to the nearest integer and decimal places are lost. Any value that is not between 0 and 255 is lost completely and replaced with a blank field.

Data Loss When Changing Data Type

If you change the data type of a field, all data that cannot be held in the new field type is lost. For example, if you change a text field to a number field, any character in the text field that is not a number is lost.

Adding a Primary Key

If you designate an existing field as a primary key, any records with duplicate data in that field are discarded because a Primary Key must have a unique value in each field.

Making a Backup Copy

When modifying a table design, it is good practice to copy the existing table to a temporary table to have a backup incase a mistake is made. To do this, select the object name and select **Copy** from the Edit menu (or press **Ctrl-C**); and then choose **Paste** from the Edit menu or press **Ctrl-V** to paste the object with a new name.

For example, highlight TEACHSLF, press **Ctrl-C**, then **Ctrl-V**. Access will prompt you for a new name. Enter **TEACHSL2** and press **Enter**. Now you can modify TEACHSLF with TEACHSL2 as a backup copy.

Utilities like this will be covered in detail in chapter 12.

Closing a Table

To close a table in either Datasheet View or Design View, choose **Close** from the File menu or choose **Close** from the Table window's Control menu. Access prompts you to save any changes you made in the table's data or design.

To Sum Up

In this chapter, you created a database file and designed a table.

You learned that you must look carefully at the application you are working with *before designing the table* to decide what data you need and how to break it up into fields. You now know to make sure that the fields in your table are in a one-to-one relationship, so that you do not have to use a multi-table database, and that it is best to give an Access table one field that is its primary key.

To design the table, you use the Table window in Design View and specify what fields the table should have. You enter the name and data type of each field in the table and properties such as Field Size for some fields. After you design the table, you save it and name it using Access naming conventions.

Now that you have created a sample table, you can go on in the next chapter to work with data.

Working with Data

*I*n the last chapter, you created a sample table named Contractors, and you learned how to display it in Design View and Datasheet View. Now you are ready to work with the table in Datasheet View to add, edit, and view data. Often, you can make it easier to add data by creating data-entry forms, which you learn about in later chapters. However, working in Datasheet View is the easiest way to work with many database applications and is a common way of working with tables. In this chapter, you learn to:

❑ use the Access editor to add and edit data

❑ move among records you have already added

❑ delete records

❑ use shortcuts that save data entry time

❑ search for records containing specific data

❑ search using partial values and wildcard characters

❑ modify data quickly

❏ move, hide, resize, and freeze columns for easier viewing

❏ change fonts and row sizes to create more attractive datasheets

❏ print datasheets

Adding and Editing Data

You learned in the last chapter to open and close a table. To open a table, highlight the name of the table you want in the Database window and then click the **Open** button, or press **Enter**. You can also double-click the name to open the table.

If you are working with several types of objects, you may have to select the **Table** button in the Database window to display a list of tables.

N O T E

To close a table, select **Close** from the File menu or select **Close** from the table window's Control menu.

You also learned that you can switch between Design View and Datasheet View by using the toolbar or by choosing **Table Design** and **Datasheet** from the View menu.

You already know how to work with the table in Design View to define the fields that make up the table and specify their properties. In this chapter, you work with the table in Datasheet View to add, edit, and view data. When you first open a table, it is displayed in Datasheet View, so you can enter data.

Data Entry Basics

You use the Access editor to add new records or modify existing records. Before you learn more about the editor, though, you should be familiar with a few general ways of working with records.

WORKING WITH RECORDS

As you enter data, these three graphics are displayed in the *record selector box*, which is to the left of the fields in the datasheet:

❏ *Asterisk*—Access automatically adds blank records to the end of the table as you add data. The blank record is marked with an asterisk in the left column to indicate that it will not be saved when you close the table.

❏ *Arrowhead*—If you highlight a blank record, the asterisk is replaced by an arrowhead to indicate it is the current record.

❏ *Pencil*—When you begin entering data in a record, the arrowhead is replaced by a pencil to indicate changes have been made but not yet saved.

N O T E

You can also make any record the current record by moving the cursor to one of its fields. The easiest way to do this is by clicking on a field.

Figure 3.1 shows the asterisk and pencil graphics.

FIGURE 3.1   DATA ENTRY GRAPHICS.

You can select a record by clicking its record selector box. When you move the pointer to this box, it is displayed as a right-pointing arrow, and when you click it, all the fields in the record are highlighted, as shown in Figure 3.2. You can also select records by choosing **Select Record** from the Edit menu to select the current record, or **Select All Records** from the Edit menu to select all the records.

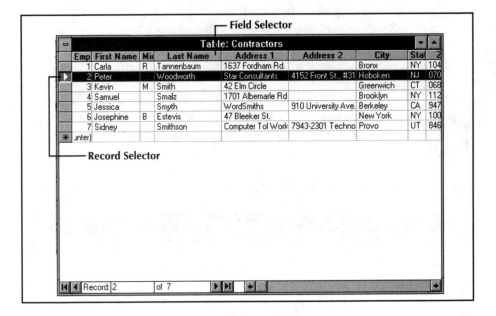

FIGURE 3.2   SELECTING A RECORD.

You can select groups of records in the following ways:

❏   Click the record selector box of one field, hold down the mouse button, and drag up or down across the boxes of adjacent records to select all these records.

❏   Select a record, and hold down the **Shift** key while you click the record selector box of another record to select the two records and all the records between them.

You can also select columns in much the same way you select records. Later in this chapter, you learn how to work with columns and to select blocks of data by clicking and dragging over them.

These graphics and these methods of selection make it easy to add new records and modify or delete existing ones, once you have learned to use the Access editor.

The Access Editor

Editing data in Access is a bit different from editing text in other Windows applications.

In Access, as in other Windows applications, you can select (highlight) text, and it will be replaced by anything you type or be deleted if you press **Del** or the **Backspace** key. You can also place an insertion point in the text, so that text is inserted at that point. Using the insertion point also enables you to use the **Del** key to delete a single character to its right, and the **Backspace** key to delete a single character to its left.

If you are working with an insertion point and press the **Ins** key, you toggle from *insert mode* to *overwrite mode*, and each character you type replaces a character of the existing text. You can press **Ins** again to toggle back to insert mode.

Special Keyboard Behavior

The Access editor allows you to use the keyboard in some ways that are different from other Windows applications, which makes it easier to move around tables of data.

In most Windows applications, if text is selected (highlighted), you deselect it by pressing any of the cursor movement keys—the **Arrow** keys, **Home**, **End**, **PgUp**, or **PgDn**. In Access, these keys are used to move among records and fields.

If you use the keyboard to move the highlight to a field, the data in that field is selected. As in other Windows applications, anything you type replaces the selected text. However, pressing any of the cursor movement keys moves the highlight to another record or field, and the highlight is *not* replaced with an insertion point.

For example, in other Windows applications, pressing the **Left Arrow** key deselects text and places an insertion point at the left of the text. In Access, pressing the **Left Arrow** key moves the highlight one field to the left, and selects all the data in that field.

By default, the data in fields is always selected as you use the keyboard to move through datasheet. To place an insertion point in the field using the keyboard, press **F2**. You can then use the cursor movement keys to move the insertion point within the field. Use the Left or Right Arrow keys to move one character left or right, and the Home or End key to move to the beginning or end of the data in the field.

The **F2** key is a toggle. If you are working with an insertion point, you can press it again to select (highlight) the text in the field.

N O T E

Table 3.1 summarizes the use of all of the cursor movement keys when there is selected text or an insertion point. Whenever you use one of these keys to move to another field, the data in that field is selected, and you must press **F2** if you want to use an insertion point again.

TABLE 3.1   CURSOR MOVEMENT KEYS IN DATASHEET VIEW.

KEY	SELECTED DATA	INSERTION POINT
Left, Right arrow	Moves one field left or right	Moves one character left or right
Up or Down arrow	Moves one record up or down	Moves one record up or down
Ctrl-Left arrow, Ctrl-Right arrow	Moves one field left or right	Moves one word left or right
Ctrl-Up arrow, Ctrl-Down arrow	Moves to top or bottom of column	Moves to top or bottom of column
PgUp, PgDn	Scrolls up or down one screen	Scrolls up or down one screen
Ctrl-PgUp, Ctrl-PgDn	Scrolls left or right one screen	Moves to beginning or end of field
Home, End	Moves to first or last field of record	Moves to beginning or end of field
Ctrl-Home, Ctrl-End	Moves to first or last field of table	Moves to beginning or end of field
Tab	Moves to next field	Moves to next field
Shift-Tab	Moves to previous field	Moves to previous field
Enter	Moves to next field	Moves to next field

If you use the mouse to highlight the field, you can either select the data in the field or place an insertion point in the field, as you do with other Windows applications. Click on a field for an insertion point or double-click a field to select the data in it. To find the field you want, scroll through the data using the scroll bars at the side and bottom of the Table window, as you do with other applications.

Changing Keyboard Behavior

If you are not comfortable with keyboard behavior that is different from other applications you are accustomed to, you can easily change Access' default keyboard behavior.

Choose **Options** from the View menu to display the Options dialog box, and select **Keyboard** from the Category box to display the options shown in Figure 3.3. Select options from the drop-down lists for each item you want to change.

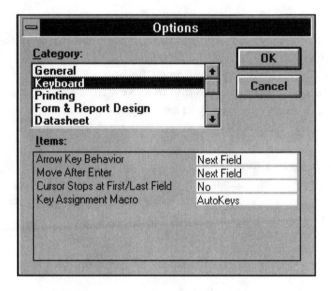

FIGURE 3.3 THE OPTIONS DIALOG BOX.

The **Arrow Key Behavior** drop-down list gives you the options **Next Field** (the default) and **Next Character**. Select **Next Character** to have the arrows act as they do in other Windows applications: deselecting the field and placing an insertion point in it rather than moving you to the next field. Other cursor movement keys also work as usual. For example, Home and End move you to the first or last field of the record.

The Move After Enter drop-down list gives you three options. Next Field is the default. Select **Next Record** to move the highlight down one record when you press **Enter**. Select **No** and pressing **Enter** will have no effect.

The Cursor Stops at First/Last Field drop-down list lets you determine whether you can use the Left and Right arrow keys to move among records. By default, **No** is selected. If you are in the last field of a record, you can use the Right arrow key to move to the first field of the following record, and likewise if you are in the first field of a record, you can use the Left arrow key to move to the last field of the previous record. If you select **Yes**, you cannot move among records in this way. The Left or Right arrow key moves the highlight to the beginning or end of a record and no further.

Adding and Modifying Records

To add a new record to the table, move the highlight to the blank record that Access automatically adds to the end of the table, which is marked with an asterisk. Add the data to it using the editor techniques described previously. In a table that has many records, you might find it useful move the highlight to the new record by choosing **GoTo** and then **New** from the Records menu. As a shortcut for this menu selection, you can click the **New** tool (which has an asterisk on it), or press **Ctrl-+** (hold down the **Ctrl** key and press the **+** key).

To edit an existing record, move the highlight to the record, and change the data in it using the editor techniques described previously. Methods for moving among existing records and finding a specific record are described later in this chapter.

 When you move to the record, a right arrowhead is displayed in the selection box to show that it is the current record.

N O T E

DATA ENTRY MODE

Sometimes it is more convenient to add new records without displaying the records already in the table. To do this, choose **Data Entry** from the Records menu. Access hides all the existing records in the table and displays a blank record, as shown in Figure 3.4. You make entries in the usual way, but only the new data you enter in the table is displayed.

To display all the records again, choose **Show All Records** from the Records menu.

FIGURE 3.4   DATA ENTRY MODE.

CANCELING AN ENTRY

When you begin to make a new entry or edit an existing record, the pencil is displayed to the left of the record. This indicates that the record has been changed but not saved.

As long as the pencil is displayed, you can cancel all the changes in the current field by pressing **Esc**. Pressing **Esc** a second time cancels all the changes you made in the record.

NOTE

SAVING AN ENTRY

Changes you make to a record are automatically saved when you move the highlight to another record, so there is usually no need to explicitly save your data.

If you want to save the current record while you are still working on it, you can do so by choosing **Save Record** from the File menu by clicking the **Save Record** tool on the toolbar (which has a picture of a floppy disk and a pencil writing), or by pressing **Shift-Enter**.

DELETING A RECORD

To delete a record, select it and then choose **Delete** from the Edit menu, or press the **Del** key. You can also select multiple records and delete them all in the same way.

In either case, Access displays the dialog box shown in Figure 3.5, telling you the number of records you deleted and giving you the opportunity to confirm or cancel your change.

FIGURE 3.5   CONFIRMATION DIALOG BOX.

SPECIAL CONSIDERATIONS FOR DATA ENTRY

Generally you enter values into fields using the Access editor described earlier in this chapter. There are a few data types that are entered differently than others, however.

Yes/No fields

You may type the values **yes**, **no**, **true**, **false**, **on**, or **off** in a Yes/No field. The capitalization of your entry is not important.

You may also enter a number in a Yes/No field. Access interprets **0** as **No** and any other number, positive or negative, as **Yes**. If you enter a decimal, Access rounds it to the nearest integer before interpreting it this way, so that **.4**, for example, is **No**.

SHORTCUT

The quickest way to enter data in a Yes/No field is to enter **0** for No and **1** for Yes.

Whatever you enter is displayed in the display format of Yes/No fields. By default, the format is **Yes** and **No**.

Memo Fields

Memo fields are entered and edited in the much same way as ordinary text fields. You can enter an indefinite amount of text, and scroll through the field to view it.

If you want to enter more than one paragraph in a memo field, you can press **Ctrl-Enter** to add a line break, since pressing **Enter** will move you to the next field rather than beginning a new paragraph. Once you have added multiple paragraphs, you can use the Up and Down arrow keys to move among them when you are working with the insertion point, and you can use the Left and Right arrow keys to move within each paragraph. If you use the Up arrow when the insertion point is in the first paragraph, however, or the Down arrow when it is in the last paragraph, the highlight moves to the previous or next record.

It is difficult to work with multiparagraph memo fields in Datasheet View. If you have lengthy memo fields, you should create a form to work with them, using the methods covered in Chapters 5 and 7.

OLE Object Fields

Object Linking and Embedding (OLE) lets you store objects from other Windows applications, such as pictures, sounds, spreadsheets, or videos, in Access databases. A common use of OLE is to store pictures of people in a database, along with their names and addresses.

Because OLE is a powerful and advanced technique that can be used in many ways, it is discussed at length in Chapter 12.

DATA ENTRY SHORTCUTS

In addition to the methods described previously, there are a few shortcuts that can save you data entry time.

Copying Data from the Previous Record

You can copy data from the same field of the previous record by pressing **Ctrl-'** or **Ctrl-"**. (Hold down the **Ctrl** key and type either a single or double quotation mark.)

Inserting the Current Date or Time

To insert the current date, press **Ctrl-;**. To insert the current time, press **Ctrl-:**.

Inserting Default Values

If you have defined a default value for a field (using the Default Value property described in Chapter 2), you can enter it in the field by pressing **Ctrl-Alt-Spacebar**. (Hold down both the **Ctrl** and **Alt** keys and then press the **Spacebar**.)

The default value is entered in the field automatically when the record is created, but you may want to use this key combination to reenter the default value in a field that you edited earlier.

Cutting, Copying, and Pasting

You can also use the usual Window editor functions—cut, copy, and paste—to save time when you are entering data.

Select (highlight) the text you want to remove. Then choose **Cut** from the Edit menu or press **Ctrl-X**. The text is placed in the Windows clipboard, an area of memory used to store data temporarily. If you select a record or a number of records and choose **Cut** from the Edit menu, Access asks for confirmation, just as it does when you delete records, since you are removing the records from the table.

To copy text, select it and then choose **Copy** from the Edit menu, or press **Ctrl-C**. The text remains in its current location, and a copy is also placed in the Windows clipboard.

You can paste the contents of the clipboard in any location you choose. Move the insertion point to the new location, and choose **Paste** from the Edit menu, or press **Ctrl-V**. Whenever you use cut or copy, however, you must remember that the clipboard holds only one piece of data at a time. When you cut or copy something else, it replaces any data that is already in the clipboard.

SHORTCUT

Copying and pasting are particularly useful if you select an entire record. Click the selection arrow to the left of a record to select all the fields of that record, then select **Copy** from the Edit menu to place the entire record in the clipboard. You can copy a name and address out of an Access table in this way, and then paste it in a letter in a Windows word processing program.

Paste Append

In addition to the ordinary Paste command, Access has a Paste Append command that creates a new record containing the contents of the clipboard.

If you are entering a new record with data similar to an existing one, you can select and copy the existing record, as described above, and then choose **Paste Append** from the Edit menu to add a second copy of that record to the end of the table. You can then edit the second record as necessary.

You can also select and copy a record from a different table and then return to the current table and use the Paste Append option to add it to the table. When you append a record to a datasheet in this way, Access pastes data into the columns of the table in the same order they appear in the original table, regardless of the names of the fields. If the fields are not in the same order in the two tables, you can use the methods described later in this chapter to move the columns of the datasheet you are appending data to, so that they match the order of the columns in the datasheet that you are copying data from.

SHORTCUT

As you learned earlier, you can also select multiple records in a table by clicking and dragging the mouse through their selection boxes. You can choose **Copy** from the Edit menu to copy them all, and then choose **Paste Append** to add them all to a table.

Undoing the Last Change

Another common Windows editor function is also useful in data entry. You can choose **Undo** from the Edit menu or click the **Undo** tool to undo the last change you made.

For example, if you move the highlight to a field to select the data in that field, and then mistakenly type a letter, that letter replaces the existing entry in the field. You can click **Undo** to restore the original entry to the field.

In many Windows applications, you can undo only the last change you made, but Access also lets you undo all the changes to a record or field that has not yet been saved. Choose **Undo Current Field** or **Undo Current Record** from the Edit menu to undo changes. The option on the Edit menu changes depending on whether Access can undo several changes in several fields in the current record or only in the current field. The Undo Current Record tool on the toolbar is equivalent to this menu option.

N O T E

The option is no longer available after you have saved changes by moving the highlight to another record or by choosing **Save Record** from the File menu.

MOVING AMONG RECORDS

After you have entered data, you can move among the fields of existing records by using the cursor movement keys described earlier in this chapter. Using the mouse, simply click a field in the record that you want to make the current record. If necessary, use the scroll bars as described in the section on Windows basics in Appendix B to display the record you want.

To move quickly among records, choose **GoTo** from the Records menu to display a submenu with these choices:

❏ *First* moves to the first record in the table.

❏ *Last* moves to the last record in the table.

❏ *Next* moves to the next record after the current record.

❏ *Previous* moves to the record before the current record.

❏ *New*, as you learned earlier, moves to the blank record marked by an asterisk at the end of the table.

Access also has four arrow tools on the lower border of the Table window in Datasheet View that are equivalent to the GoTo commands.

The *record indicator*, in the center of the record tools, displays the number of the current record. You can change this record number to move to a different record. Double-click the record number or press **F5** (or click it to add an insertion point). Type a new record number and press **Enter** to make the new record the current record.

Figure 3.6 illustrates the record tools and indicator.

If you are working with a large table, you will probably find it easier to use the Find option to move to the record you want.

N O T E

The Find option is discussed later in this chapter, but before you look at it, you should add some data to your sample table to consolidate what you have learned already.

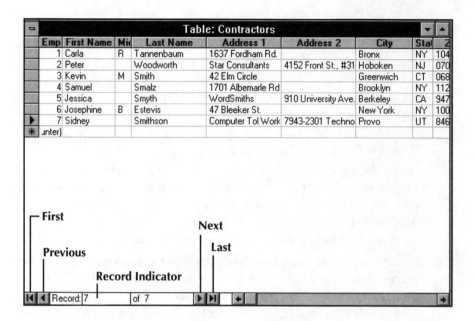

FIGURE 3.6 THE RECORD TOOLS AND INDICATOR.

Adding Sample Data

Now, let's add some sample data to the table you created in Chapter 2. This will get you accustomed to the methods of data entry used in Access and will provide sample data to use for future exercises when you produce forms and reports and work with a relational database.

1   If necessary, open the **Contractors** table in Datasheet View. To make it easier to use all the fields, click the Table window's **Maximize** button so it fills the entire screen.

2.   The employee number is entered automatically, so press **Tab** to move the highlight to the First Name field and type **Carla**. Notice that as soon as you begin to make an entry, the pencil is displayed to the left of the first record, a new record with the asterisk to its left is added to the table, and the employee number **1** is entered for the first record.

3.   Press **Tab** and type **R** in the Middle Initial field. Press **Tab** and type **Tannenbaum** in the Last Name field. Press **Tab** and type **1637 Fordham Rd.** in the Address 1 field. Press **Tab** twice to skip Address 2,

and in the City field, type **Bronx**. Press **Tab** and in the State field, type **NY**. In the Zip field, type **10423**.

4. Press **Tab** to move to the Job Category field. Notice the field description you entered when you defined the table, "Type P for Programmer, W for Writer or C for Clerical," is displayed in the status bar. Type **P**. Press **Tab** to move to the Hourly Pay field, and type **95**. Notice this number is displayed as $95.00 because it is a currency field, and is displayed by default in this format.

5. Leave the Date Available field blank and press **Tab** to move to the Emergencies field. Type **true** and press **Tab**. Notice the value is displayed as Yes. Now press the **Left arrow** key to move back to the field, with the entry selected, and type **1** to replace the original entry. This is the quickest way to enter a value in a Yes/No field.

6. In the Notes field, type **Low level database programming in C language**. Notice how the memo field scrolls to hold an indefinite amount of text, as shown in Figure 3.7. Press **Tab** to move to the next record. Access saves the first record as it makes the second record the current record.

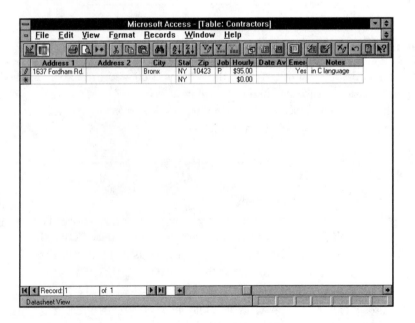

FIGURE 3.7   ENTERING TEXT IN A MEMO FIELD.

Now that you have gotten a feel for how to move among fields, you should enter the data listed below, so you have a few more sample records in the table to work with in later exercises.

Do not enter values in parentheses. The employee numbers are entered automatically in the Counter field, and they are included in parentheses to make it easier to keep track of the records as you enter them. Likewise, (none) simply means there is nothing to enter in the field.

Employee Number	(2)
First Name	Peter
Middle Initial	(none)
Last Name	Woodworth
Address 1	Star Consultants
Address 2	4152 Front St., #314
City	Hoboken
State	NJ
Zip	07030
Job Category	P
Hourly Pay	80
Date Available	7/1/94
Emergencies	No
Notes	Programs the user interface in C
Employee Number	(3)
First Name	Kevin
Middle Initial	M
Last Name	Smith
Address 1	42 Elm Circle
Address 2	(none)
City	Greenwich
State	CT
Zip	06830
Job Category	W
Hourly Pay	55

Date Available	(none)
Emergencies	Yes
Notes	Designed and wrote manual for our financial analysis software

Employee Number	(4)
First Name	Samuel
Middle Initial	(none)
Last Name	Smalz
Address 1	1701 Albemarle Rd. Apt. D-14
Address 2	(none)
City	Brooklyn
State	NY
Zip	11226
Job Category	C
Hourly Pay	9
Date Available	(none)
Emergencies	Yes
Notes	(none)

Employee Number	(5)
First Name	Jessica
Middle Initial	(none)
Last Name	Smythe
Address 1	WordSmiths
Address 2	910 University Ave.
City	Berkeley
State	CA
Zip	94709
Job Category	W
Hourly Pay	50
Date Available	9/1/94
Emergencies	No

Notes	Complete manual writing service
Employee Number	(6)
First Name	Josephine
Middle Initial	B
Last Name	Estevis
Address 1	47 Bleeker St.
Address 2	(none)
City	New York
State	NY
Zip	10010
Job Category	P
Hourly Pay	90
Date Available	12/01/94
Emergencies	Yes
Notes	Programs user interface in C or Pascal
Employee Number	(7)
First Name	Sidney
Middle Initial	(none)
Last Name	Smithson
Address 1	Computer Tool Works
Address 2	7943-2301 Technology Parkway
City	Provo
State	UT
Zip	84601
Job Category	P
Hourly Pay	150
Date Available	(none)
Emergencies	No
Notes	Provides customized functions for financial calculations in C, Pascal, Xbase, and COBOL

Now that you have finished entering the data, your table should look like the one in Figure 3.8.

FIGURE 3.8 SAMPLE DATA IN THE CONTRACTORS TABLE.

Finding Records

It is common to want to find a record based on its contents. There are two ways you might want to do this:

- ❑ *Find a single record*—for example, look up a person by name
- ❑ *Isolate a group of records*—for example, find all the people in your table who are programmers

In this section, you look at *finds*, which are used to look up a single record. Chapter 4 discusses *queries* and *filters*, which are used to find a group of records.

This is the simplest way to find a single record:

1. Place the cursor in a field that contains the data you want to search for. Choose **Find** from the Edit menu to display the Find dialog box, shown in Figure 3.9. You can also click the **Find** tool, which looks like a pair of binoculars, to display the dialog box.

FIGURE 3.9   THE FIND DIALOG BOX—LABEL TOOL.

2.   Enter the value you are searching for in the **Find What** text box. You can enter text and/or numbers.

3.   Click the **Find First** button to find the first occurrence of the value in that field, or click the **Find Next** button to find the next occurrence of the value in the field.

4.   If the record you have found is not the one you want, continue to click the **Find Next** button until you reach the record you want. The dialog box remains open until you select the **Close** button.

If you begin the search by clicking **Find Next**, then Access lets you continue the search at the beginning of the table after it reaches the end so that you can scan the entire table.

If you are searching for the record of someone whose last name is Smith and you think the record is near the beginning of the table, for example, place the cursor in the Last Name field, enter **Smith** in the Find What text box, and click the **Find First** button to go to the first Smith in the table. If that is not the right person, click the **Find Next** button repeatedly until you get to the right Smith. When you find the right person, click the **Close** button to close the Find dialog box and return to the table, with that record as the current record.

If Access cannot find the record, it displays a message saying it has reached the end of the dynaset. You learn about dynasets in Chapter 4.

N O T E

Find Options

In addition to this simple search, there are a few other options in the Find dialog box.

COMPLETE OR PARTIAL MATCH

By default, Access looks for a complete match. The value you enter in the **Find What** text box must be the same as the entire entry in the field.

You can use the Where drop-down list to search for these types of partial matches:

❏ *Select Start of Field* finds all records that begin with the value you entered. For example, if you search for the last name *Smith*, Access would find records that have Smithson or Smithe as the last name, as well as Smith.

❏ *Select Any Part of Field* finds records that have the value anywhere in the field. This is very useful, for example, if you are searching for an address and you remember only the street name, not the street number.

SEARCHING ALL FIELDS

By default, the Find option searches for the value you entered only in the current field, the field where the cursor was when you began the search. To make this clear, the title of the dialog box is **Find in field:** followed by the field name.

If you select the **All Fields** button, Find searches for the value in all the fields of the table. The title of the dialog box changes to **Find** to make this clear.

Searching all fields is slower than searching only the current field, so you should use this option only if you have some special reason to.

FIND DIRECTION

By default, Access searches down through the table, from the first to the last record. You can select the **Up** or **Down** button to change the direction of the search.

MATCH CASE

By default, finds do not distinguish between upper and lower case letters. If you search for Smith, for example, you will also find records with SMITH and smith in them.

Select the **Match Case** check box if you want to find records with the text capitalized exactly as it is where you entered it.

SEARCHES BASED ON FORMAT

By default, the value you enter must match the value in the table. Select the **Search Fields as Formatted** check box if you want to search for the value as it is displayed, based on the display format you specified for the field.

For example, ordinarily you would search for a date by entering something like **11/15/94** in the Find What text box. If you select this option, you could search for that same date by entering **15 Nov 94**, assuming you formatted the date field so it is displayed in that way.

This option slows down the find, and you should use it only if you have some special reason to.

NOTE

Finds Using Wild Cards

Rather than entering an exact value in the Find What text box, you can use the wild card characters shown in Table 3.2 as part or all of the value you are searching for.

TABLE 3.2   WILDCARD CHARACTERS FOR FINDS.

CHARACTER	MEANING	EXAMPLE
?	Matches any single character	Sm?th matches Smith, Smyth, Smeth, etc.
*	Matches any number number of characters	Sm* matches Smith, Smyth, Smithson, Smythers, etc.
[ ]	Matches all options enclosed in brackets	Sm[iy]th matches Smith or Smyth but not Smeth
[!]	Matches all options not enclosed in brackets	Sm[!i]th matches Smyth or Smeth but not Smith
[–]	Matches a range of characters	[a-d]* matches any value beginning with a, b, c, or d.

Find and Replace

Access includes a Find and Replace feature, which gives you a quick way of changing records on the basis of their content.

Choose **Replace** from the Edit menu to display the Replace dialog box shown in Figure 3.10. As you can see, all the controls in this dialog box are the same as controls in the Find dialog box, with one exception. This dialog box also has a Replace With text box, where you can enter a new value to replace the one in the Find What text box.

```
┌─────────────────────────────────────────────────────────────┐
│ ─        Replace in field: 'Last Name'                       │
│                                                              │
│  Find What:   [                      ]     [ Find Next ]     │
│  Replace With: [                     ]     [  Replace  ]     │
│  ┌─Search In──────────────────────┐                         │
│  │ ● Current Field   ○ All Fields │        [ Replace All ]   │
│  │                                │                         │
│  │ □ Match Case   ☒ Match Whole Field │    [  Close  ]      │
│  └────────────────────────────────┘                         │
└─────────────────────────────────────────────────────────────┘
```

FIGURE 3.10   THE REPLACE DIALOG BOX.

You can select **Find Next** to go to each occurrence of the Find What value. When you see the value, you can select **Replace** to replace it with the Replace With value and go to the next occurrence, or you can select **Find Next** to go to the next occurrence without replacing the current one. You can select **Replace All** to replace all the occurrences of the value without confirmation, or select **Close** at any time to close this dialog box.

As an example of how the Replace feature can be used, consider a telephone area code region that has added another area code. Some of the records in your database maintain the old code, while others need to be changed to the new code. You could enter **212** in the Find What text box and **718** in the Replace With text box. Then, as you go through the table, you can decide whether to select **Replace** to change the area code in the record or select **Find Next** to go on without changing the area code.

Indexed Finds

Finds are faster if the field you are searching is indexed. If you often search for the last name, for example, you should create an index on the last name field.

As you saw in Chapter 2, you can create an index based on a single field by selecting Yes as the Indexed property for that field in Design View. Indexes are discussed in detail in Chapter 4.

Finds versus Queries

The Find and Find and Replace options are relatively simple because they are based on a value in a single field. In contrast, queries let you find records based on much more complex criteria. For example, a query can be based on the content of many fields or on a comparison of values in fields with the criteria in the query. Queries are discussed in detail in Chapter 4. In Chapter 10, you will look at Action Queries, which give you a more powerful way of changing data.

N O T E
Finds are usually the fastest way of finding a specific record when you need to look up a record by last name or by the content of some other field.

Changing the Format of the Table

Often, you can view data more conveniently when you rearrange the table. Chapters 5 and 7 discuss forms, which are useful when you want to work with one record at a time, but simple changes in the table's format are more effective when you want to work with multiple records.

Working with Columns

The main limitation of Datasheet View is that you usually cannot see all the fields of a record. This can be a nuisance, for example, if you want to look at a list of names and phone numbers. The name fields may disappear beyond the left edge of the screen as you are scrolling right to see telephone number.

To resolve this problem, you can move or resize your table's columns. You must select columns before manipulating them in some of these ways.

SELECTING COLUMNS

Before you can move or resize your columns, you must select them. The way that you select columns is similar to the way you select fields.

To select a single column, simply click its field selector—the field name at the top of the column. When the pointer is on the field selector, it becomes a down arrow. You can then select the column by clicking on it and highlighting it, as shown in Figure 3.11.

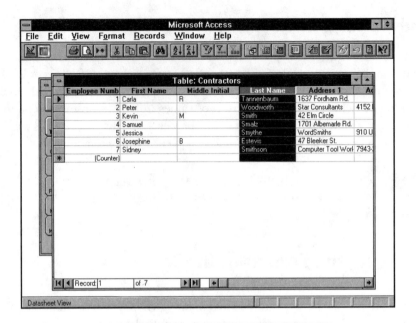

FIGURE 3.11   THE LAST NAME COLUMN IS SELECTED.

To select multiple columns, select a single column, hold down the **Shift** key, then select another column. The two columns you clicked and all the columns between them are highlighted showing that they are selected. You can also select multiple columns by clicking and dragging through the column selectors of all of them.

MOVING COLUMNS

Moving columns gives you one easy way to view names and phone numbers. You just have to move the phone number field left so it is next to the name fields.

You can move either one column or several adjacent columns. In either case, you must begin by selecting the column(s).

NOTE

To move a single column, click and drag the column's field selector to move it. The pointer will be displayed with small square at its base, as it is when you use the drag-and-drop feature of other Windows applications. Do not release the mouse button until the pointer is at the location where you want the column.

Access displays a heavy line to show that the column will be placed to the left of the column where the pointer is when you release the mouse button.

You move multiple columns just as you do single columns. Select a group of adjacent columns. Then click and drag the field selector of any of the selected columns to the new location.

RESIZING A COLUMN

Sometimes, you can view all the fields you want to see only if you make the columns smaller. It may be convenient, for example, to display just the first letter of first names. There are also times when you want to widen a column to see more of the data in a field than Access displays by default.

Resizing Using the Mouse

It is easy to resize a column with the mouse. Just place the mouse pointer at the right edge of a field selector on the line that divides it from the next column. The pointer is displayed as a vertical bar with arrows pointing left and right. You can then click and drag the right edge of the column left to make the column narrower or right to make it wider.

Resizing by Entering Column Size

You can also resize columns using the menu. Select a column, and then select **Column Width** from the Format menu to display the Column Width dialog box shown in Figure 3.12. Enter a number in the Column Width text box that is the number of characters you want displayed in the field.

FIGURE 3.12   THE COLUMN WIDTH DIALOG BOX.

If you enter anything except the default width, the Standard Width checkbox is deselected. You can select it at any time to enter the default width in the Column Width text box.

If you select multiple columns before you select **Column Width**, they are all resized to the size you enter.

HIDING COLUMNS

Hiding columns you do not need is sometimes even more convenient than moving columns. You can move through the datasheet without unnecessary fields getting in your way.

Hiding Selected Columns

To hide columns, select the column or the group of adjacent columns you want to hide. Then choose **Hide Columns** from the Format menu. The selected columns will disappear.

The Show Columns Dialog Box

You can hide columns more selectively or you can make hidden columns reappear by choosing **Show Columns** from the Format menu. The Show Columns dialog box will display as shown in Figure 3.13.

FIGURE 3.13   THE SHOW COLUMNS DIALOG BOX.

This dialog box lists the names of all of the fields in the table, with a checkmark to the left of the ones that are currently displayed. Select fields in this list, then select the **Hide** button to hide them. To show fields that are hidden, select the **Show** button to display them in the datasheet again. When you have made all the changes you want, select the **Close** button.

FREEZING COLUMNS

Sometimes it is convenient to freeze columns so that they are always displayed, even as you scroll right to see additional fields. For example, you might want to display the First Name and Last Name fields permanently at the left edge of the table as you scroll right to see all the other data.

To freeze columns, select the column or the adjacent columns you want to freeze and choose **Freeze Columns** from the Format menu. The frozen columns are automatically moved to the far left of the table. They continue to be displayed even if you scroll through all the fields of the table.

To unfreeze columns, choose **Unfreeze All Columns** from the Format menu. When you do this, the columns that had been frozen are still displayed at the far left of the table. You can move them back to their original location using the techniques described in the section "Moving Columns," earlier in this chapter.

Other Format Changes

There are a few other methods of customizing the datasheet that you might sometimes find convenient such as changing fonts, resizing rows, and hiding gridlines. They are particularly useful when you want to print the table.

FONTS AND STYLES

Choose **Font** from the Format menu, to display the Font dialog box shown in Figure 3.14. You can select the typeface, style, and size of the font used for all the data in the datasheet.

FIGURE 3.14   THE FONT DIALOG BOX.

Select a typeface, such as Arial or Times Roman, from the Font list. The type-faces you have available depend on the fonts you have installed under Windows. Use the **Font Style** list to specify whether the type should be bold, italic, bold italic. Select **Regular** to remove these effects. Select the **Underline** checkbox to underline the text.

Use the Size list to select the size of the font in points (the unit of measure used for type size, equal to 1/72 of an inch). Some fonts, such as TrueType fonts, (displayed in the font list with a TT to their left) are scalable, and they are available in more sizes than can be displayed in the list. Type in a point size in the Size text box to use a size that is not listed.

RESIZING ROWS

You resize the height of rows in much the same way you resize a column. Move the pointer to the line between any two record selector buttons. The pointer becomes a horizontal line with arrows pointing up and down. Click and drag up to reduce the row height or drag down to increase the row height. The height of all rows will be changed.

Alternatively, select **Row Height** from the Format menu to display the Row Height dialog box shown in Figure 3.15. Enter the height in points in the Row Height text box.

FIGURE 3.15   THE ROW HEIGHT DIALOG BOX.

Select the **Standard Height** check box to automatically enter the height of the standard size in the Row Height text box. The standard size depends on the font you are using. After changing font size, you can select **Standard Size** to resize all rows to fit the new font, if they are not resized automatically.

GRIDLINES

Select **Gridlines** from the Layout menu to remove the lines that separate rows and columns. This option is a toggle, and if you have already removed these lines, you can select it again to restore the lines.

Saving Datasheet Settings

Choose **Save** from the File menu to save changes to the table's layout. If you close the Table window without saving changes, Access displays the dialog box shown in Figure 3.16. Select **Yes** to save changes.

FIGURE 3.16 ACCESS PROMPTS YOU TO SAVE LAYOUT CHANGES.

These methods of saving changes are similar to the ways that you save your data in other Windows applications, but as you know, data you enter in Access is saved automatically as you move the highlight from record to record. In Access, you use these methods to save changes in the design of objects—in this case, changes in the layout of the table.

Resizing Columns in the Sample Table

You have may have noticed that the width of your table makes it inconvenient to work with, since you must scroll back and forth to see different fields. Yet some of its columns are much wider than they need to be to display the data they hold. You can make the table easier to use by narrowing these columns as follows:

1.   Place the mouse pointer on the right edge of the title of the employee number column, so it is displayed as a vertical line with arrows pointing left and right. Hold down the mouse button and drag left to narrow the column, until it is the right width to display the employee number, as shown in Figure 3.17.

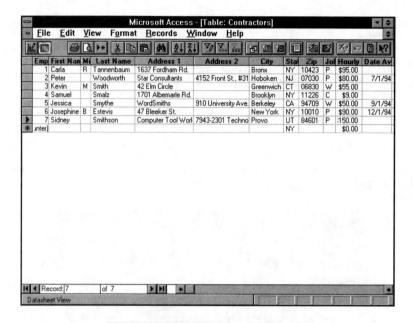

FIGURE 3.17   NARROWING THE COLUMNS.

2. Likewise, narrow the **First Name** column a bit. Click and drag the **Middle Initial** column so it is just large enough for a single letter, and narrow the remaining columns so they are just large enough for their data, as shown in Figure 3.17. Now you can see most of the fields for each record.

3. Choose **Save** from the File menu to save these settings.

In the future, when you open the table, it will have these column widths.

Printing the Datasheet

The ReportWizards let you create sophisticated printed reports easily, but it is even easier to print the datasheet.

For many purposes, printing the datasheet is as useful as printing a report. For example, if you want to print out names and telephone numbers to call the people on your list, you can rearrange the columns, if necessary, so the telephone number column is next to the name columns. You can then select these three columns and print them.

The Print Dialog Box

Before you print a datasheet, select the rows or columns that you want to print if you do not want to print the entire table. Sometimes it is necessary to print only some columns to fit the table on a page.

If you think it will make the table easier to read, you can also change the font and remove the gridlines, as described earlier in this chapter.

Then choose **Print** from the File menu to display the Print dialog box shown in Figure 3.18. This Print dialog box is similar to the dialog box used for printing in other Windows applications.

FIGURE 3.18 **THE PRINT DIALOG BOX.**

The Print Range area lets you select how much of the table you want to print. You can print it all, print the area of the table that is selected, or print only certain pages, beginning with the page number you enter in the From text box and continuing through the page number you enter in the To text box.

The Print Quality drop-down list lets you select the resolution of the printout. On some printers, you can print a rough draft more quickly with lower resolution and print only the final draft in higher resolution. The options displayed in this drop-down list depend on the capabilities of your printer.

If you select the **Print to File** checkbox, Access places the contents of the table and all the printer codes needed to print it in a disk file. The printer codes included in this file depend on the printer named at the top of the Print dialog box. After you select **OK**, Access displays the Print To File dialog box, shown in

Figure 3.19, which lets you name the file. You can include a drive and path name in the file name. Anyone who has the proper printer can print this file using the DOS command **Copy <filename> PRN**, even if they do not have Access.

Print To File

Output File Name:

OK

Cancel

FIGURE 3.19   THE PRINT TO FILE DIALOG BOX.

In the Print dialog box, enter the number of copies you want to print in the **Copies** text box. If you print more than one multipage datasheet, the **Collate Copies** checkbox is selected by default, so that each copy of the datasheet is printed from beginning to end before the next one is printed. If you deselect this checkbox, all the copies of page one will be printed, then all the copies of page two, and so on.

The Print Setup Dialog Box

If necessary, you can select the **Setup** button of the Print dialog box to display the Print Setup dialog box shown in Figure 3.20. You can also display this dialog box at any time by choosing **Print Setup** from the File menu.

Select the printer you want to use from the drop-down list in the Printer area. Next, select the orientation of items on the page from the Orientation area.

When you are printing database tables, it is often useful to select **Landscape**, which prints across the longer dimension of the paper, so an entire record fits on one line.

N O T E

In the Paper area, select the **Paper Size**, and if your printer has more than one paper tray, select the **Source**. Enter the margins in the **Margin** text boxes at the bottom of the dialog box.

FIGURE 3.20   THE PRINT SETUP DIALOG BOX.

You can also choose **Print Preview** from the File menu, or click the
Print Preview tool to display the table in the Print Preview Window
shown in Figure 3.21. Print Preview lets you see exactly how the table
will look when it is printed. Then choose **Print** from the File menu, or click the
Print tool to print the table.

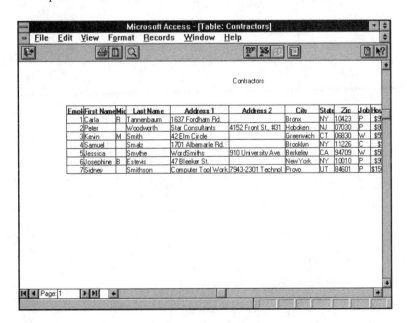

FIGURE 3.21   THE TABLE IN THE PRINT PREVIEW WINDOW.

Reports are automatically displayed in the Print Preview window rather than in Datasheet View, and so it is discussed in detail in Chapter 5.

To Sum Up

In this chapter you learned to work with a table in Datasheet View. You began with the basics of data entry, including how to add and delete records, how to use the Access Editor to edit records, and how to move among the records of the table. Then you learned to use finds to search for specific records, and to use find and replace to change data quickly.

You learned to change the appearance of the datasheet in ways that make it easier to work with on the screen—by moving, hiding, resizing, and freezing its columns. You also learned how to change a datasheet's fonts to make it more attractive. And, finally, you leaned how to print a datasheet.

In Chapters 2 and 3, you learned all you need to know about tables. You can now proceed to Chapter 4, which describes another Access object, the query.

ACCESS

Chapter 4

Querying and Sorting Your Data

*Y*ou have already learned how to use finds to locate a single record. In this chapter, you learn to use filters and simple queries, called *Select Queries*, to isolate groups of records.

In this chapter you learn about:

- ❏ the definition of a *dynaset*
- ❏ creating and saving a query
- ❏ specifying fields the query will display
- ❏ specifying the sort order of records the query will display
- ❏ entering criteria to specify the records the query will display
- ❏ using comparison operators in criteria to locate a range of values
- ❏ entering multiple criteria using a logical AND and a logical OR
- ❏ creating quick reports by designing a query and printing the dynaset

❑   creating a filter for a table

❑   saving a filter as a query

❑   performing a quick sort of a table

❑   creating indexes based on single or multiple fields

Queries

Queries are independent objects. Filters are not independent objects: they are attached to tables, forms, or reports. Yet you define filters in much the same way you define simple queries. In this chapter, you learn about queries first, and then you can easily apply the same methods to defining filters.

Select queries are based on a single table, and they let you specify which fields and records of a table are displayed. Access also lets you use queries in more powerful ways to join several tables in a relational database. These queries are discussed in Chapter 6 and advanced queries, such as Action Queries, which let you modify the data in tables, are covered in Chapter 10.

This chapter describes Quick Sorts as well as sorts done through queries. Since you can speed up queries and sorts by using indexes, this chapter concludes with a general discussion of indexes in Access.

The Dynaset

Query is the object listed below Table in the Database window, and queries can often be used instead of tables. For example, a form or a report can be based on a table or on a query. Either the table or the query contains the set of fields and records displayed by the form or report.

A query, however, lets you enter criteria to specify which fields and records are displayed and what order they are displayed in. You can create a query, for example, to display only the name and address fields of people from New York, with the records in alphabetical order by name.

A query displays a subset of all the fields and records in a table (or, when you work with relational databases, in multiple tables). Any changes you make in the data displayed by the query is also changed in the table. Because of this dynamic relationship between the query and the tables it is based on, the subset of data displayed by the query is called a *dynaset*.

The Query Window

Before looking at how to create and use a query, take a quick look at the Select Query window shown in Figure 4.1 to get a general idea of its features.

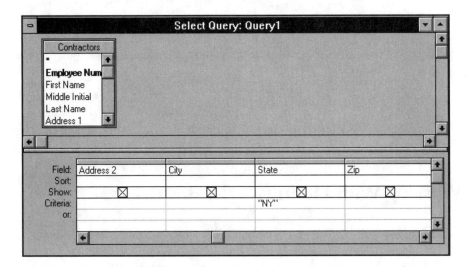

FIGURE 4.1   THE SELECT QUERY WINDOW.

As you can see, the panel in the top half of this window contains a list of all the fields in a table. As you can see the fields from our Contractors sample table are shown in Figure 4.1. When you work with relational databases, you can add multiple field lists here, and then join them. When you are working with a single-table database, however, you should have only one field list here.

The bottom half of the Select Query window includes what is called the *Query By Example* (QBE) grid, which has the following features:

❑   The first line lets you specify which fields are included in the dynaset that results from the query.

❑   The second line lets you specify which fields to sort the query on.

❑   The third line lets you specify which fields to display.

❑   The remaining lines let you enter criteria to determine which records are included in the dynaset.

This is called Query By Example because the criteria consist of examples of the data you want to result from the query. In Figure 4.1, for example, the criterion NY is entered under the State field, so only records with the value NY in that field will be included in the resulting dynaset.

You can select, move, and resize columns in this grid just as you do in a table.

❏ Click the selector box above a column to select it, and then click or drag it to move it.

❏ Move the pointer to the right edge of the selector box, and it is displayed as a vertical line with arrows pointing in both directions. You then can click and drag the line to resize the column.

Working With Queries—The Basics

You work with queries just as you do with any object:

❏ To create a new query, select the **Query** button in the Database window and the select the **New** button.

❏ To open an existing query in Datasheet View, select the **Query** button in the Database window, select the query name in the list box, and then select the **Open** button.

❏ To open an existing query in Design View, select the **Query** button in the Database window, select query name in the list box, and then select the **Design** button.

Once a query is open, you can switch between Datasheet View and Design View by choosing **Query Design** or **Datasheet** from the View menu. Alternatively, you can click the **Design View** or **Datasheet View** tool on the toolbar.

N O T E

Queries also generate commands in *Structured Query Language* (SQL). You can view these commands at any time by choosing **SQL** from the View menu or by selecting the SQL View tool that is added to the toolbar when you are working in the Select Query window. SQL is useful for programmers but is not covered in this book.

The QueryWizards

When you create a query, Access displays the New Query dialog box shown in Figure 4.2. You can choose whether to use QueryWizards or to create a New Query yourself by defining it in the Select Query window. The QueryWizards let you create advanced queries, and so they will be discussed in chapter 10.

FIGURE 4.2   THE NEW QUERY DIALOG BOX.

Creating a New Query

After you select the **New Queries** button to define the query yourself, Access displays the Add Table dialog box to let you select the tables or queries to include as field lists in the Select Query window.

SHORTCUT

To quickly create a new query based on a single table or query, select a table or query in the Database window. Select **New** and then **Query** from the File menu or select the **New Query** tool from the toolbar. Access bypasses the Add Table dialog box and opens the Select Query window with the table or query in it. There are also menu options and tools, shown in Figure 4.3, for creating other objects in the same way.

FIGURE 4.3   TOOLS FOR CREATING NEW OBJECTS.

Saving a Query

When you are working with a query you can choose **Save** from the File menu at any time to save your work.

The first time you save your work, Access displays the Save As dialog box shown in Figure 4.4 so you can enter a name for the query. Enter a name up to 64 characters, following the usual Access naming conventions.

FIGURE 4.4   THE SAVE AS DIALOG BOX.

NOTE

If you close a query without saving all changes, Access prompts you to save the query.

RENAMING A QUERY

Choose **Save As** from the File menu to display the Save As dialog box and rename the query. Access creates a second copy of the original query with the new name.

REUSING A SAVED QUERY

After you have saved a query, you can reuse it.

❑ Select the **Query** button in the Database window to display query names.

❑ Select the query you want and select **Open** (or double-click the query name) to open the Query window with an updated dynaset for that query.

Field Lists

It is best to add the field lists you need to the Select Query window when you first create the query. In the single-table queries you work with in this chapter, you should have no trouble doing this. However, when you begin working with more complex queries, you may sometimes find it useful to add or remove field lists as you work with the table.

THE ADD TABLE DIALOG BOX

When you create a query by selecting the **New** button, Access displays the Add Table dialog box shown in Figure 4.5. You can then select the tables or queries that will be the basis of the new query.

❑ Select **Tables**, **Queries**, or **Both** by clicking the **View** buttons at the bottom of this dialog box.

❑ Select a table or query name from the list box and select the **Add** button, or double-click a table or query name.

A list of the fields for that table or query is placed in the Select Query window, and you can include any of these fields in the result of the query.

FIGURE 4.5   THE ADD TABLE DIALOG BOX.

When you are working with a relational database, you can base queries on two or more tables. You can continue selecting tables and queries from this list until all you want are added to the Query window. When you are done, click the **Close** button to close this dialog box.

With a simple database, you should add only one table to the Select Query window and then close the Add Table dialog box.

As you learned earlier, you can also include a table in the Select Query window without using the Add Table dialog box. Select the Table name, choose **New**, and then **Query** from the File menu, or click the **New Query** tool.

ADDING AND REMOVING TABLES

You can change the tables or queries that are displayed in the Select Query window at any time:

❏ To add new tables or queries to the window, choose **Add Table** from the Query menu to display the Add Table dialog box. Use it to add existing tables or queries to the query window, just as you do when you are first creating the query.

❑ To remove a table or query from the Select Query window, first select it by clicking on one of its fields to highlight it. Then choose **Remove Table** from the Query menu.

WARNING

When you remove a table from the Select Query window, the fields you included in the query are also removed. This can result in the loss of a considerable amount of work. As a precaution, *save the query before removing the table*. Then, if removing the table has unanticipated effects, you can close the query window without saving that change.

Selecting Fields to View

There are three ways to add a field from the field lists to the QBE grid so that a particular field is included in the result of the query:

❑ Click the Field name in the field list, and while holding down the mouse button, drag the field name to one of the Field cells in the QBE grid. If there is already a field name in the cell, the new one replaces it, and moves existing fields to the right.

❑ Click a field cell in the QBE grid to display a drop-down list, of the fields in all the field lists in the Select Query window. Select a field from this list to place it in that cell.

❑ Click a field cell in the QBE grid. Then type in a field name.

ADDING MULTIPLE FIELDS

There may be times when you want to include all the fields in the result of the query. For example, you may want the query to isolate specific records but you want all the feilds of those records. For this reason, Access gives you an easy way to place all the fields in the QBE grid.

First, select all the fields in the field list. The easiest way to do this is to double-click the field list's title bar. Then, click and drag any of the fields from the field list to the first field cell. All of the fields will be placed in field cells.

You can also include any number of fields from the field list. First, select the fields you want in the field list. Clicking a field generally selects it and deselects other fields, but you can select multiple fields in two ways:

❑ Hold down the **Ctrl** key when you click a field to select it without deselecting other fields.

❑ Click one field, then hold down the **Shift** key and click a second field. All the fields between the first and last fields will be selected. This method is a quick way of selecting fields that are adjacent to each other in the field list.

Once you have selected all the fields you want, click and drag any of them to one of the field cells, and they will all be placed in field cells, beginning with the cell that you dragged to.

ADDING ALL FIELDS: THE ASTERISK

Field lists in the Select Query window always contain an asterisk, which represents all fields.

If you click and drag the asterisk to a field cell, the QBE window displays the table name followed by an asterisk in that cell, as shown in Figure 4.6. You can also select the table name followed by the asterisk from the field cell's drop-down list or type it in the field cell.

NOTE

When you run the query, all fields from that table will be included in the resulting dynaset.

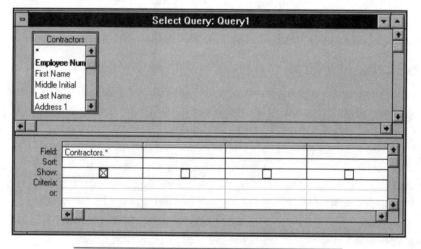

FIGURE 4.6   USING THE ASTERISK TO INCLUDE ALL FIELDS.

Using the asterisk is different in a couple of ways from the method of including all fields discussed in the previous section. If you use the asterisk, all fields will be included in the dynaset even if you change the structure of the table to add new fields. If you add individual field names, on the other hand, then you must manually add new fields if you modify the structure of the table.

The asterisk makes your work easier in this way, but it does make it a bit more difficult to sort or enter criteria for the fields, as you see later in this chapter.

N O T E

Generally, adding individual field names is the easiest way to work with a single table. The asterisk is useful when including all fields from additional tables in a relational database.

Inserting, Deleting, or Moving Fields and Columns

The fields in the dynaset are displayed in the order they appear in the QBE grid.

You can insert a field in any location in any Field cell in the grid simply by clicking and dragging it from the field list to the location you want. The field already in that location and all the fields to its right will move right.

You can also manipulate fields after adding them to the QBE grid just as you manipulate fields in tables. Click and drag the border between the field selector box above the Field name cell to resize the columns.

Click the **Field Selector box** to select a column, as shown in Figure 4.7. Once you have selected a column, you can move it by clicking and dragging the field selector right or left.

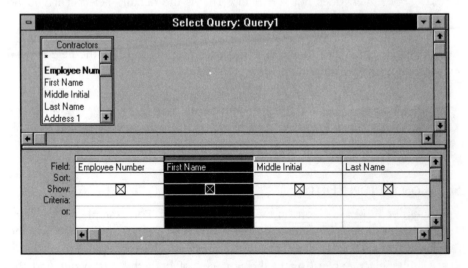

Figure 4.7   Selecting a field in the QBE grid.

You can delete the selected column by choosing **Delete** from the Edit menu, or by pressing the **Del** key. You can also place the cursor in the column and choose **Delete Column** from the Edit menu.

To insert a new column or row, choose **Insert Column** or **Insert Row** from the Edit menu. You can also delete a row by choosing **Delete Row** from the Edit menu.

Specifying Sort Order

Queries let you specify the order in which the records are displayed in the dynaset.

To sort records based on a single field—for example, to sort records in Zip Code order—click the **Sort cell** under that field. Then click the **Sort** drop-down list to display these options:

❑ *Ascending* sorts records from the lowest to the highest value in the field. In text fields, sorts are in normal alphabetical order; in number fields sorts are from the smallest to the largest number; and in date fields, sorts are from the earliest to the latest date.

❑ *Descending* sorts records from highest to lowest value.

❑ *(not sorted)* does not sort fields. This is the default. Select it if you no longer want to sort on a field that you sorted on previously.

Access displays the word Ascending or Descending in the cell if the field is used in a sort and leaves it empty if it is not used in a sort.

SHORTCUT

You can speed up a sort you use frequently by creating an index based on the sort field or fields. Indexes are discussed later in this chapter.

SORTS ON MULTIPLE FIELDS

You may need to base a sort on more than one field. For example, if you want to alphabetize records by name, you need to sort on both the last name and the first name fields to make sure that Aaron Jones comes before Zazu Jones. To do this, simply select **Ascending** in the Sort cell of both the *Last Name* and the *First Name* fields.

When you sort on multiple fields in this way, Access uses the leftmost field as the basis of the sort and uses fields to its right as tie-breakers when values in the leftmost field are the same. Thus, to sort by name, you must arrange the fields so the last name is to the left of the first name.

You can also combine ascending and descending sorts. For example, if you want the records sorted by state in descending order from Wyoming to Alaska, and the records within each state sorted alphabetically by name, make State the leftmost field and select **Descending** in its Sort cell. Make Last Name and First Name the next two fields and select **Ascending** in their Sort cells.

THE ORDER OF FIELDS

You have seen that Access bases sorts on the leftmost field and uses fields to the right only as tie-breakers. For this reason, when you close the Select Query window, Access moves the sort field or fields left, if necessary, to make them the leftmost columns of the QBE grid.

Hiding Fields

The Show checkbox is useful if you use the asterisk to include all the fields in a table. When you do this, you must also include fields individually if you want to enter criteria for them or to sort on them. Add them in the way discussed earlier in this chapter.

When you run the query, each of these fields would normally be displayed twice in the dynaset, once because of the asterisk and once because it is included in a column of its own. To avoid this repetition, you click the **Show** checkbox in the field's own column and the X is no longer displayed.

NOTE

Except for this special case, you generally want to show all the fields you add to the QBE grid, and so the Show checkbox is automatically checked when you add a field to the grid.

Entering Criteria

You can enter a simple criterion, a value for a single field to match, in the following ways:

❑ *Number, Currency, or Counter fields* enter a number without currency signs or number separators. For example, enter **3000** rather than **3,000**.

❏ *Text field* enter the value you want to search for. When you leave the cell, Access automatically puts quotation mark **(")** delimiters around it. For example, if you type **NY** as the criterion for the *State* field, Access will display it as **"NY"**. You can also include the quotation marks when you enter the text. These queries are not sensitive to capitalization. If you enter the criterion **"NY"** for example, the query will also find any states that were entered in lower case as ny.

❏ *Date fields* enter the value you want to search for. When you leave the cell, Access automatically puts pound sign **(#)** delimiters around it, as shown in Figure 4.8. You can enter dates in number or text form, but the month, day, and year should be in the same order defined in the Windows International Panel. In the United States, for example, you can enter **1/1/94**, **Jan 1 94**, **1-Jan-94**, or any other valid American date order. Access will display any of these as **#1/1/94#**.

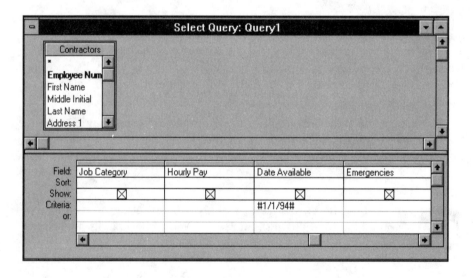

FIGURE 4.8   ACCESS AUTOMATICALLY ADDS DELIMITERS.

❏ *Yes/No fields* enter the criterion **Yes**, **True**, **On**, or **1** to search for Yes. Enter **No**, **False**, **Off**, or **0** to search for No.

Later in this chapter, you learn about complex criteria you can use in queries.

Running the Query

After you have finished filling out the QBE grid, you must run the query to produce its dynaset. You can do this by selecting **Run** from the Query menu or clicking the **Run** tool, which has an exclamation point on it.

You can also run the query by switching to Datasheet View. Either choose **Datasheet** from the View menu or click the **Datasheet** tool.

After taking a moment to process the query, Access displays a datasheet with the fields, records, and sort order that you specified in the query.

A Sample Query

In the rest of this chapter, you look at the more complex criteria you can enter to determine which records are displayed in the query.

First, though, you should get a bit of hands-on experience by creating sample queries based on simple criteria. The simplest criteria, as you learned at the beginning of this chapter, are examples of the value that you want in that field in the dynaset. For example, to display all the records of people from New York State, enter **NY** in the **Criteria cell** of the State field.

Try creating a sample query that displays names and addresses of contractors who live in New York state, sorted alphabetically by name.

1. Select the **Query** button on the Database window, and then select the **New** button. When Access displays the New Query dialog box, select the **New Query** button.

2. Access opens the Select Query window and displays the Add Table dialog box, with Contractors already selected. Select the **Add** button. A field list for the Contractors table is added to the Select Query window, as shown in Figure 4.9. Select the **Close** button of the Add Table dialog box.

3. Click the **Maximize** button of the Select Query window to make it easier to work with. Double-click the title bar of the Contractors field list to select all the fields. Click and drag any of the selected fields to the first Field cell in the QBE grid to add all the fields to it.

4. Scroll right to view the Notes field, click the selector box above this column to select it, and press the **Delete** key to delete it. In the same way, delete the Emergencies, Hourly Pay, and Job Category columns. Scroll left and delete the Employee Number column in the same way.

FIGURE 4.9 ADDING THE TABLE.

5   To sort alphabetically by name, you must make Last Name the first column of the query. Click the selector box of the Last Name column and
release the mouse button. Now that the column is selected, click the
selection box again, hold down the mouse button, and drag left to make
it the first column.

6. Click the **Sort** box of the Last Name field, and use its drop-down list to
select **Ascending**. Likewise, select **Ascending** for the First Name and
Middle Initial fields.

7. Scroll right so you can see the State field, and in its first **Criteria** cell,
type **NY**. Click another field, so you can see that Access adds the quotation mark delimiters around this criterion.

8. Choose **Save Query** from the file menu. Access displays the Save As
dialog box. As the Query Name, enter **Address List of Contractors
from New York**.

9. If you want, you can narrow some of its columns to make the QBE grid
easier to see and to work with in the future. Do it as you did with the
table in the exercise in Chapter 3. Click and drag the right edge of a column's selector box to narrow it. The query design with narrowed
columns is shown in Figure 4.10.

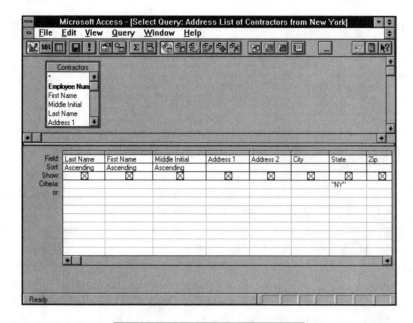

FIGURE 4.10   THE FINAL QUERY DESIGN.

10. Click the **Datasheet View** tool, and access displays the results of this query. Click the **Restore** button to display this window in its normal size, as shown in Figure 4.11.

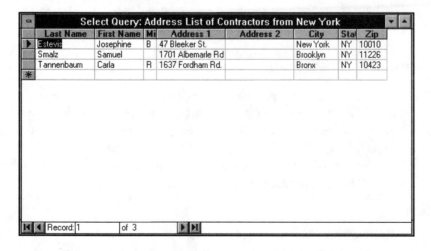

FIGURE 4.11   THE RESULT OF THE QUERY.

Only the name and address fields are displayed, all the state fields have the value NY, and the records are alphabetized by name.

More Complex Queries

Now that you have looked at all of the basics of creating a query with a simple criteria, you can look at more complex criteria that can add more power to your query. There are two major ways in which you can use criteria more powerfully:

❏ You can use a criterion based on an *expression* (a special type of formula) rather than on a simple value such as NY. You can use expressions to find values greater or less than the value you specify, for example, and you can use them to do queries based on the current date rather than entering a specific date.

❏ You can use multiple criteria for a single query. Rather than simply finding records in the state of New York, for example, you can find records for New York and New Jersey, or you can find only the people in New York who are programmers.

Because you have learned how to use the Select Query window, the examples that follow show only the design of the query, without step-by-step instructions on how to create each query.

You should have no trouble creating and running the following query designs on your own, and you should do so, at least for some of the queries, to become more familiar with how queries work.

Expressions in Queries

Expressions are a complex topic discussed at length in Chapter 8. In this chapter, we look at a few features of Access expressions that are useful in queries. Though Access includes an *Expression Builder*, which helps you to create complex expressions, the expressions you need for most queries are so simple that it is easier to type them in than to use the Expression Builder. For this reason, the Expression Builder is also described in Chapter 8.

LITERALS

So far, you have used only the simple criterion "NY" in queries. This sort of criterion is called a *literal*, because it is the actual, literal value that you are searching for.

You have already seen that:

❑ *text literals* must be surrounded by the " (quotation marks) delimiter.

❑ *date literals* must be surrounded by the # (pound sign) delimiter.

❑ *number literals* do not need delimiters and must not include the currency sign or number separators.

In Queries, Access automatically adds necessary delimiters to literals.

Constants

Access also has a few special literals called *constants*, which are often useful in queries. Do not use delimiters for constants.

You have already looked at Yes, True, No, and False, which are used as criteria in Yes/No fields. For example, to find all contractors who are available for emergencies, use the query shown in Figure 4.12.

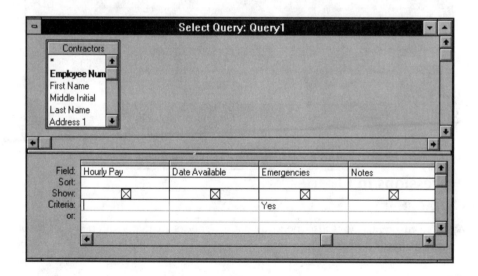

FIGURE 4.12 A QUERY FOR A LOGICAL FIELD.

Finding Empty Fields

In addition, Access uses the constant *Null* for empty fields. You can enter it as a criterion for a field to find all records that have nothing entered in that field.

In your sample database, for example, you do not enter a value in the Date Available field unless contractors tell you they are not available. You can find all the contractors who have never said they are unavailable by using the query shown in Figure 4.13. Access automatically adds the operator *Is* when you use the criterion *Null*. Note though that this query would not find contractors who were unavailable previously and now are available. To do that, you would have to use a query with a logical *OR*, which is discussed later in this chapter.

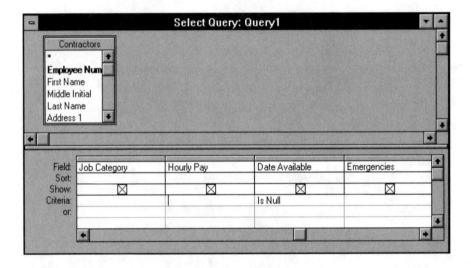

FIGURE 4.13   A QUERY TO FIND AN EMPTY FIELD.

OPERATORS

Apart from literals, you also need to use operators in many queries. Operators let you search for more than a single value.

Comparison

It is most common to use a simple literal criterion such as "NY" when you are search a text field. When you are searching fields of other data types, you often want to find a range of values rather than an exact match. To do this, you use the *comparison operators* shown in Table 4.1.

TABLE 4.1 THE COMPARISON OPERATORS.	
OPERATOR	MEANING
=	Is equal to
>	Is greater than
>=	Is greater than or equal to
<	Is less than
<=	Is less than or equal to
<>	Is not equal to

You are probably familiar with these operators from mathematics, but you should bear in mind that, in Access, they can be used with text and dates as well as with numbers.

For example, to display records for all the contractors who were not available previously and will be available by the third quarter of 1994, you can use the query shown in Figure 4.14. The criterion **<#10/1/94#** isolates records with an available date that is earlier than October 1, 1994, but as you can see in Figure 4.15, it does not include records that do not have a value entered in this field. To display all contractors who are available at that time, you would have to use a logical *OR*, discussed later in this chapter.

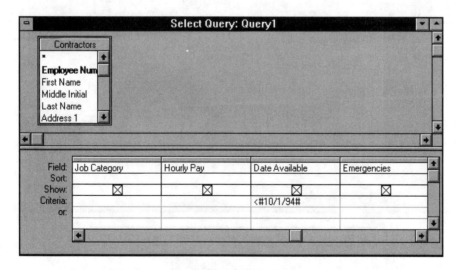

FIGURE 4.14   USING A COMPARISON OPERATOR IN A DATE FIELD.

Select Query: Query1										
Address 1	**Address 2**	**City**	**Sta**	**Zip**	**Job**	**Hourly F**	**Date A**	**Emerg**		**N**
▶ Star Consultants	4152 Front St., #31	Hoboken	NJ	07030	P	$80.00	7/1/94	No	Program
WordSmiths	910 University Ave.	Berkeley	CA	94709	W	$50.00	9/1/94	No	Complet
＊						$0.00			

Record: 1   of 2

FIGURE 4.15   THE RESULT OF THE QUERY.

It is often useful to use the <> (is not equal to) operator with text values. For example, you can use this operator to find all contractors who do not live in New York, as shown in Figure 4.16.

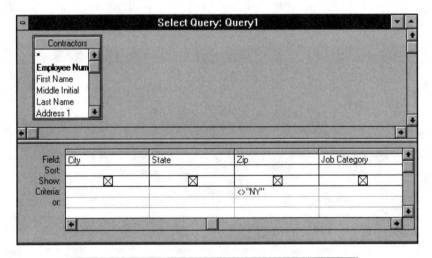

FIGURE 4.16 USING A COMPARISON OPERATOR IN A TEXT FIELD.

You can omit the = operator. The criterion "NY" is exactly equivalent to the criterion ="NY".

SHORTCUT

You can also omit the delimiters around the literal in any of these queries. Access adds them just as it does when only the literal is used as a criterion.

Between...And Operator

Access has another operator it classifies as *miscellaneous* rather than comparison, but it is a very useful addition to the comparison operators.

You can use the *Between...And* operator to find a range of values. For example, to find the records for all contractors who become available during the third quarter of 1994, you can use the criterion **Between #10/1/94# And #12/31/94#**.

This operator finds a range that includes the two values you entered in it. In the example, it would include records with the dates 10/1/94 and 12/31/94 and all those records with dates in between.

As you learn later in this chapter in the section "Logical AND," you can create an equivalent query using the comparison operator: *>= #10/1/94#* and *<= #12/31/94#*, but *Between ... And* is usually easier to use.

Wildcards: The Like Operator

Two wildcard characters you use with Searches (Finds) can also be used with constant values in queries:

❏   * represents any group of characters

❏   ? represents any single character

You must include the *Like* operator with these wildcard characters. When you enter a value that includes a wildcard in a criterion cell, however, Access automatically adds Like, just as it automatically adds delimiters. This, if you want to find all last names beginning with A, you can enter the criterion **A*** in the **Last Name** field. Access automatically displays this as **Like "A*"** when you leave the cell.

Searching for Part of Field's Value

Remember that the Find dialog box, discussed in Chapter 3, has the search options Start of Field, or Any Part of a Field, and Match Whole Field. In queries, you can use the * (asterisk) wildcard as the equivalent of these options. To match the start of a field, add the * after the criterion, and to match any part of a field, include the * before and after the criterion.

For example, to find everyone in a table who lives on Main St., you can enter the criterion ***Main*** in the Address field. As always, Access adds the Like operator and delimiters.

Querying Memo Fields

You almost always must use the * operator in order to query memo fields.

N O T E

For example, to find all contractors who program the user interface, use the query shown in Figure 4.17. Use the criterion ***interface*** to isolate all records that have the word "interface" anywhere in the memo field. As always, Access adds the Like operator and delimiters.

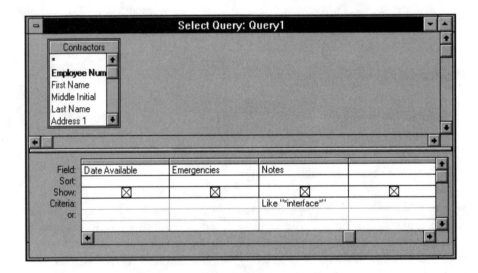

FIGURE 4.17   QUERYING A MEMO FIELD.

Arithmetic Calculations

Expressions can also include calculations using arithmetic operators. Table 4.2 includes the most useful of these operators, which are similar to symbols used in arithmetic and other computer programs.

TABLE 4.2	THE ARITHMETIC OPERATORS.
OPERATOR	MEANING
+	Addition
–	Subtraction
*	Multiplication
/	Division

The addition and subtraction operators can be used to perform calculations on dates. Numbers used in date calculations refer the number of days added to or subtracted from a date.

FUNCTIONS

Access functions are discussed in Chapter 8. In this chapter, we look at just one function that is particularly useful in queries.

The function *Date( )* returns the system date of your computer, which is the current date if your computer's clock/calendar is working properly.

Like all functions, *Date( )* must include the open and close parentheses after it to show Access that it is a function and not a text literal.

This function is invaluable in queries you use to identify records with time limits that have passed. For example, Figure 4.18 shows a query to identify contractors who have become available as of the current date. Using the Date( ) function, which automatically represents the current date, is obviously much easier than reentering the current date each time you run the query.

You can also do calculations using the *Date( )* function, as you can with other date values. For example, if you changed the criterion in the previous query to **< Date( ) + 30** instead of **< Date( )**, you would find all contractors who had already become available or would become available in the next 30 days.

The query in Figure 4.19 is even more precise. You can enter the criterion **Between Date( ) And Date( ) + 6** to isolate the records of contractors who are becoming available today or in the next six days. You could use this query to do a regular weekly mailing to all the contractors you expect to become available in the coming week.

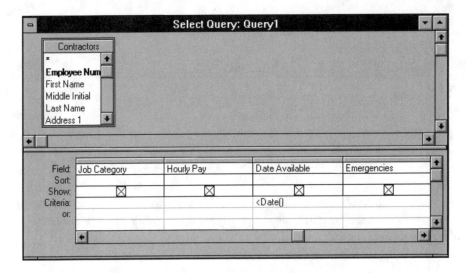

FIGURE 4.18   A QUERY USING THE *Date*( ) FUNCTION.

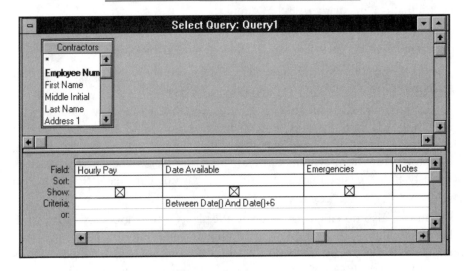

FIGURE 4.19   A QUERY USING DATE ARITHMETIC.

OBJECT NAMES

Access expressions can also include object names, such as names of fields and tables. For example, you can use field names for queries of relational databases where you want to compare the value in a field of one table with a value in another.

Using Multiple Criteria

Now that you have looked at how to use expressions to enter more powerful criteria in a single cell of the QBE grid, you should learn how to enter criteria in multiple cells.

There are two ways that multiple criteria may be used:

❑ *Logical AND* includes the record in the dynaset only if all the criteria are true.

❑ *Logical OR* includes the record if any one of the criteria is true.

Notice that *AND* and *OR* are used in a more precise sense here than they are in ordinary conversation. Ordinarily, for example, you could say you are looking for people from New York *or* New Jersey or just as easily say that you are looking for people from New York *and* New Jersey.

However, you must use a logical *OR* to find records from either state. The record qualifies if it has NY or NJ in the State field. If you used a logical *AND*, a record would qualify only if it had both NY and NJ in the State field, which is impossible.

Logical *AND* is *exclusive*. For each new criterion you add, there will be fewer records that match all the criteria.

Logical *OR* is *inclusive*. For each new criterion you add, there will be more records that match at least one criterion.

Logical *AND*

To search for records with values in more than one field, simply enter all the criteria under the appropriate fields on the Criteria line. Access considers this a logical AND, and it finds only those records that meet all the criteria.

For example, to find records of people who live in New York and who are also programmers, use the query shown in Figure 4.20. Access isolates only those records that meet both criteria.

Logical *OR*

To search for records that have several values in a field, list the first value in the criteria field, and each additional value in an *OR* field.

For example, you can find all of the contractors who are currently available by using the query shown in Figure 4.21. Under the Date Available field, type

Null in the *Criteria* field and **< Date ( )** in the *or* field. This query isolates records that have no entry in the Date Available field or an entry that is earlier than the current date.

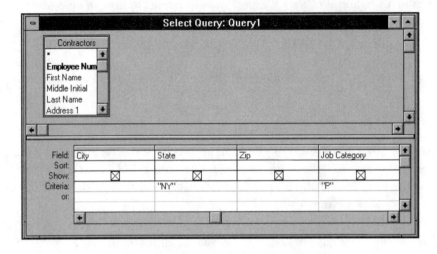

FIGURE 4.20 A QUERY USING A LOGICAL *AND*.

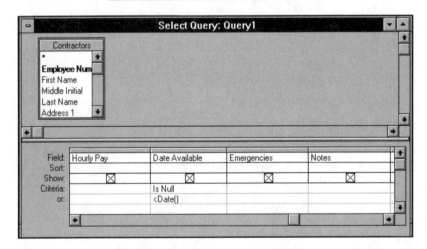

FIGURE 4.21   A QUERY USING A LOGICAL *OR*.

COMBINING *AND* AND *OR*

You can combine logical *AND* with logical *OR* by entering several rows of criteria, each with criteria entered under several fields.

For example, Figure 4.22 shows a query to find all the people who are currently available, are programmers, and are available in an emergency.

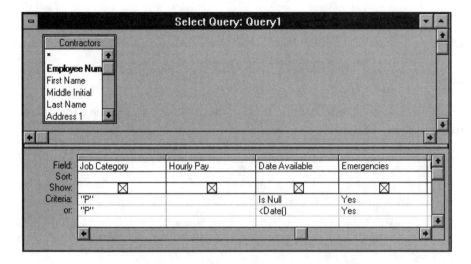

FIGURE 4.22   A QUERY COMBINING AND WITH OR.

In this sort of query, Access reads each row and finds only the records that match all the criteria on the row. Thus, the query finds the records that match all the criteria in any row.

THE LOGICAL OPERATORS

You can create most queries you want by entering criteria in the QBE grid as described above. However, there are cases where it is easier or more powerful to use logical operators, which are listed in Table 4.3.

TABLE 4.3   THE LOGICAL OPERATORS.

OPERATOR	MEANING
And	Both criteria must be true to match
Or	Either criterion must be true to match
Xor	One of the criteria but not both must be true to match
Not	The criterion must be untrue to match

The *Xor* operator is used in programming and advanced expressions.

The *Not* operator reverses the expression that follows it. If an expression is true but is preceded by Not, it matches all records where the expression is false. If an expression is false and is preceded by Not, it matches all records where the expression is true. For example, *Not Between Date( ) and Date( ) + 6* would match all dates that are not in the next week.

The And Operator

You must use the And operator if you want to enter two criteria for a single field.

This can be used to isolate a range of values, in the same way that the Between...And operator does. For example, the query in Figure 4.23 finds contractors who become available in the week beginning today. The value in the Date Available field must match both criteria. It must be greater than or equal to (>=) the current date and also less than or equal to (<=) date( ) + 6. This is equivalent to the criterion Between Date( ) And Date( ) + 6, which you learned about earlier.

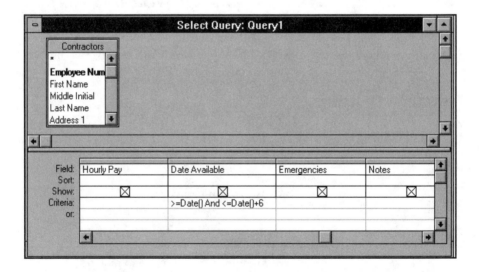

FIGURE 4.23   USING THE AND OPERATOR TO FIND A RANGE OF VALUES.

You could not enter this query by using different cells of the QBE grid to represent the logical AND. It requires the And operator.

Use the logical And operator with comparison operators to find a range of values. Do not use the And operator with two literals. For example, you will not find any records if you use the criterion *NY And NJ* in the State field because there are not any records that have both NY and NJ entered in that field.

The Or Operator

The Or operator is used as a convenience. If you are combining logical AND with logical OR, it is easier to use the Or operator than it is to rewrite all the criteria for several fields.

For example, Figure 4.24 shows two ways of finding all the people who live in New York, New Jersey or Connecticut; are programmers; and are available in an emergency.

In a query like this, which combines many conditions, it is easier to use the Or operator than to enter all the data in each row.

Field:	State	Zip	Job Category	Hourly Pa	Date A\	Emergencies
Sort:						
Show:	☒	☒	☒	☒	☒	☒
Criteria:	"NY"		"P"			Yes
or:	"NJ"		"P"			Yes
	"CT"		"P"			Yes

Field:	State	Zip	Job Category	Hourly Pa	Date A\	Emergencies
Sort:						
Show:	☒	☒	☒	☒	☒	☒
Criteria:	"NY" Or "NJ" Or "CT"		"P"			Yes
or:						

FIGURE 4.24   THE OR OPERATOR IS EASIER TO USE THAN MULTIPLE ROWS.

The Quickest Reports: Printing the Dynaset

In Chapters 5 and 9, you learn to create presentation quality reports. However, if you need to print a report for your own use, the quickest way is by doing a query and printing the dynaset.

After running the query and displaying it in Datasheet View, you can manipulate the datasheet as you do a table in Datasheet View. You can use the Format menu to change font, row height, column width, and to hide, show, freeze, and unfreeze columns, using the same methods that you learned in Chapter 3.

You can also print the dynaset by choosing **Print** from the File menu. Use the Print and Print Setup dialog boxes exactly as you do when you are printing a table, as described in Chapter 3.

Filters

As you know, queries are independent objects, listed in the Database window along with tables and other objects.

There are times when it is easier to incorporate the features of a query into another object rather than creating a query as a separate object. By using a *filter*, you can incorporate the features of a query into a table or form, without creating a separate query object. The filter is temporary and is discarded when you close a table or form, unless you save it as a query.

NOTE

If you have used a filter before doing a Find, Access will search through only the records that are still displayed. If Access cannot find a record you know you entered, it is probably because you have used a filter.

To work with a filter, display the table or form window you want it to be based on. When working with filters, you can use the Edit Filter/Sort, Apply Filter/Sort, and Show All Records options from the Records menu. You can also use the equivalent toolbar tools shown in Figure 4.25.

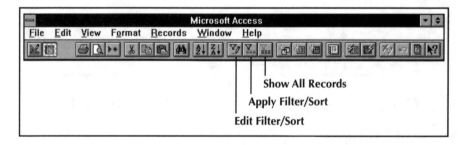

FIGURE 4.25   TOOLS FOR WORKING WITH FILTERS.

Using a Filter

To create a new filter or edit an existing one, display the object it applies to and choose **Edit Filter/Sort** from the Records menu. Access displays the Filter window shown in Figure 4.26.

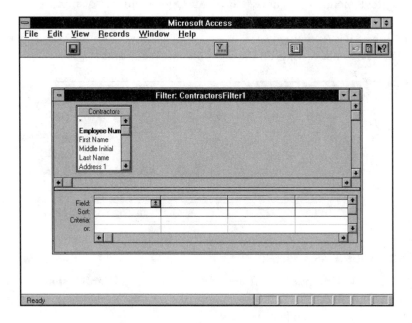

FIGURE 4.26   THE FILTER WINDOW.

As you can see, the Filter window is almost identical to the Select Query window. It automatically includes a field list with the fields of the underlying table or query. You can add the fields to be displayed to columns, specify the fields to sort on, and enter criteria to determine which records are displayed just as you do when you are designing a query.

After you have designed the filter, you must apply it by choosing **Apply Filter/Sort** from the Records menu. You can also click on the Filter window with the right mouse button to display a shortcut menu from which you can select **Apply Filter/Sort**. A filter is not applied automatically when you close the Filter window.

You can remove the filter by selecting **Show All Records** from the Records menu. This option restores the original order of the records and displays all records and fields.

SAVING A FILTER AS A QUERY

Filters are temporary and are lost when you close the object they are based on. If you think a filter will be useful in the future, you can save it as a query.

To save it, click on the Filter window with the right mouse button to display the shortcut menu, and choose **Save As Query**. Access displays the Save As Query dialog box shown in Figure 4.27. Enter the name for the query, as you do with all the Save As dialog boxes in Access. This new query will be displayed in the Database window and can be used like any other query.

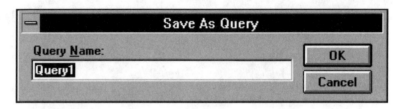

FIGURE 4.27   THE SAVE AS QUERY DIALOG BOX.

USING A QUERY AS A FILTER

Rather than designing a filter from scratch, you can use an existing query as a filter. The query must be a Select Query based solely on the table or query you want to apply it to as a filter.

❑ Click on the Filter window with the right mouse button to display the shortcut menu, and choose **Load from Query**. Access displays the Applicable Filter dialog box shown in Figure 4.28, with a list of queries that can be applied as filters to this object.

❑ Select a query from this list and select **OK**. The Filter window is automatically filled in with the same definition as that Query window. Then you can apply the query in the usual way.

Quick Sorts

If you only want to change the sort order of the records temporarily and not enter criteria, the easiest way of doing it is by using a *Quick Sort*. Figure 4.29 shows the Quick Sort tools and the table sorted alphabetically by last name.

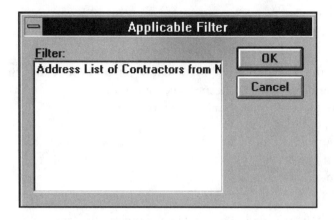

FIGURE 4.28   THE APPLICABLE FILTER DIALOG BOX.

FIGURE 4.29   A QUICK SORT BASED ON LAST NAME.

To do a quick sort, put the cursor in any record in the field you want the sort to be based on. Then do the following:

❏ Click the **Sort Up** tool (or choose **Quick Sort** and then **Ascending** from the Records menu) to sort the records in ascending order.

❏ Click the **Sort Down** tool (or choose **Quick Sort** and then **Descending** from the Records menufrom the Records menu) to sort the records in descending order.

The Sort Up tool has an *A* at its top and a *Z* at its bottom, while the Sort Down tool has a *Z* at its top and an *A* at its bottom, indicating the order of the sort.

N O T E

This sort is only temporary and is lost when you close the table.

Using Indexes

There are times when you should index a table to speed up a query or sort. To know when to create an index, you should understand a bit about how they work.

What is an Index?

An *index* of a database table is very much like an index of a book.

A book's index is an alphabetical list of topics in the book, with the page number for each. It is easier to look up the topic in the index and then go the page it is on than it is to look through the entire book page by page until you find the topic.

Likewise, a table's index is an ordered list of all the values in a field (or several fields) of the table, with pointers to the record where each value appears. For example, an index could be an alphabetical list of all the last names in a table, with a pointer to the record in which each name appears. It is faster for Access to look up the last name in the index and then go to the record it points to than to read through every record in the table until it finds the name.

The primary key of an Access table is automatically indexed, and Access can use this index to speed up many of its operations. That is why it encourages you so strongly to include a primary key in each table.

You can also create indexes for other fields that are used in finds, query criteria, or Sorts. If you create the index, Access uses it to speed up performance.

Advantages and Disadvantages of Indexing

Why doesn't Access just create indexes automatically when you do a find or query, so they are ready to reuse when you do the find or query again?

There is a disadvantage to creating too many indexes. When you enter or edit data, Access automatically updates indexes, and it takes a tiny amount of time to update each. If you have a few indexes, you do not notice the time it takes to update them. Updating occurs more quickly than you can type. If you have a large number of indexes in a table with many records, however, the time it takes to update them slows down Access enough that you find yourself waiting as you do data entry.

For this reason, you should create indexes for only those fields that are the basis of finds, queries, and sorts that you use frequently.

If you are always looking up people by last name, for example, you should index on the last name field to speed up the find.

If you often print mailing labels in Zip Code order and reports in alphabetical order by name, you could create an index on the Zip field and another on the Last Name and the First Name field.

However, you should not create indexes for finds, sorts, or queries that you do only occasionally.

NOTE

Indexing a Single Field

To create or remove an index based on a single field, open the table in Design View and select a value for the Indexed property. There are three options for this property:

- ❏   *No* means there is no index based on the field. This is the default.
- ❏   *Yes (Duplicates OK)* creates an index based on the field and lets you enter the same value in any number of records in the field.
- ❏   *Yes (No Duplicates)* creates an index based on the field and does not let you enter a value in the field if that value has already been entered in another record.

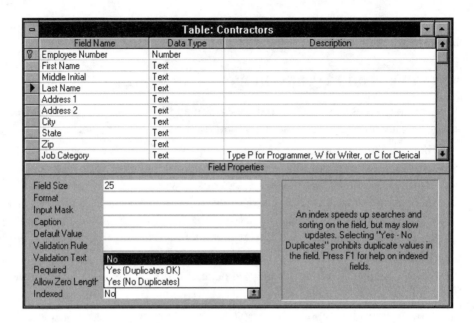

FIGURE 4.30   INDEXING ON A SINGLE FIELD.

You cannot create indexes for Memo, Yes/No or, OLE Object fields.

N O T E

Yes (No Duplicates) is the type of index that is used for the primary key. You must enter a unique value for the primary key in each record. When you designate a field as a primary key, it is automatically given this index property, and you cannot change its index property as long as it remains a primary key.

You should select **Yes (Duplicates OK)** to speed up searches and sorts based on the field.

Indexes you create in this way are included in the Indexes window, which is discussed next.

Indexing on Multiple Fields

To create an index based on multiple fields, display the table in Design View, and choose **Indexes** from the View menu or click the **Indexes** tool. The Indexes window is displayed, as shown in Figure 4.31.

FIGURE 4.31   THE INDEXES WINDOW.

Enter a name for the index in the Index Name column. Use the drop-down list in the Field Name column to select a field on which to base the index. Use the drop-down list in the Sort Order column to specify whether the field should be indexed in **Ascending** or **Descending** order. Continue selecting Field Names and Sort Orders in the rows below the Index name. All field names and sort orders that do not have an index name are used as part of the index whose name is above them. As with sorts, the first field used is the primary field that the index is based on, and fields that follow are used as tie-breakers.

In Figure 4.31, for example, there is a primary key, an index named Names, and an index named Zip. Names is based on the Last Name, First Name, and Middle Initial fields, and is used to speed up alphabetical sorts by name. All these fields are part of the Names index because they do not have their own entries in the Index Name column.

Index Properties

You can set the following index properties in the Index window:

❑ *Primary Key*: the index is the primary key. Only one index can have this property.

❑ *Unique*: unique values must be entered in the field. This property is equivalent to selecting Yes (No Duplicates) when you create the index.

❏ *Allow Nulls*: a value must be entered in the field if you select No for this property. It cannot be left blank. This property is automatically No for the Primary Key.

To Sum Up

In this chapter, you learned to use Select Queries. These are the most important type of query in Access because they can be used instead of tables as the basis of reports or forms.

The result of a Select Query is a *dynaset*. The fields and records that you specify are a *dynamic subset* of the table, and changes you make in them are also made in the original table.

You learned to use the Query window in Design View to specify which fields are included in the dynaset, and to use the column of the QBE grid under each field to specify whether that field should be displayed or used as the basis of sort order. You also learned to enter simple or complex criteria under the fields in the QBE grid to include only fields that have certain values in those fields in the dynaset.

Finally, you learned about Quick Sorts, Filters, and Indexes, which use the same concepts as Select Queries.

In the next chapter, you learn to create forms and reports.

Fast Forms,
Graphs, Reports,
and Mailing Labels

*I*n Chapters 1 through 4, you learned to design tables, add and edit data, and use queries to define what data is displayed. In this chapter you learn to use forms and reports to define how data is displayed.

When you design a form or report, you control how your data is laid out. Forms are used primarily to display and edit data on the screen, and reports are designed primarily to be printed. In this short chapter, you learn:

❏   to create AutoForms

❏   to create single-column forms

❏   to create tabular forms

❏   to create simple graphs

- ❑ to create single-column reports
- ❑ to create tabular reports
- ❑ to create mailing labels
- ❑ to work with forms and reports from the Database Window
- ❑ to work with the Print Preview window

Like other database management programs, Access includes windows that let you design custom forms and reports. You can control the exact location of fields and add the text and graphic enhancements you want in the design. Access also has a feature that is missing from other database management programs: the Form and ReportWizards let you fill out dialog boxes and then do the work of designing a form or report for you.

These wizards are sophisticated enough that many users can get by without designing custom forms or reports. For this reason, custom forms and reports are covered in Chapters 7 and 9 in Part II of this book. Part I is meant to let you work with Access as easily as possible, and so this chapter covers Access' AutoForms and AutoReports and its FormWizards and ReportWizards, which you can learn about almost effortlessly.

Using Forms

As you know, you can view and enter data directly in Access tables. However, this is sometimes inconvenient because you usually cannot see all the fields of a record at the same time.

Forms let you redesign the display to make it easier to view on the screen. Though you can print forms—they sometimes are a valuable addition to your printed reports—they are meant primarily to be viewed on the screen.

The easiest form to use is the *AutoForm*, which you can create by clicking a single button. The FormWizards let you create more sophisticated forms very easily, including bar graphs, pie graphs, and other graphics. Access considers graphs to be forms because they are meant to be displayed on the screen, though they can also be very valuable as printed output.

AutoForms

An AutoForm, as you can see in Figure 5.1, displays the fields of each record one above another, rather than side by side, as they are displayed in the

Datasheet View of a table or query. This form lets you see all or most of the fields of a record displayed on the screen, though it does not let you view many records at a time, as a table does.

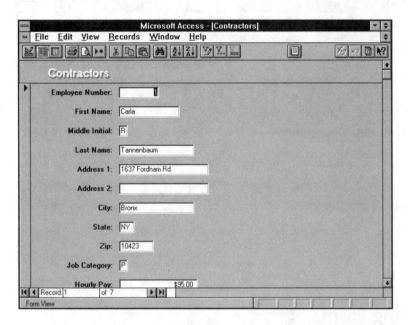

FIGURE 5.1 THE AUTOFORM FOR THE CONTRACTORS TABLE.

To create an AutoForm, simply select the table or query in the Database window that you want it to be based on and click the **AutoForm** tool shown in Figure 5.2.

FIGURE 5.2 THE AUTOFORM TOOL.

You should create an AutoForm, so you have it to look at while you read about the features of the Form window in the next section:

1. If necessary, open the Database window or click the **Table** button. Select the **Contractors** table in the Tables list.

2. Click the **AutoForm** tool. After taking a moment to generate it, Access
    displays the AutoForm for this table, as shown in Figure 5.3.

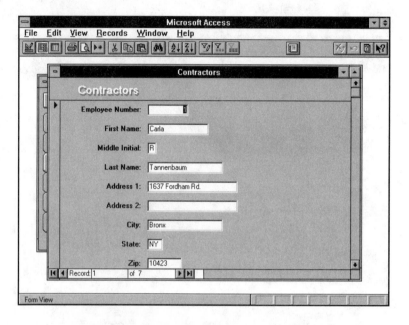

FIGURE 5.3   CREATING AN AUTOFORM.

3. Choose **Save** from the File menu. Access displays the familiar Save As
    dialog box. As the Form Name, type **Contractors: AutoForm** and press
    Enter.

If you scroll down, you will see that the AutoForm automatically creates a
checkbox for the Emergencies field, as this is the easiest way of entering data in
a Yes/No field.

Creating and Using Forms

Apart from AutoForms, you create and use forms in the same way you do other
objects. First, you must click the **Form** button of the Database window to display the Forms list, and then use the Database window's buttons:

❑ To create a new form, click the **New** button.
❑ To use an existing form, select it and select the **Open** button.

❏ To change the design of a form (using the methods described in Chapter 7), select it and select the **Design** button.

You also save and name forms as you do other objects, using the File menu and then **Save**, and then the Save As dialog box.

When you create a new form in this way, Access displays the New Form dialog box, shown in Figure 5.4.

FIGURE 5.4   THE NEW FORM DIALOG BOX.

First you must use the drop-down list in this dialog box to select the table or query that the form is based on. Then select the **Blank Form** button to create a custom form from scratch (using the methods described in Chapter 7), or select the **FormWizards** button to have Access design the form for you.

As with other objects, you can also create a form by selecting a table or query in the Database window and selecting the **New Form** tool (or choosing **New** and then **Form** from the File menu). Access displays the New Form dialog box with that table or query already entered in its drop-down list.

It is important to remember that a form can be based on a query as well as on a table. If you want to specify which records are displayed in a form or to specify their sort order, begin by creating a query that includes the appropriate records, using the methods described in Chapter 4. As you will see, you can also add a filter to a form, as you do to a table, which acts as a temporary Query.

THE FORMWIZARDS

Each of the FormWizards is a series of dialog boxes which let you enter information that is used to generate your form.

When you select the **FormWizards** button, Access displays a dialog box that lets you choose among the wizards available to design different types of forms.

Once you select one of these, Access displays a series of FormWizard dialog boxes such as the one shown in Figure 5.5. Each of these lets you make choices to specify certain features of the form and includes directions on how it is used.

FIGURE 5.5   USING A FORMWIZARD.

Each dialog box has the same buttons at the bottom which you use to navigate among all the dialog boxes of the FormWizard:

❑ *Next >* displays the next dialog box. Select this button after you have filled out each dialog box. When you get to the last one in the sequence, this button is dimmed.

❑ *< Back* displays the previous dialog box, so you can change specifications you entered earlier.

❑ *Finish* leaves the Wizard and creates the form.

❑ *Cancel* leaves the Wizard and discards your work.

❑ *Hint* provides help on the current dialog box.

The final dialog box of any FormWizard has radio buttons that let you generate the form and display it with data or display it in Design View, so you can customize its design. Design View is covered in Chapter 7. By default, the form is displayed with data when you select the **Finish** button.

After the FormWizard generates a form, you must save and name it in the usual way. Select **Save** from the File menu, and enter the new name in the Save As dialog box, following the usual Access naming conventions that you used to name a table.

Types of Form

When you begin creating a new form and select the **FormWizards** button, Access displays the dialog box shown in Figure 5.6, which lets you choose among the available FormWizards.

FIGURE 5.6   CHOOSING A FORMWIZARD.

If you select **AutoForm**, Access does not display any additional dialog boxes. It automatically creates a form that is identical to the AutoForm.

The Main/Subform wizard is used when you are working on relational databases. The main form holds the fields from one table and includes a subform area with fields from the second table. This wizard is covered in Chapter 6.

The other wizards—which let you create forms with fields one above another, forms with fields side by side, and graphs—are covered next.

SINGLE-COLUMN FORMS

A single-column form has fields arranged one above the other, like an AutoForm, but the wizard lets you specify which fields are included, what order they are displayed in, and the graphic style and title the form has.

This FormWizard begins by displaying the dialog box shown in Figure 5.7, which lets you select the fields to include in the form. Select a field in the **Available fields** box and click the > button to move it to the **Field order on form** box, or click the >> to move all the fields. When you move a field in this way, it is removed from the Available fields list.

FIGURE 5.7   CHOOSING THE FIELDS TO INCLUDE.

Likewise, you can select a field in the **Field order on form** box and click < the button to remove it from this box and restore it to the **Available fields** box. Select the << button to remove all the fields and start over.

You also can double-click a field to move it to or remove it from the **Field order on form** list.

SHORTCUT

As its name implies, the order of the fields in the Field order on form box determines their order in the form. Many FormWizards and ReportWizards have a similar field picker dialog box.

Next, the wizard displays a dialog box with radio buttons that let you choose the graphic style you want for your form. The options are *Standard*,

Chiseled, Shadowed, Boxed, and *Embossed.* Access displays the style you select in the magnifying glass in this dialog box.

Finally, the wizard displays the dialog box shown in Figure 5.8, which lets you enter a title for the form. Virtually all FormWizards and ReportWizards have this same final dialog box.

FIGURE 5.8   THE FINAL DIALOG BOX.

If you select the **Open CueCards** checkbox, Access automatically displays cue cards to help the user when this form is opened. Most forms are simple enough to use that this is not necessary.

If you select the **Modify the form's design** radio button, the form will be displayed in Design View when you click the **Finish** button to create it, so that you can customize its design. It is common to begin creating custom forms and reports by using a wizard, and then make further changes to them in Design View.

Figure 5.9 shows a form created by this wizard that has a shadowed style.

TABULAR FORMS

The wizard that you use to create tabular forms displays the same dialog boxes as the wizard that you use to create single-column forms.

Use them in the way described in the previous section to specify the fields included in the form, the order in which they are displayed, the graphic style of the form, and so on.

When you generate the form, this wizard creates a form with the fields side by side and multiple records visible. Figure 5.10 shows a form created by this wizard that has an embossed style (which is the default style used on forms).

FIGURE 5.9   A SINGLE-COLUMN FORM.

FIGURE 5.10   A TABULAR FORM.

GRAPHS

When you select Graph after creating a new form, Access displays the GraphWizard. Graphs you can create using Access wizards have many advanced features that are beyond the scope of this book, but it is very easy to create simple graphs.

This wizard begins with a dialog box that lets you select fields from the table to use as the basis for the graph. You must choose at least one numeric field with the values to be graphed, though you may also graph multiple numeric fields. You may also select a field to use as the labels for the graph. For example, you might add the Hourly Pay and Last Name fields from the Contractors table to produce a graph of contractors' pay rates, with their last names used as labels.

Simply add these fields to the **Fields to be graphed** list and click the **Next >** button. The following dialog boxes let you choose what calculation you want and what type of graph you want, as shown in Figure 5.11, and let you add a title and legend to your chart. Access generates the graph and displays it in its default style.

These features are all easy to use. For example, it is obvious, simply by looking at the illustration, how you use it to select chart type.

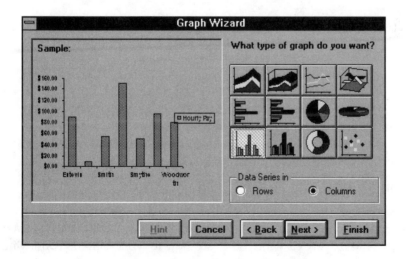

FIGURE 5.11   THE CHARTWIZARD.

Figure 5.12 shows the default graph of contractors' hourly pay rates. You can create this graph effortlessly, simply by adding the **Hourly Pay** and **Last Name** fields to the GraphWizard's **Fields for Graph** list, and keeping the default settings for the other dialog boxes.

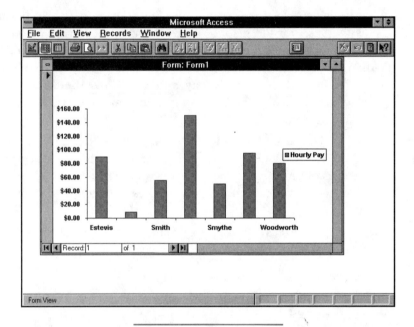

FIGURE 5.12   A SIMPLE GRAPH.

The final dialog box contains a checkbox that you can select to display cue cards with information on how to customize the graph.

Working with Data in the Form Window

Given what you already know about working with the table and Query windows, it should be very easy for you to see how to work with the Form window after you are done creating a form, simply by looking at its toolbar and some of its other features, shown in Figure 5.13.

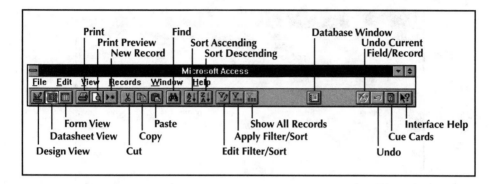

FIGURE 5.13   THE TOOLBAR FOR THE FORM WINDOW.

SWITCHING AMONG VIEWS

Notice that the toolbar includes a Form View tool on its left, in addition to the usual Design View and Datasheet View tools that you are familiar with from working with the Table Window.

❑ Click the **Design View** tool (or choose **Form Design** from the View menu) to work with the Form window in Design View so you can move objects, add graphics, and so on. It should *not* be confused with the Design View tool for the Table window, which lets you change the definitions and properties of fields. Chapter 7 covers Design View for forms.

❑ Click the **Form View** tool (or choose **Form** from the View menu) to switch back to Form View.

❑ Click the **Datasheet View** tool (or choose **Datasheet** from the View menu) to display the form as a table, as shown in Figure 5.14. Notice that Access displays the same toolbar when you display the form in Datasheet View as it does when you are in Form View. You can work with a form in Datasheet View just as you do in Form View. Though it is displayed as a table, you should not confuse a form in Datasheet View with a table in Datasheet View.

N O T E

It is easiest to work with most simple, single-table databases by creating an AutoForm and using it as the main object you work with. Then you can use these tools to toggle easily from Form View to Table View, and it is usually most convenient to be able to work with both of these at different times.

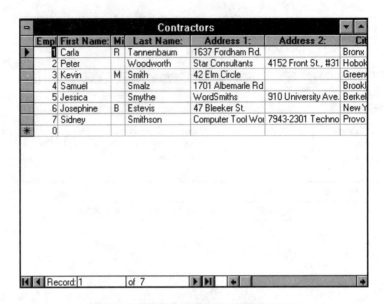

FIGURE 5.14 A FORM IN DATASHEET VIEW.

PRINTING THE FORM

To print the form, simply click the **Print** tool or choose **Print** from the File menu. Access displays the Print dialog box (covered in Chapter 3), as it does when you print a table or a query.

Before printing the form, you may want to click the **Print Preview** tool or choose **Print Preview** from the File menu to display the form in the Print Preview window, as shown in Figure 5.15. As you can see, the Print Preview window has its own toolbar. Because it is more common to print reports than forms, this toolbar is covered later in this chapter. You can close this window in any of the usual ways to return to the Form window.

OTHER FEATURES OF THE FORM WINDOW

Other features of the Form window are the same as those of the Table window, and are described next.

The Toolbar

You are already familiar with the remaining tools of the Form window:

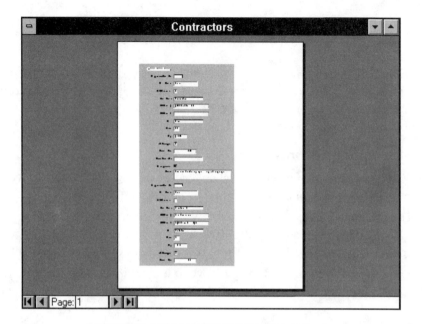

FIGURE 5.15   A FORM IN PRINT PREVIEW MODE.

❑   Click the **Save Record** tool (or choose **Save Record** from the File menu) to save changes on a record while you are still working on it, rather than waiting for Access to save the changes automatically when you switch records.

❑   Click the **New Record** tool (or choose **GoTo**, and then **New** from the Records menu) to add a new record.

❑   Click one of the two quick **Sort** tools (or choose **Quick Sort** from the Records menu) to do a quick sort of the records.

❑   Click the **Filter** tools (or choose **Edit Filter/Sort**, **Apply Filter/Sort**, or **Show All Records** from the Records menu) to add a filter, edit a filter, or remove the filter and show all records. You use filters with forms just as you do with tables, as described in Chapter 4.

❑   Click the **Database Container** tool (or choose **Database** from the Window menu) to display the Database window.

❑   Click the **Undo Current Field/Record** tool (or choose **Undo Current Field/Record** from the Edit menu) to restore the previous value in the current field or record.

❏ Click the **Undo** tool (or choose **Undo** from the Edit menu) to undo the last editing change you made.

The only difference between the toolbar for forms and tables is that the tables have tools that let you create a new query, form, or report and an AutoForm or AutoReport. These are omitted from the Form window's toolbar because you cannot create forms, reports, or queries based on forms.

Moving among Records

You also navigate among records when you are using a form just as you do when you are using a table, as described in Chapter 3.

Use the record indicator and arrow tools at the bottom of the window (or the equivalent **GoTo** commands in the Records menu) to move to the first record, previous record, next record, last record, or a record whose number you enter.

From the Edit menu, use **Find** to move to a record based on the contents of a field, and **Replace** to change the contents of a field, just as you do with a table.

Creating a Sample Form

To get a feel for the FormWizards, you should try creating a simple but useful sample form, which includes all the fields of the Contractor table except for the Employee Number field. Since the employee number is in a counter field, which is entered automatically, this form could be used by people who routinely enter and look up data, to make sure that they do not change an employee number by mistake.

1. If necessary, close the AutoForm you created earlier or click the **Form** button to display the Form list in the Database window. With the Form list displayed, select the **New** button of the Database window.

2. In the New Form dialog box, use the **Select A Table/Query** drop-down list to select **Contractors**, and click the **FormWizards** button. Then, select **Single Column** as the FormWizard you want and select **OK**.

3. The first dialog box lets you select the fields. Click the **>>** button to add all fields to the form. Then, with the **Employee Number** selected in the **Field order on form** list, select the **<** button to remove it from the form. Click the **Next >** button.

4. In the next dialog box, select the **Chiseled** style for the form, and click the **Next >** button.

5. In the next dialog box, enter the title **Contractors Data Entry**, and click the **Finish** button to create the form.

6. Click the **Maximize** button of the Form window to display all the fields of the new form, as shown in Figure 5.16. Choose **Save Form** from the File menu. When the Save As dialog box is displayed, enter **Contractors Data Entry** as the form name and select **OK**. Try using this form, and then close the Form window when you are done.

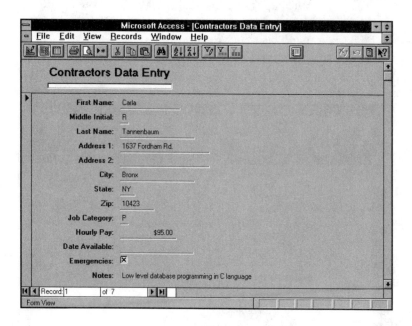

FIGURE 5.16   THE NEW FORM.

Using Reports

In Access, a report is any output designed specifically to be printed. Thus, the ReportWizard lets you create mailing labels as well as other types of printed reports.

Because a report is meant to be printed, Access displays it in the Print Preview window when you view it. Because you cannot display them in Datasheet View, you cannot edit data displayed in reports, as you do data in tables, queries, and forms.

The Print Preview window is the same as the window that is displayed when you are viewing a table, query or form in Datasheet View and you choose **Print Preview** from the File menu (or click the **Print Preview** tool). It is described at length at the end of this chapter.

AutoReports

You can create an AutoReport in the same way that you create an AutoForm. Select the table or query in the Database window that you want it to be based on and click the **AutoReport** tool.

As you can see in Figure 5.17, an AutoReport simply lists the field names and the contents of the fields one above another.

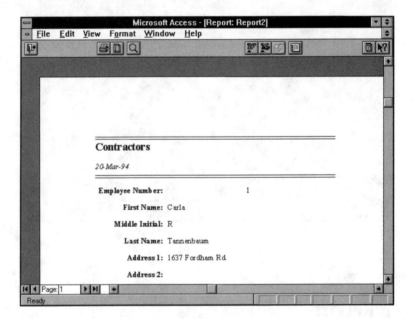

FIGURE 5.17   THE AUTOREPORT ON THE CONTRACTORS TABLE.

Because this layout is not easy to read, the AutoReport feature is not generally useful for reports on tables. It can be very useful, however, if you create a query that includes only a few fields you want to display and use it as the basis of the AutoReport. Of course, you can also use the query to specify which records to include in the report and their sort order.

Creating and Using Reports

You create and use reports in the same way you do forms and other objects, with the difference that, because they are meant to be printed, you view their contents in the Print Preview window rather than in Datasheet View.

After you click the **Report** button of the Database window to display the Report list, the Database window has the following buttons:

❑ *New* creates a new report.

❑ *Preview* opens an existing report, and displays it in the Print Preview window.

❑ *Design* lets you change the design of a report (using the methods described in Chapter 7).

You save and name reports as you do other objects, by choosing **Save** from the File menu.

When you click the **New** button, Access displays the New Report dialog box, shown in Figure 5.18, which is like the New Form dialog box. As with forms, you use the drop-down list in this dialog box to select the table or query that the report is based on. Then click the **Blank Form** button to create a custom form from scratch (using methods described in Chapter 7), or select the **FormWizards** button to have Access design the form for you.

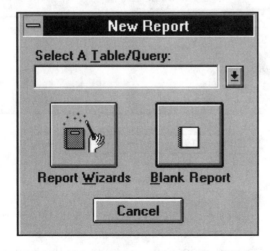

FIGURE 5.18 THE NEW REPORT DIALOG BOX.

As with forms, you can also create a report by selecting a table or query in the Database window and selecting the **New Report** tool (or choosing **New**, and then **Report** from the File menu) to display the New Report dialog box with that table or query already entered in its drop-down list.

N O T E

You will often want to base a report on a query rather than on a table, in order to specify which records are displayed in a form or to specify their sort order. Begin by creating a query that includes the appropriate records, using the methods described in Chapter 4. For example, you might want to create a report just for the hours worked by contractors who are programmers. You would begin by creating a query with **"P"** as the criterion in the Job Category column of the QBE grid, and use this query as the basis of the report.

Types of Report

When you select the **ReportWizards** button in the New Report dialog box, Access displays the dialog box shown in Figure 5.19. You can then choose among the available Wizards.

FIGURE 5.19 SELECTING A REPORTWIZARD.

If you select AutoReport, it immediately creates a report like the AutoReport described above.

To create the types of reports described later in this chapter select an option in the drop-down list. A series of dialog boxes is displayed which you navigate using the same methods described in the section on the FormWizards earlier in this chapter.

SINGLE-COLUMN REPORTS

A single-column report displays field names and their contents one above the other. The wizard you use to create it is similar to the one you use for a single-column form.

The first dialog box lets you specify which fields will be included and what order to put them in, and the second dialog box lets you specify sort order.

The styles you can select in the next dialog box include **Executive**, **Presentation**, and **Ledger**. You an also specify line spacing, and choose **Portrait** or **Landscape** orientation. Landscape orientation, with the longer dimension of the paper used as its width, lets you get more fields across the page, and is useful for many reports.

The final dialog box, shown in Figure 5.20, lets you specify whether each new record should begin on a new page and whether the title should be printed on each page, two features that are useful for printing output. Its other features are like the features of the final dialog box of the FormWizard.

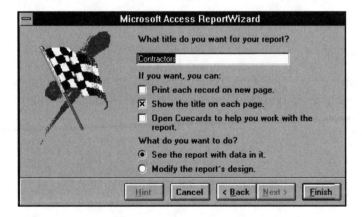

FIGURE 5.20   USING THE REPORTWIZARD.

Figure 5.21 shows a single-column report in Executive style that includes the names and addresses of your contractors.

TABULAR REPORTS

A tabular report, like a tabular form, displays the fields of each record side by side. This is the type of report that is most commonly used to print out the data in a table.

FIGURE 5.21   A SINGLE-COLUMN REPORT.

The dialog boxes of this wizard are the same as the ones used to create a single-column report. You define the report by selecting the fields, sort order, style, and so on. Because the fields are displayed side by side, printing in landscape orientation is selected by default.

In addition, the final dialog box has a **See all the fields on one page** checkbox. You should generally select this, so that Access narrows the columns to fit all the fields within the width of the page.

N O T E

Figure 5.22 shows a tabular report in Presentation style that includes the names and addresses of your contractors. Notice that it uses landscape orientation, so that all the fields fit on the page.

GROUPED REPORTS WITH TOTALS

The Groups/Totals ReportWizard is powerful enough to create reports with records divided into groups based on the content of specific fields, with subtotals of numeric fields for each group, and with a final total of numeric fields for the entire table.

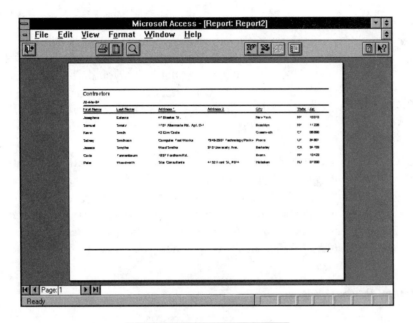

FIGURE 5.22   A TABULAR REPORT.

If you do not include fields to group on, the report provides only grand totals for the entire table or query it is based on.

You can select a single field to group on, and the report provides subtotals for that group and a grand total for the table. For example, you could produce a report on your contractors that groups them by job category.

You can also use multiple groups. For example, you can produce a report on contractors that groups them by state and, within each state, groups them by city and, within each city, groups them by zip code. You can use up to four groupings nested within each other in this way. The report includes a grand total, subtotals, and sub-subtotals for all groups. This wizard automatically includes subtotals and totals for all numeric fields you include in the report.

As with many other wizards, its first dialog box lets you select the fields to be included in the report. The second lets you select up to four fields to group by. The third lets you select the style of the report. The fourth lets you enter a title for the report and also includes the other usual features of the final dialog box of a wizard, such as letting you enter a title for the report.

NOTE

When you are creating this sort of report, remember that all numeric fields you include, even employee number, will be totaled for each group and for the entire report, unless you choose them as the field to group by. Do not include numeric fields that you do not want totaled, (such as the Hourly Pay field in the sample application) unless you plan to customize the report using the techniques covered in Chapter 9, *Designing Custom Reports*.

Grouped reports are useful when you are working with relational databases, where you have a second table with many records for each in the first table. In Chapter 6, you add a second table to the sample application, with the hours worked for each employee, and you create a report grouped by employee that totals the number of hours worked for each employee. Chapter 6 covers relational databases and includes an exercise where you create a grouped report using this ReportWizard.

Summary ReportWizard

The Summary ReportWizard is like the Groups/Totals ReportWizard, and includes the same dialog boxes. The difference is that the final report displays lines with only subtotals and totals, not the individual values of numeric fields in each record.

Like grouped reports, summary reports are very useful when you are working with relational databases.

Mailing Labels

When you select mailing labels as the ReportWizard to use, Access displays the dialog box shown in Figure 5.23. Though it looks similar, this dialog box works differently than the field selectors that you looked at earlier, as it actually lets you lay out the label, rather than just specifying fields.

You move individual fields to the **Label appearance** box in the usual way. Double-click a field in the **Available fields** box or click it and click the > button to move it. You also remove it in the usual way.

In addition to adding fields, however, you also add spaces and punctuation marks simply by clicking the buttons that represent them. You add text by typing it in the text box and clicking the **Text->** button. You indicate when a new line begins by clicking the **NewLine** button. If you do not add spaces or new lines, fields will simply be put next each other on the same line in the Label appearance box.

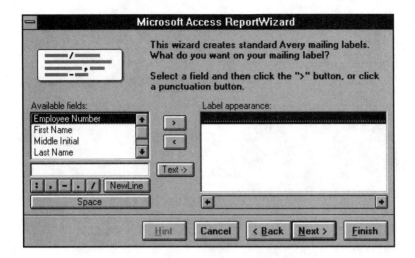

FIGURE 5.23 **LAYING OUT MAILING LABELS.**

Typically, then, you would create a mailing label by adding the first name field, adding a space, adding the middle initial field, adding a space, adding the last name, adding a space, and adding a newline field to complete the first line, before you add the address on the second line.

If you add so many fields to a line that they do not fit in the width of the Label appearance box, you can use the scroll bar under it to view them.

The second dialog box lets you select a field or fields to sort by—usually zip code or last and first name.

The third dialog box lets you specify the dimensions and type of label form you are using, as shown in Figure 5.24.

As you can see, each label in the list box is identified by the following:

❏ *Avery number* is the product number on the package of Avery labels

❏ *Dimensions* is the size of each individual label

❏ *Number across* is the number of labels next to each other on a line

Avery is the most popular brand of label. Most users will simply be able to look at the number on their Avery label packages to see which number to choose. If you use another brand, however, you will almost certainly be able to find a label of the dimension and number across that you need.

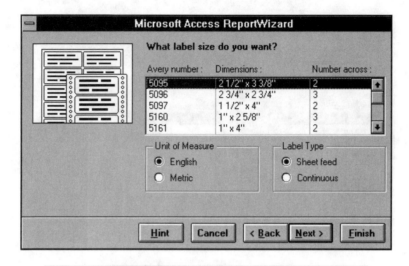

FIGURE 5.24 SPECIFYING THE DIMENSIONS AND TYPE OF LABEL FORM.

The radio buttons below the list box offer the following options:

❑ *English:* dimensions are in inches.

❑ *Metric:* dimensions are in millimeters.

❑ *Sheet feed:* the labels are on forms that are fed into the printer one sheet at a time. This is generally used for laser printers.

❑ *Continuous feed:* the labels are on forms that are on a continuous strip. This is generally used for tractor-feed printers.

The items available in the list box change as you select different radio buttons to include the Avery labels that use that unit of measure and are that type.

The next dialog box lets you specify the typeface of the label, as shown in Figure 5.25. The options that it includes depends on the fonts that you have installed in Windows. The final dialog box simply lets you display the labels in the Print Preview window or in Design View and to specify whether they run with cue cards. Unlike other wizards, it does not let you enter a title, as this is not appropriate for mailing labels.

Creating a Sample Report

Most of the ReportWizards should be very easy for you to use, particularly if you did the exercise earlier in this chapter using the single-column FormWizard, which has dialog boxes similar to many ReportWizards. Chapter 6 has an exercise using the Groups/Totals ReportWizard, which has more advanced features.

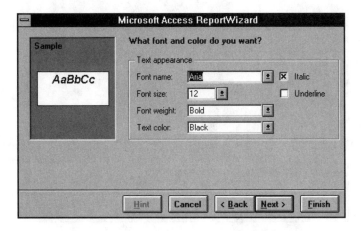

FIGURE 5.25 SELECTING THE TYPEFACE OF MAILING LABELS.

You should try doing an exercise using a ReportWizard to create mailing labels, because this wizard works a bit differently than the others, and you will need it in most practical applications.

1. Begin with the Database window open and the Reports list displayed. Select the **New** Button. When Access displays the New Report dialog box, use the drop-down list to select **Contractors** as the table that the report is based on, and select the **ReportWizards** button. In the next dialog box, select **Mailing Label** as the wizard you want, and select **OK**.

2. Access displays the first dialog box of the ReportWizard for mailing labels. Double-click the **First Name** field to add it to the Label appearance box. Click the **Space** button. Double-click the **Middle Initial** field, click the **Space** button, and double-click the **Last Name** field.

3. You have finished adding the first line of the label, so you must click the **NewLine** button. Then scroll down in the Available fields list, and double-click the **Address 1** field. Again, click the **NewLine** button, and then double-click the **Address 2** field.

4. One more line is needed in the label. Click the **NewLine** button. Then double-click the **City** field. Click the **Comma** button. Click the **Space** button. Double-click the **State** field. Click the **Space** button. Double-

click the **Zip** field. You have added all the necessary fields and other characters to the label, as shown in Figure 5.26. Click the **Next >** button.

FIGURE 5.26 THE FIELDS NEEDED IN THE LABEL.

5. In the next dialog box, double-click the **Zip** field to add it to the Sort order dialog box, assuming that you are doing a bulk mailing that you want sorted in zip code order. Click the **Next >** button.

6. The next dialog box lets you choose label size. If you want to try printing these labels, look at the Avery number or the dimensions of your mailing label forms and choose the label size accordingly. Otherwise, you can use the default Avery number **5095**, which is a common size for two-column labels. Click the **Next >** button.

7. In the next dialog box, you can try changing fonts if you want, or leave them as the default. Remember not to use a font size so large that the fields do not fit on a label.

8. Select **Next >** and you will see that you have reached the final dialog box of this wizard. Select **Finish** to view the labels in the Print Preview window.

9. Choose **Save** from the File menu. In the Save As dialog box, enter **5095 Mailing Labels** and select **OK**. (Of course, if you created different size labels, you should name them accordingly.)

10. Look at the labels in Print Preview, as shown in Figure 5.27. Notice that Access does not leave a blank line when a record does not have an Address 2 field. It automatically adjusts the spacing for either three or

four line addresses. When you are done, close the Report window to
return to the Database window.

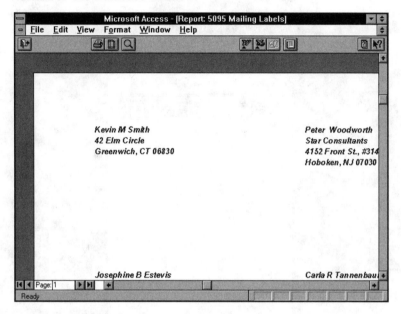

FIGURE 5.27 **THE LABELS IN THE PRINT PREVIEW WINDOW.**

The Print Preview Window

The Print Preview window displays an object just as it would appear if it were
printed. You can display tables, queries, and reports in the Print Preview window by choosing the File menu, then **Print Preview** or clicking the
Print Preview tool. It is covered here because reports are displayed in
Print Preview by default.

Figure 5.28 shows a table in the Print Preview window. When the pointer is
on the table, it is displayed as a magnifying glass, as in the illustration. The
report can be displayed in actual size or in a size small enough that you can see
a full page in the window. It toggles between these two views when you click it.

Clicking the **Zoom** tool has the same effect as clicking the page with
the magnifying glass pointer.

NOTE

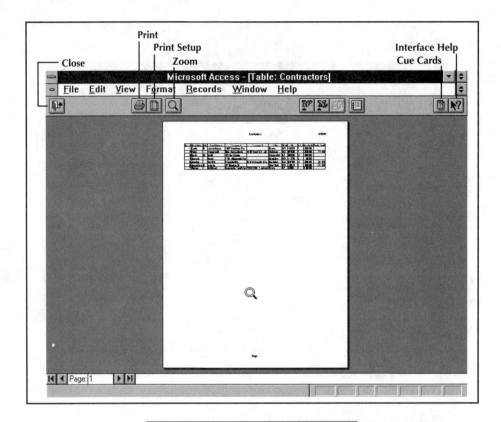

FIGURE 5.28   THE PRINT PREVIEW WINDOW.

Choose **Close** from the File menu or click the **Close** tool to close the Print Preview window.

Choose **Print** from the File menu or click the **Print** tool to display the Print dialog box (which was discussed in Chapter 3), and print the object displayed in the window.

Choose **Print Setup** from the File menu or click the **Print Setup** tool to display the Print Setup dialog box, which was discussed in Chapter 3.

To Sum Up

In this chapter, you learned to create AutoForms and to use the FormWizards to create single-column forms, tabular forms, and graphs. You also learned to use the ReportWizards to create single-column reports, tabular reports, and mailing labels. Part II of this book includes chapters on designing custom forms and reports, but many users will find that the wizards are powerful enough to create all the forms and reports they need.

Now you have learned about all the different objects that you need to know about to manage your own data. Chapter 6 teaches you how to use these objects when you are working with more complex data, that requires you to use multi-table databases.

Relational Databases

*I*n this chapter, you learn to store more complex data by using multiple tables that are related to each other with common key fields. This is called a relational database. First you learn about general database design, so you understand the types of relationships that can exist between tables. Then you learn the techniques used in Access to join the tables of a relational database. In this chapter, you learn about these topics:

- ❏ what a many-to-one relationship is
- ❏ how the primary key and foreign key fields are used in the two tables in a many-to-one relationship
- ❏ when it is best to use a one-to-many rather than a many-to-one relationship
- ❏ what a many-to-many relationship is
- ❏ how to break down a many-to-many relationship into two many-to-one relationships

163

❑ how to create a default relationship in Access

❑ how to enforce referential integrity in Access

❑ when to use the three different join types available in Access

❑ how to create queries based on relational databases

❑ how to use the ReportWizards to create grouped and summary reports on relational databases

❑ how to use the Main/Subform wizard to create a form that displays a one-to-many relationship

Database Design

Before you can do any hands-on work with a relational database in Access, you must have some basic understanding of database theory. Before you can do anything practical, you need to understand enough theory to know how to break up the data into different tables, which you then relate to each other using a common key field. In database terminology, this is called *normalizing data.*

This book does not cover the technical rules of normalization, which are discussed in textbooks on database theory. Instead, it gives you some simple common-sense guidelines, which are easy to apply once you understand why multitable databases are sometimes necessary and once you understand the two basic types of relationships that require multitable databases—the *many-to-one* and the *many-to-many* relationship.

Single-Table Databases

When you were first designing your sample Contractors table, you learned that you must be sure there is a one-to-one relationship between each field and the record.

In the sample table you have used so far, each record contains data on a contractor. When you designed it, you had to make sure that each field contained data that applied only once to each contractor. You saw that each contractor has one first name, one last name, one address, one wage rate, and one availability date.

You assumed that everyone works as a programmer, a writer, or clerical help, but not as more than one of these. Therefore, this information was also in a one-to-one relationship with the record and could be kept in a single field. If some people did more than one of these jobs, you could have designed the table differently. Instead of one Job Category field, you could have created three Yes/No fields—one for Programmer, one for Writer, and one for Clerical—so that you could select more than one for some contractors.

One-to-One Relationships

It is possible to break up data like this into several tables and to relate them. You could conceivably keep each contractor's name and address in one table and the other information on this contractor in a second table. Both tables would have the Employee Number field as their primary key, which would be used to relate them, so you could get all of the information on each contractor.

Though it is possible to create a database with this sort of one-to-one relationship between tables, it is usually easier and more effective to keep all the data in one table.

Access, like other database programs, makes it possible to join tables in a one-to-one relationship, but this is useful only in special cases. For example, you might use it to join two tables made to record data on your employees for two different applications, which you have some special reason for combining.

When you are designing an application, however, you should keep this sort of data in a single table.

Many-to-One Relationships

As you learned in Chapter 2, there is information on contractors that you need for this application that you cannot store in a single table. Billing data is a good example. Since each contractor sends a bill periodically—say, at the end of the month—you will get many bills for each contractor. Each time you get a bill, you will have to enter the billing date, the number of hours worked, and other billing data.

This billing data is in a many-to-one relationship with the records in your contractor file. You must record many bills for each contractor.

As you learned in Chapter 2, it is impossible to enter this data in the same table as the contractor's name and address. If you included fields for billing date and hours worked in the same record as the contractor's name and address, it would be easy to enter the date and hours of the first bill, but how would you enter the data on the second bill you got?

You might try adding a new contractor record to hold this data, but then you would have to reenter all the basic data name and address data for a contractor each time you got a bill.

You might try adding new fields to the table called Billing Date 2, Hours Worked 2, Billing Date 3, Hours Worked 3, and so on, but then you would have an unwieldy table with many empty fields for contractors who work on fewer jobs. You also you would have trouble producing reports summarizing billing data kept in fields with different names.

In this chapter, you learn the right way to record this data. You create a separate table for it, called the Billing table, which has fields for the employee number, the billing date, the hours worked, and so on. As you know, each record in the Contractor table also has an Employee Number field. You can see in Figure 6.1 how these key fields are used to relate the two tables in a many-to-one relationship.

FIGURE 6.1   A MANY-TO-ONE RELATIONSHIP.

The figure shows just a bit of the data that would actually be in the Billing table, the bills for Employee Number 1 to Employee Number 4 for the first three months of 1994. For the sake of simplicity, it does not show all the fields.

The arrows make it easy for you to see how Access can use the key field to look up the record in the Contractors table that goes with each record in the Billing table. The Billing table includes fields for Employee Number, Billing Date, and Hours Worked. By finding the record with the same employee number in the Contractors table, you know the name and address of the person who worked those hours.

USING KEY FIELDS

The key field is used differently in these two tables, and by looking carefully at how this relationship works, you can understand how the two different types of key field work.

The Primary Key

Now that you see how the Contractor table fits into a relational database, you can understand why its primary key, the Employee Number field, must be unique to each record.

If the Billing table has a record of January's bill for employee number 1, there must be only one record in the Contractor table with that Employee Number. If you were ready to pay that January bill and two records in the Contractor table had that same Employee Number, you would not know who to make out the check to.

When you are joining two tables that are in a many-to-one relationship, the key field that you use in the table on the "one side" of the relationship must be the primary key of that table. It must be unique, so you can look up a record in that table. You need to find only one record in the table that has that value in the key field. There can only be one contractor who sends each bill.

The Foreign Key

On the other hand, the Employee Number field in the Billing table is not the primary key for that table, and it is not unique in each record.

The key field used in the table that is on the "many side" of a many-to-one relationship cannot possibly be unique for each record. By definition a one-to-many relationship can always have more than one record in this table with the same key as each record in the "one table" it is related to. There can be many bills from each contractor.

The Billing table can have its own primary key, called something like Bill Number, but it cannot use the Employee Number field as its primary key. The Employee Number field is the primary key of another table and is used to relate the Billing table to that other table.

In Access, this is called a *foreign key*, to emphasize that it is a primary key of another table.

Valid Values in Key Fields

The primary key and the foreign key have different criteria for their validity.

As you know, the primary key must be unique and must be entered in each record. When you designate a field as a primary key, Access automatically makes sure that the value you enter in that field meets these criteria.

When you are using a field as a foreign key, the value must be present in the other table and must be entered in each record.

For example, if you enter **1** in the Employee Number field of the Billing table, there must also be a record with Employee Number 1 in the Contractors table. If you enter an employee number that does not correspond to one in the Contractor table, or if you do not enter an employee number in the Billing table at all, then you will not be able to look up the name and address of the person to send the check to.

You can make Access check the validity of entries in a field that is a foreign key as it checks the validity of the primary key field. This is known as checking for *referential integrity*. In other words, Access checks to make sure that there is some record in the other table that the foreign key *refers* to.

ONE-TO-MANY RELATIONSHIPS

One other point that you should know about this sort of relational database is that sometimes it is most convenient to work with it as a one-to-many relationship rather than as a many-to-one relationship.

Rather than using the table on the "many side" as the primary table of the database and looking up a record in the table on the "one side" that corresponds to each of its records, as shown above in Figure 6.1, you will sometimes find it easier to use the table on the "one side" as the primary table of the database and look up a record in the table on the "many side" that corresponds to each of its records, as shown in Figure 6.2.

Contractors Table				Billing Table		
EmpNo	Name		etc.	EmpNo	Bill Date	Hours
1	Carla	Tannenbaum	...	1	1/31/94	95.5
				1	2/28/94	32.0
				1	3/31/94	150.5
3	Kevin	Smith	...	3	3/31/94	28.5
4	Samuel	Smalz	...	4	2/28/94	162.5
				4	3/31/94	22.0

FIGURE 6.2   A ONE-TO-MANY RELATIONSHIP.

If you compare these two figures, you will see that you can use exactly the same tables in either a many-to-one or a one-to-many relationship, and that there is no difference in the use of the primary and foreign key fields in the two tables. There is one significant difference between the two types of relationship, however.

If you are working with a many-to-one relationship, you can find a single record in the table on the one side that matches each record in the table on the many side. You can find Name and Address fields in the Contractors table, for example, for each record in the Billing table. Thus, you can join the two tables into a single table, as shown in Figure 6.3.

Bill Date	Hours	Name		etc.
1/31/94	95.5	Carla	Tannenbaum	...
2/28/94	32.0	Carla	Tannenbaum	...
3/31/94	150.5	Carla	Tannenbaum	...
3/31/94	28.5	Kevin	Smith	...
2/28/94	162.5	Samuel	Smalz	...
3/31/94	22.0	Samuel	Smalz	...

FIGURE 6.3   JOINING TWO TABLES THAT ARE IN A MANY-TO-ONE RELATIONSHIP.

If you compare this joined table with Figure 6.2, you will see that creating the joined table is just a matter of following the arrows from each record in the Billing table and filling in the blank spaces with the data from the Contractor table. Of course, the joined table has repetitious data, but you can fill in the extra data for each of its records.

In Access (as in some other database management programs), you can use a query to join two tables that are in a many-to-one relationship to produce a result like the one shown in Figure 6.3. The employee numbers do not have to be included, since you can see right in the query's result which person each bill applies to. In fact, since you can arrange the fields in a query in any order, you can easily display names in the left columns and the billing data at the right.

On the other hand, if you are working with a one-to-many relationship, you cannot find a single record in the table on the many side that matches each record in the table on the one side. There are several records in the Billing table for each Name and Address field in the Contractors table. Thus, you cannot join the two tables in a table that looks like Figure 6.3. Instead, you must display one record from the Contractors table (or other table on the one side) with several records from the Billing table (or other table on the many side) below it.

In Access, you can display this sort of relationship by using the Form/Subform wizard, which was mentioned in Chapter 5. By now, you should see why it is that the form holds data from the Contractors table, and the sub-form has multiple lines to hold the corresponding records of the Billing table. This is what you need in a one-to-many relationship.

Later in this chapter, you learn how Access works with relational databases using both queries and the Form/SubForm wizard. They should be easy for you to understand now that you know the database theory behind them.

Many-to-Many Relationships

Not all applications are based on the sort of one-to-many relationship that you have looked at so far. Some are based on a many-to-many relationship.

Consider an example similar to the one you have been looking at so far. Imagine that you run a referral agency for contractors, matching them with employers and billing the employers for their work. This involves a many-to-many relationship, because each contractor can work for many different employers, and each employer can hire many different contractors over the course of the years. You need tables with data on each contractor and on each employer, but you cannot relate these to each other using the one-to-many and many-to-one relationships discussed previously.

It is easy to come up with other examples of many-to-many relationships. For example, students and classes in a school have this relationship. Each student can take many different classes, and each class can enroll many different students.

When two tables are in a many-to-many relationship, you must work with them by breaking down the relationship into two separate one-to-many relationships. This involves creating a third table that is in a one-to-many relationship with both of the two original tables.

In the case of the contractor referral business, you would create a Billing table, like the one shown in Figure 6.4. Like the previous example, this includes the work of employee numbers 1 to 4 during the first three months of 1994. As you can see, those four people happened to work for only two different employers during that time. Employer number 25 needed more people during the beginning of the period, and employer number 14 needed more toward the end of the period.

Billing Table

Employee No.	Employer No.	Bill Date	Hours
1	25	1/31/94	120.5
1	25	2/28/94	23
1	14	2/28/94	52.5
1	14	3/31/94	94.5
3	25	1/31/94	48
4	25	2/28/94	62
4	14	3/31/94	56

FIGURE 6.4   A THIRD TABLE TO LINK TWO TABLES THAT ARE IN A MANY-TO-MANY RELATIONSHIP.

This Billing table has two foreign keys. The Employee Number field is the primary key of the Contractor table, just as it was in the previous example. In addition, the Employer Number field is the primary key of a table that holds data on employers.

Notice that you can relate this Billing table to the Contractors table by using a one-to-many relationship (or a many-to-one relationship) just as you did in the previous example, as shown in Figure 6.5. You could find how many hours each employee worked exactly as you did in the previous example.

FIGURE 6.5   ONE HALF OF THE MANY-TO-MANY RELATIONSHIP.

Looking at the data in the illustration, you can see that you could also add a bit of information on the employers they worked for, since each record in the Billing table has a foreign key that refers to only one record in the Employer table. You could print a report to send out with employees paychecks that not only lists the hours they worked each month, but also includes the name of the employer (or employers) they worked for. Looking at the illustration, you can see that you could look up one Employee Name for each Employee Number.

You could also use the same methods to join this Billing table with an Employer table, as shown in Figure 6.6. The Employer table would hold all the data on each employer, including the employer number and name, address, contact person, and so on. This table can be joined in a many-to-one or one-to-many relationship with the Billing table, just as the Employee table is.

Employer Table			Billing Table			
EmpNo	Name	etc.	Employee No.	Employer No.	Bill Date	Hours
14	ABC Inc.	...→	1	14	2/28/94	52.5
			1	14	3/31/94	94.5
			4	14	3/31/94	56
25	XYZ Ltd.	...→	1	25	1/31/94	120.5
			1	25	2/28/94	23
			3	25	1/31/94	48
			4	25	2/28/94	62

FIGURE 6.6 THE OTHER HALF OF THE MANY-TO-MANY RELATIONSHIP.

Looking at the illustration, you can see how easily you could use this one-to-many relationship to produce a list of the hours worked for each employer, so that you know how much to bill them. Because the records in the Billing table also have employee numbers, you could also pull in data from the Employee table. For example, you could send a bill with the name of the employee next to the hours that person worked.

You can always treat a many-to-many relationship between two tables as two many-to-one relationships in this way. You just need to create a third table whose records include the primary key fields from the two other tables, plus any other data that is in a many-to-one relationship with those tables.

For example, students and classes are in a many-to-many relationship with each other. Each student takes many classes and each class has many students enrolled in it. If you had a table with students (each with a student number, name, and so on), and a table with classes (each with a class number, number of credits, room, days, and times in session, and so on), you could link them with a table of enrollments, each of which has the student number and the class number.

The Enrollments table is in a many-to-one relationship with the Students table. Each student has many enrollments, but each enrollment involves one student. Likewise, the table is in a many-to-one relationship with the Classes table. Each class has many enrollments, but each enrollment involves one class.

What other data would you need in the Enrollments table? It would also hold the student's grade for that class. The grade is in a many-to-one relationship with classes and students. Each student gets many grades, and each class has many grades for its students. Grade is in a one-to-one relationship with the Enrollments table. There is one grade given out for each enrollment of a student in a class.

More Complex Relationships

There are also more complex databases that must be broken down into more than three tables. Like many-to-many databases, however, these can all be broken down into a number of one-to-many relationships.

An example is a database recording sales. Each salesperson deals with many customers, and each customer deals with many salespeople. This many-to-many relationship can be broken down into two one-to-many relationships, like the one above. You need a Salesperson table, with Employee Number as its key field, a Customers table, with Customer Number as its key field, and an Invoice table with fields Employee Number, Customer Number, Date and other information about each sale. The Invoice table would also have an Invoice Number field as its own primary key. With these three tables, you could easily print out a list of when each customer made purchases and when each salesperson made sales, just as you would with the Contractor and Employer database previously described.

However, you also need to record all the products sold in each sale, how many of each is sold, the price of each, and so on. Any number of products could be sold in each sale, so products are in a many-to-one relationship with invoices. The usual way to handle this relationship is to create a separate

Invoice Line table, which includes fields for the invoice number, the price of each product, the quantity sold of the products, and other data. Use the Invoice Number field to join the Invoice Line table with the Invoice table. You could print out the heading of the Invoice, which includes:

❑ the date from the Invoice table

❑ the customer's name, which you find by looking in the Customer table for the record whose primary key is the same as the customer number in the Invoice table. This is a typical many-to-one relationship, as there are many invoices for each customer.

❑ the salesperson's name, which you find by looking in the Employee table for the record whose primary key is the same as the employee number in the Invoice table. This is also a typical many-to-one relationship, as there are many invoices for each salesperson.

Under this heading, you could print all the lines of the invoice, which you find by looking in the Invoice Line table for all the records that have this invoice number as their foreign key. This is a typical one-to-many relationship, as there are many invoice lines for each invoice.

You would also want to include the product's name in each line of the invoice. You probably already would have a Product table, with product number, product name, product cost, and other data on each product. If you include the product number as a foreign key in each invoice, you can pull in the product name from the Product table. This is a typical many-to-one relationship, as there can be many invoice lines that include each product.

As you can see, this example includes many different types of data stored in many tables that must be related to one another. However, it is finally broken down into a number of typical one-to-many and many-to-one relationships.

However complex the database, you can always break it down in this way into a number of many-to-one relationships.

Normalization Made Easy

The technical rules of data normalization, which are covered in more advanced textbooks on database theory, are useful in complex cases, but in most cases you can do just as well by using the three common-sense rules you learned in this chapter:

1. Be sure there is a one-to-one relationship between each table and all of the fields in it. The entity represented by each record in the table should have the data in each field recorded for it only once. For example, an employee has only one address and one zip code, so these fields can go in the Employee table, but an employee sends many bills, so these cannot go into the Employee table.

2. If there is a one-to-many relationship between the table and some data, put this data into a second table, which includes the primary key of the first table as its foreign key. For example, to record the employee's bills, create a Billing table that includes the Employee Number field as a foreign key.

3. Break up a many-to-many relationships between two tables into two many-to-one relationships by creating a third table that includes the primary keys of both of the original tables as its foreign keys. For example, if each employee bills many customers and each customer pays many employees, then the Employee table and the Customer table are in a many-to-many relationship, and you need a Billing table with both the Employee Number and Customer Number fields as foreign keys.

If you keep looking for one-to-many and many-to-many relationships where you must break the data down into separate tables, and if you use common sense, you can generally normalize even complex data.

Since the data is always normalized into a series of tables with many-to-one relationships, you can work with even complex data using the techniques that you learn in the following examples, where you use Access to create many-to-one and one-to-many relationships.

Relational Databases in Access

Access gives you a number of ways of defining relationships. For example, you can use the Query window to define a relationship among tables that is used as the basis of that single query.

In general, however, you should begin by using the Relationship window to define the relationship among tables that are the fundamental to your database, such as the relationship between the Employee table and the Billing table in your sample application, so they are used as the default relationship when you work with the tables.

Creating a Default Relationship

To create a default relationship, open the database and select **Relationships** from the Edit menu or click the **Relationships** tool. The first time you do this, Access displays the Add Table dialog box, shown in Figure 6.7, which lets you choose the tables or queries that you want to include in the Relationships window. Double-click a table or select a table and click the **Add** button to add it to the window.

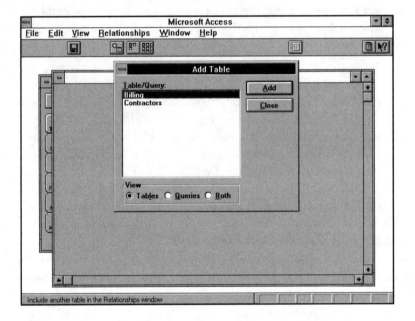

FIGURE 6.7   ADDING THE TABLES.

When you are done, close the Add Table dialog box to display the field lists for the tables, as shown in Figure 6.8. Notice that name of the field that is the primary key for each table is displayed in darker type.

WORKING WITH THE TABLES

At any later time, you can add new tables to the Relationship window by choosing **Add Table** from the Relationships menu, or clicking the **Add Table** tool to display and use the Add Table dialog box again.

You can remove a table from the Relationships window by selecting it and pressing **Del** or choosing **Remove table** from the Relationships menu.

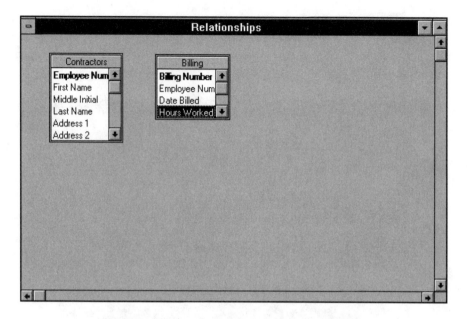

FIGURE 6.8   FIELD LISTS IN THE RELATIONSHIPS WINDOW.

You can move a table simply by clicking and dragging its title bar. It is some-times convenient to move tables in complex databases to make it easier to see the connections between them.

CREATING THE RELATIONSHIP

To create the relationship, click and drag from one of the fields that it is based on to the other. For example, in the sample application, you would click and drag the Employee Number field of the Contractor table to the Employee Number field of the Billing table.

NOTE   You should begin dragging from the field that is the primary key of the table on the "one side" of the relationship. In the sample application, you should be sure to drag the Employee Number field from the Contractors table to the Billing table. The table that you begin drag-ging from is called the *primary table* of that relationship. As you will see, you must use the "one table" as the primary table in order to enforce referential integrity.

When tables are joined in this way, Access displays a line connecting the fields that the join is based on, as shown in Figure 6.9. Notice the number 1 near the

Contractors table, and the symbol ∞ near the Billing table, indicating that this is a one-to-many relationship. There can be an indefinite number of Billing records associated with each Contractors record. This is sometimes called *Graphical System Relationships*, since you display the relationships graphically.

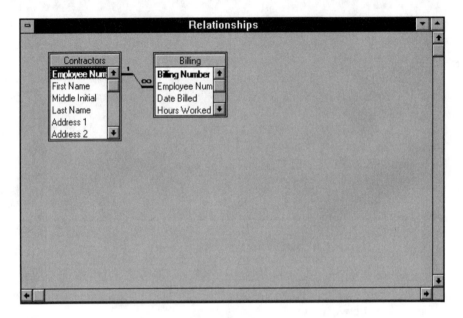

FIGURE 6.9 ACCESS DISPLAYS THE JOIN.

DEFINING THE RELATIONSHIP

When you first create a relationship in this way, Access displays the Relationships dialog box shown in Figure 6.10.

If you want to change the definition of the relationship, you can display this dialog box at any time by double-clicking the line that represents the relationship or by clicking the line to select it and choosing **Edit Relationship** from the Relationships menu.

The primary table or query of the relationship is listed on the left, and the table or query that is related to it is listed on the right.

One To Radio Buttons

The One To radio buttons let you specify if this is a one-to-one or one-to-many relationship.

FIGURE 6.10   THE RELATIONSHIPS DIALOG BOX.

As explained in the section "One-to-One Relationships" earlier in this chapter, this relationship should only be used in special cases where you are relating tables from different applications, or where there is an extraordinary reason for breaking up data into two tables with a one-to-one relationship. Ordinarily, if there is a one-to-one relationship, it is best to keep the data in a single table.

You should always use the One To radio buttons to choose a One-to-many relationship.

NOTE

Notice that you can not specify a many-to-many relationship here. As explained in the section "Many-To-Many Relationships" earlier in this chapter, you must break this sort of relationship up into two one-to-many relationships.

Enforce Referential Integrity

As explained earlier, in one-to-many relationships, the primary key in the "one table" has to be unique in each record, and the foreign key in each record of the "many table" has to be present as the primary key in one of the records of the "one table."

For example, the Employee Number field had to be unique in each record in the Contractor table, and each record of the Billing table had to have an Employee Number field that was present in some record of the Contractor table, so you could find the name of the person who worked those hours.

A record in the "many table" whose foreign key does not refer to any record in the "one table" is sometimes called an *orphan record*. If you select the **Enforce Referential Integrity** checkbox, Access will automatically make sure that there are no orphan records in the "many table." Access will not let you do the following:

❏ add a record to the related table unless there is a record with that number in the primary table.

❏ change a value in the primary key field of the primary table if there are records in the related table that use that value as their foreign key.

❏ delete a record from the primary table if there is a record in the related table that refers to it.

NOTE   Notice that this feature can work only if you use the table on the "one side" of the relationship as the primary table and the table on the "many side" of the relationship as the related table. That is why, when you create a relationship, you should click the **primary key** in the "one table" and drag it to the foreign key in the "many table." You must make the "one table" the primary table to use this checkbox.

Unless you have some special reason not to, you should select the **Enforce Referential Integrity** checkbox to make sure you do not enter invalid foreign keys by mistake.

Notice that this checkbox only protects the integrity of the foreign key in the related table and does not protect the integrity of the primary key in the primary table. For example, it would not prevent you from entering the same value as the employee number in two records of the Contractor table. To prevent this error you should use a counter field (or some other field with a unique index) as the primary key.

Cascade Update and Delete

If you select the Cascade Update or Cascade Delete checkboxes, Access will overrides the usual protections for relational integrity in the following ways:

❏ If you select Cascade Update Related Fields, you will be able to edit the primary key field in the "one" table, and Access will automatically make the same change to the foreign key in the "many" table, so the records will still be related.

❏ If you select Cascade Deleted Related Records, you will be able to delete records in the "one" table even if there are related records in the "many" table. Access will automatically delete the related records in the "many" table, so it will not have orphan records.

WARNING

After a cascading update or delete, the database will still have relational integrity, but there may have been changes to many records in the many table without the user knowing it. Though this feature can sometimes be useful in applications, it should be used with great care, since you may delete or modify records in the "many" table automatically, without knowing it. Non-programmers should avoid Cascade Updates and Deletes, since they override many of the protections built into Access.

You can accomplish the same thing more safely by using an action query. Include the key fields from both of the related tables in the query form, and use the action query to change them both. Using this method to change the data forces you to change the values in the key field of the many table or to delete records from the many table explicitly, rather than doing it automatically. Action queries are covered in Chapter 10.

Join Type

If you select the **Join Type** button, Access displays the Join Properties dialog box, which lets you specify which records are included in the joined database.

As you can see in Figure 6.11, the radio buttons in this dialog box give you three options.

FIGURE 6.11   THE JOIN PROPERTIES DIALOG BOX.

It is obvious how to use these buttons if you are working with a one-to-one relationship. You can include only records that are in both tables or all the records that are in one or the other table.

Join Properties for One-to-Many Relationships

When you are working with a one-to-many relationship, however, the descriptions in the dialog box are a bit confusing, particularly because they refer to the primary and related tables in the relationship that you created with Access rather than to the "one table" and the "many table" in the logical relationship between the tables.

Assuming that you make the "one table" the primary table, as you must to enforce referential integrity, have the following options:

1. Include only records that are in both tables. There will be a record in the joined database only if there is a record with that key in both tables. In the example, there must be a record with the same Employee Number in both the Contractor table and the Billing table for it to be included. If there is a contractor who has not billed or if there is a bill without a contractor to send it to, it is not included. Note that if there were no errors in data entry, there would not be any record in the Billing table without a record in the Contractors table that represents the person who sent you the bill.

2. Include all records from the "one table" and only the records from the "many table" that are related to it. In the example, you would include all records from the Contractor table and only the records from the Billing table that have a related record in the Contractor table. Note that if there were no errors in data entry, this would be all of the records in the Billing table, since each record in this table must have a related record in the Contractors table. Thus, this option would include all the contractors, whether they sent bills or not.

3. Include all records from the "many table" and only the records from the "one table" that are related to it. In the example, this would include all records from the Billing tables and only the records in the Contractor table that are related to it. Thus, this option would include records on the contractors who have sent bills but would leave out the contractors who did not send bills.

When you are working with an ordinary one-to-many relationship, with the "one table" as the primary table, options 1 and 3 in the Join Properties dialog box should be equivalent. In the sample application, both would display only the contractors who sent bills, and not the other contractors. The difference between the two is that option 1 would hide records where there is a bill without a contractor and option 3 would not.

NOTE

Since there should never be a bill without a contractor, the two options should give you the same result. If there were an error, though, and there were a bill without a contractor, option 3 would include this bill and option 1 would hide it. In an ordinary one-to-many relationship, the only difference between the two options is that option 1 hides your errors and option 3 reveals them. It is always better to use option 3, so that your errors do not go undetected. Access does well enough at enforcing referential integrity that errors should not appear, but in the rare cases where errors do slip in, it is best to know that they are there.

When to Use Different Join Properties

The important choice you must make in the Join Properties dialog box is between option 2 and option 3.

If you are using a typical one-to-many relationship with referential integrity enforced, option 2 will include all records in both tables, and option 3 will leave out the records in the "one table" with no equivalent in the "many table." Which of these you should use depends on your reason for joining the tables.

For example, if you want to pay your bills, you should select option 3, and display only the records of contractors who have sent bills.

On the other hand, if you want to produce a report that lets you look generally at how much work your contractors have done, you would probably want to select option 2, so you could also see which contractors have not worked.

You can choose whichever of these is most convenient as the default. You may have to change this property in some forms, queries, or reports.

THE DATA TYPE OF THE FOREIGN KEY

Access gives you a great deal of flexibility in designing key fields. When you create the most common type of relationship, however, a many-to-one relationship with referential integrity enforced, your options become more limited.

As you know, it is usually best to use a counter as the data type of a primary key. If you want to relate a foreign key to a primary key in another table that is a counter and enforce referential integrity, you should make it the Number Data type with the Long Integer length.

WARNING

If you use any other data type, Access displays a rather confusing error message saying that key fields must be the same data type to enforce referential integrity. You will create endless problems for yourself if you try to do as the message says and make the foreign key a Counter. Access considers the Long Integer to be the same data type as the Counter because they are both integers of the same size.

Creating a Sample Database

Now that you have enough of a grounding in database theory and in the methods that Access uses to create relationships, it should be very easy for you to create a sample relational database.

In this section, you create a second table, define its default relationship to the Contractors table, and enter sample data in it. Then, in later parts of this chapter, you use this sample database in exercises to create queries, reports, and forms for relational databases.

CREATING THE BILLING TABLE

First, you must define the Billing table that you will relate to the Contractors table. Since this table was used as an example in the general discussion of database design in the section "One-To-Many Relationships "earlier in this chapter, you have already done most of the analysis needed to design this table. However, the examples did not require you to think about precisely what fields should be in the sample table.

The table needs an Employee Number field as its foreign key and fields for Billing Date and Hours Worked, as shown in the examples. Though it was left out of the example for the sake of simplicity, the table should also have a Billing Number field as its primary key, since Access generally works most efficiently if each table has its own primary key.

Finally, though you might not realize it at first, this table should also have an Hourly Pay field, like the Contractors table, so you can multiply the Hours Worked field by the Hourly Pay field to find the total pay for the period.

At first, you might think you could multiply the Hours Worked field by the Hourly Pay field in that person's record in the Contractors table. This would only be possible if you are sure that the hourly pay will never change. If a contractor ever changed pay rates and you changed the value in the Hourly Pay field, you would no longer be able to calculate the total pay earned during past periods.

The Hourly Pay field in the Contractor's table is the pay rate at the current time, and it can be kept in this table because each contractor has only one current pay rate. However, you also have to record the contractors pay rates over time, and this is in a many-to-one relationship with the contractor table, because each contractor can have many different pay rates over the years.

You do not need a separate field for total pay earned, because this can be calculated from the values in the Hours Worked and Hourly Pay fields. In Chapter 8, when you learn about expressions, you will to see how to add this sort of calculated field to a form or report.

To create the Billing table, do the following:

1. Open the **Teachslf** database or display its list of tables. Select the **New** button of the Database Window, and select the **New Table** button to display the Table Window in Design View.

2. Enter the following field definitions. Notice that you use **Currency** as the data type for hours worked, even though it is not an amount of money. Its values can be entered with one or two decimal places and calculations using it need to be accurate to less than four decimal places. Thus, these calculations can be done more quickly using the Currency type.

FIELD NAME	DATA TYPE	PROPERTIES
Billing Number	**Counter**	(enter nothing)
Employee Number	**Number**	**Field Size: Long Integer**
Date Billed	**Date/Time**	(enter nothing)
Hours Worked	**Currency**	**Format: General Number, Decimal Places: 2**
Hourly Pay	**Currency**	(enter nothing)

3. Select the **Billing Number** row and click the **Set Primary Key** tool (or choose **Primary key** from the Edit menu).

4. Choose **Save** from the File menu. Access displays the Save As dialog box. Enter **Billing** as the table name and select **OK**. The table is now fully defined, as shown in Figure 6.12.

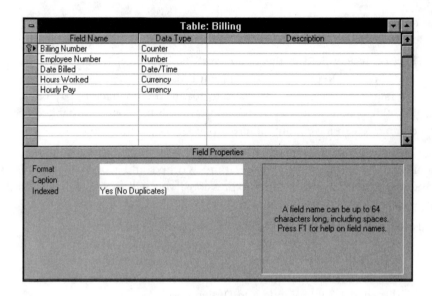

FIGURE 6.12   DEFINING THE BILLING TABLE.

5.   Double-click the Table window's Control-menu box to close the window.

RELATING THE TABLES

Now you must define the relationship between these two tables. This involves creating the most common type of relationship, a one-to-many relationship with enforced referential integrity.

Let's assume that you have a long list of contractors and you do not want to display the ones who are not currently working because you do not want these records to get in the way during data entry. Thus, you will create a default relationship that displays a record in the Contractor table only if there is a record in the Billing table related to it.

1.   Click the **Relationships** tool or choose **Relationships** from the Edit menu. In the Add Table dialog box, first double-click the **Contractors** table and then double-click the **Billing** table to add both to the Relationships window. Then select **Close**.

2.   In the Relationships window, click the **Employee Number** of the Contractors field list and drag to the **Employee Number** of the Billing table. Access displays the Relationships dialog box. Select the **Enforce Referential Integrity** checkbox, as shown in Figure 6.13.

FIGURE 6.13   DEFINING THE RELATIONSHIP.

3.   Select the **Join Type** button. In the Join Properties dialog box, select button **3**, to include all records from the Billing table and only those records from Contractors table where the joined fields are equal. Select **OK**.

4.   In the Relationships dialog box, select the **Create** button. Access displays the relationship, as shown in Figure 6.14.

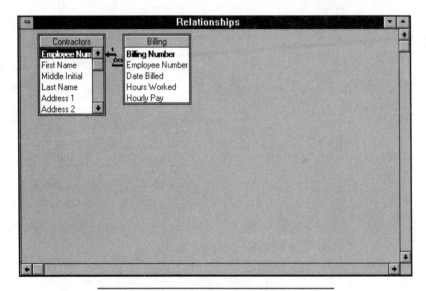

FIGURE 6.14   THE NEWLY CREATED RELATIONSHIP.

5. Select **Save Layout** from the File menu to save the changes in the Relationships window. Then close the Relationships window.

ADDING SAMPLE DATA

Now you can work with either of the tables individually, just as you always have. Try adding a bit of sample data to the Billing table:

1. Double-click the **Billing** table name to open it in Datasheet View. First, try entering invalid data, to test the way in which Access enforces referential integrity. Press **Tab** to move to the Employee Number field, and type **99**. Of course, no employee has that number in the Contractors table. Press the **Down Arrow** key to try to move to the next record. Access displays the error message shown in Figure 6.15. Select **OK**.

FIGURE 6.15   **ACCESS ENFORCES REFERENTIAL INTEGRITY.**

2. Edit the Employee Number field so it reads **1**, and continue entering the sample data listed below. (Of course, Access enters the billing number for you.)

BILLING NUMBER	EMPLOYEE NUMBER	DATE BILLED	HOURS WORKED	HOURLY PAY
1	1	1/31/94	95.5	95
2	1	2/28/94	32	95
3	1	3/31/94	150.5	95
4	3	3/31/94	28.5	55
5	4	2/28/94	162.5	9
6	4	3/31/94	22	9

3. The table should look like Figure 6.16. Double-click the Table window's control menu to close it.

Billing Number	Employee Numb	Date Billed	Hours Worked	Hourly Pay
1	1	1/31/94	95.5	$95.00
2	1	2/28/94	32	$95.00
3	1	3/31/94	150.5	$95.00
4	3	3/31/94	28.5	$55.00
5	4	2/28/94	162.5	$9.00
6	4	3/31/94	22	$9.00
(Counter)	0		0	$0.00

Record: 6   of 6

FIGURE 6.16   SAMPLE BILLING DATA.

Queries with Relational Databases

As you entered data in the Billing table, you understood that the Employee Number field linked it to the Contractor table. However, in an actual application, you would not want to look at just the Employee number in the Billing table and try to remember which person it applies to. You would want to see the contractor's name.

It is easy to display fields from both tables by using a query. Queries with relational databases are almost identical to ordinary queries. Once the related tables are included in the Query window, you add fields to the QBE list and use other features of the Query window much as you do when you are creating a query based on a single table. It is so simple that you will be able to learn how to do it simply by looking at an example.

CREATING THE QUERY

First create a query, which you will use to display all the fields of the Billing table along with the contractor's name.

This query is really just an extended version of the record in the Billing table, with the Name field as a bit of extra information, so it should use the Join Type in the default relationship. Remember that when you related the tables, you said that records in the Contractor table would be displayed only if there was an equivalent record in the Billing table.

In this case, the query will include a record for each record in the Billing table and will just add the names from the Contractor table where there is a record in the Billing table, which is just what you want. You do not want to clutter it with records for all the contractors who have not worked recently.

To define the query, simply include both tables and drag the fields you want into the QBE grid. As always, you can also use the drop-down lists in the QBE grid to select the field name. Try displaying one when you do the following exercise, and you will see that each list includes the names from both tables, beginning with the table name, followed by a dot, then followed by the field name.

1. Click the **Query** button of the Database window. When the Query List is displayed, click the **New** button. In the New Query dialog box, click the **New Query** button.

2. Access displays the Query window and the Add Table dialog box. In the dialog box, double-click the **Contractors** table and then the **Billing** table to add both to the Query window, then select **Close**. Access automatically displays the default relationship between the two, as shown in Figure 6.17.

FIGURE 6.17 ACCESS ADDS THE DEFAULT RELATIONSHIP BETWEEN THE TABLES.

3. Click the **Maximize** button to increase the size of the Query window. Double-click the title of the **Billing** field list to select all fields, then click and drag them to the first field cell of the QBE grid to place all the fields in the grid.

4. Scroll right to display blank cells in the QBE grid. Click and drag the **Last Name** and then the **First Name** fields from the Contractors field list to the QBE grid, as shown in Figure 6.18.

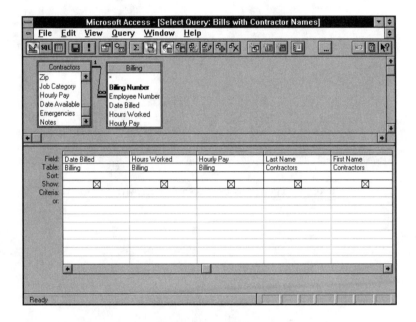

FIGURE 6.18   ADDING FIELDS FROM THE CONTRACTORS TABLE.

5. Choose **Save** from the File menu. Access displays the Save As dialog box. As the Query Name, enter **Bills with Contractor Names**, and select **OK**.

6. Click the **Datasheet View** tool. Access displays the result of the Query, as shown in Figure 6.19.

Of course, in addition to specifying which fields to include, you could have used the other features of the Query window to filter records or specify sort order, just as you do with single-table queries.

FIGURE 6.19   THE QUERY DISPLAYS THE NAME WITH EACH BILL.

Often, this sort of query looks best if you change field order, which you can do by clicking and dragging columns, as you do in any query design. In the example, you might want to move the name to the left columns and the billing data to the right. You can do this even though you still use the join property that includes all records from the Billing table and only some from the Contractor table.

WORKING WITH THE QUERY

You can add records, edit records, find values, and work with the result of this query in other ways, just as you work with any table or query in Datasheet View.

There are just a few differences that are results of the one-to-many relationship that the query is based on:

❑ If you change the Employee Number field (taken from the Billing table), the values in the Last Name and First Name fields also change, as they are looked up in the Contractor table on the basis of the Employee Number field.

❑ If you edit one of the fields taken from the Contractors table, the value changes in that table, and therefore changes in all the fields where it appears in the query.

Take a look at these two unusual features in the sample query you just created:

1. Move the cursor to the Employee Number field of the new record. Type **5** and press **Tab** to move to the next field. The first and last name automatically appear, as shown in Figure 6.20. As the Date Billed, enter **3/31/94**, and as Hours Worked enter **54**. As Hourly Pay, enter **50**.

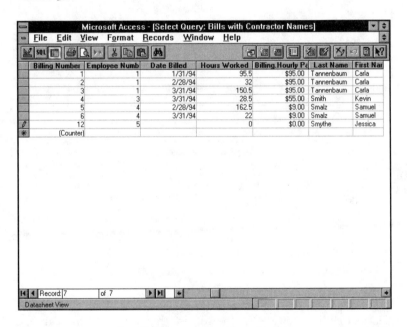

Billing Number	Employee Numb	Date Billed	Hours Worked	Billing.Hourly Pa	Last Name	First Nar
1	1	1/31/94	95.5	$95.00	Tannenbaum	Carla
2	1	2/28/94	32	$95.00	Tannenbaum	Carla
3	1	3/31/94	150.5	$95.00	Tannenbaum	Carla
4	3	3/31/94	28.5	$55.00	Smith	Kevin
5	4	2/28/94	162.5	$9.00	Smalz	Samuel
6	4	3/31/94	22	$9.00	Smalz	Samuel
12	5		0	$0.00	Smythe	Jessica
(Counter)						

FIGURE 6.20   THE FIRST AND LAST NAME FIELDS ARE ENTERED AUTOMATICALLY.

2. Move the cursor to the First Name field of record 1, and edit it so it reads **Carl** instead of Carla. Move the cursor to another record. The change is saved and the name is also changed in the next two records, as shown in Figure 6.21. Choose **Undo** from the Edit menu to get rid of the change.

Billing Number	Employee Numb	Date Billed	Hours Worked	Billing.Hourly Pa	Last Name	First Nar
1	1	1/31/94	95.5	$95.00	Tannenbaum	Carl
2	1	2/28/94	32	$95.00	Tannenbaum	Carl
3	1	3/31/94	150.5	$95.00	Tannenbaum	Carl
4	3	3/31/94	28.5	$55.00	Smith	Kevin
5	4	2/28/94	162.5	$9.00	Smalz	Samuel
6	4	3/31/94	22	$9.00	Smalz	Samuel
12	5	3/31/94	54	$50.00	Smythe	Jessica
(Counter)						

FIGURE 6.21 CHANGING THE FIELD IN ONE RECORD CHANGES THEM ALL.

SHORTCUT

You can use one of these features as a simple way of entering records in fields like the Hourly Pay field of the Billing table, where the value is copied from the other table. If you included both Hourly Pay fields in this query, the value would automatically appear in the Hourly Pay field of the Contractor table, and you could copy and paste it into the Hourly Pay field of the Employee table. You can also use Default Values, covered in Chapter 8, to enter this value automatically.

CHANGING THE RELATIONSHIP IN THE QUERY

As you learned earlier, you define the relationship you need most frequently as the default relationship between tables, but there might be cases where you want to use a different relationship as the basis of the Query.

You can select **Add Table** from the Query menu, or click the **Add Table** tool to add new tables to the Query window at any time. You can relate these tables to other tables by clicking and dragging a key field from one table to another as you do when you create a default relationship. Likewise, you can select a line representing a join and press **Del** to delete it.

It is most common to want to change the Join Properties of the relationship. You can double-click the line representing the join or you can select the line and choose the View menu, then **Join Properties** to display the Join Properties dialog box, as you did when you created the default query.

In the sample database, you might want some queries that display all the contractor records, even if there are no related billing records. Try changing the join properties in this query:

1. Click the **Design View** tool to switch the Query window to Design View. Double-click the line that represents the join (or select it and choose **Join Properties** from the View menu) to display the Join Properties dialog box.

2. Select button **2** which includes all records from the Contractors table, and select **OK**.

3. Click the **Datasheet View** tool to display the data shown in Figure 6.22, including all the names from the Contractor table. Some do not have entries in the fields taken from the Billing table.

4. As you can see, this is not a very useful way to display the data from these tables. Close the Query window and select **No** so you do not save this change in its design.

Billing Number	Employee Numb	Date Billed	Hours Worked	Billing.Hourly Pa	Last Name	First Nan
1	1	1/31/94	95.5	$95.00	Tannenbaum	Carla
2	1	2/28/94	32	$95.00	Tannenbaum	Carla
3	1	3/31/94	150.5	$95.00	Tannenbaum	Carla
					Woodworth	Peter
4	3	3/31/94	28.5	$55.00	Smith	Kevin
5	4	2/28/94	162.5	$9.00	Smalz	Samuel
6	4	3/31/94	22	$9.00	Smalz	Samuel
12	5	3/31/94	54	$50.00	Smythe	Jessica
					Estevis	Josephine
					Smithson	Sidney
(Counter)						

FIGURE 6.22   THE QUERY WITH ALL THE RECORDS FROM THE CONTRACTORS TABLE.

As you can see, when you are using a query to display fields from two tables, it is generally best to use them in the way that was described in the section "Many-To-One Relationships" earlier in this chapter. You should generally include all the records in the "many table" and look up extra data from each record in the "one table."

There are exceptions, and there might well be times when you want to use this sort of query and display all the records in the "one table," as you did in the exercise. As a general rule, however, when you are keeping all the related fields on a single line, it usually does not look right to have records with some fields blank. To include all the records from the "one table," it is generally better to use a Form/Subform form, as described at the end of this chapter.

Reports and Forms on Relational Databases

You learned in Chapter 5 that you can create a report or a form based on either a table or a query, query to specify which records appear in the Report or Form. Now you can see that you can also use a query based on multiple tables to create a report or form for a relational database.

In general, you can use the ReportWizards and FormWizards with this sort of query as you do with any query. However, you should bear in mind that, as you saw when you edited the query itself, changes you make in the "one table" in one record can also cause changes in the same field in other records, and changes you make in the foreign key of the "many table" can cause changes in the fields of the same record that are taken from the "one table."

There are a couple of features of the ReportWizards and FormWizards that were not covered in Chapter 5 because they are particularly useful when you are working with relational databases, summary and grouped reports, and forms with subforms.

SUMMARY AND GROUPED REPORTS

Because they have repetitive data, it is often useful to create summary or grouped reports on a query based on a one-to-many relationship. Both reports were discussed in Chapter 5. In the sample database, you could use either of these reports to summarize all the hours worked by each contractor.

In the exercise that follows, you create a grouped report with total hours for each contractor. You will also use this grouped report in exercises in Chapter 9, where you learn to design custom reports. The wizard used to create summary reports is almost identical to the one used to create grouped reports.

In this exercise, you include the Employee Number field in the report and use it as the field to group by. It is always best to group by a key field such as Employee Number rather than by name, as two people may have the same name. As you learned earlier, all numeric fields you include in this report are summarized, unless you use them as the field to group by. You do not include the Hourly Pay field, because you do not want the report to total all the Hourly Pay fields for each contractor and present it as if it were a meaningful summary. You can include the Employee Number field only because you are grouping on it, so it is not summarized:

1. Click the **Report** button of the Database window, and then click the **New** button. When Access displays the New Report dialog box, use the **Select A Table/Query** drop-down list to select **Bills with Contractor Names**, the query on the relational database that you just created. Then select the **ReportWizards** button.

2. In the next dialog box, select **Groups/Totals** as the wizard you want and select **OK**.

3. As the fields to include, select **Employee Number**, **Last Name**, **First Name**, **Date Billed**, and **Hours Worked**. Add them all to the **Field order on report** list, as shown in Figure 6.23, and select **Next >**.

FIGURE 6.23   INCLUDING FIELDS IN THE REPORT.

4. In the next dialog box, select **Employee Number** as the Fields to Group by. Select **Next >**. In the next dialog box, to keep Normal as the

Grouping Option, simply select **Next >**. In the next dialog boxes, to keep the default sort order and style, simply select **Next >**.

5. In the final dialog box, enter the title, **Hours Worked by Contractors**. Select the **See all the fields on one page** checkbox, and deselect the **Calculate Percent of Total** checkbox.

6. Click the **Finish** button. When Access displays the new report, select **Save** from the File menu. Enter the name **Total Hours Worked by Contractors** in the Save As dialog box and select **OK**. Scroll through the report and zoom it so you can see the entire page, as shown in Figure 6.24. When you are done, choose **Close** from the File menu to return to the Database window, and select its **Restore** button to return it to its default size.

FIGURE 6.24   THE GROUPED REPORT.

You can see that this report has the same data as the query did on the dates and hours worked by contractors, and that it also has the total hours worked by each contractor, as well as the total hours worked by all contractors.

It would improve this report if the contractors' names were included once at the beginning of the group, like the employee numbers are, rather than repeated for each record. You cannot do this using the wizard because it creates a separate group and subtotal for each field you choose to group on. In Chapter 9, where you learn to design custom reports, you will make this change.

MAIN/SUBFORM FORMS

As you saw earlier, if you use two joined tables as the basis of a query, it is usually best to take the many-to-one approach—to include all records from the "many table" and only the related records from the "one table."

You saw that it looks a bit awkward to create a query with all the records from the "one table," some with fields missing because there are no equivalent records in the "many table." The Bills with Contractors Names query did not look as good when it had all records from the Contractors table, some with blank fields for Date Worked, Hours Worked, and Hourly Pay.

The same is true of forms and reports based on this query. As a general rule, it is best to include all records from the "many table" and only related records from the "one table." There are exceptions, and you know how to change the Join properties of queries to include all records from the "one table" to accommodate them, but it is usually best to follow this rule.

If you want to use a one-to-many approach with all the fields from the "one table" and related fields from the "many table," it is generally best to use a main form and subform. The main form holds a record from the "one table," and the subform holds any related records from the many table. Because the emphasis is on the record from the "one table," it does not seem awkward when there is not a matching record from the many table.

The Main/SubformWizard makes it easy to create this sort of form. You begin by using the table you want included in the main form (the "one table") as the basis of the form. The wizard lets you specify the table to use as the subform, and relates them using the default relationship you established earlier.

WARNING

When you use this wizard, it asks you to name and save the subform. The subform must also exist as a separate form on its own, which is connected to the main form using properties discussed in Chapter 7. This subform is displayed separately in the Database window. Do not delete it from the database, or it will no longer appear in the main form. The area that had been used for the subform will be left blank instead.

Try creating a main form and a subform for the sample database:

1. Click the **Form** button of the Database window, and then click the **New** button. When Access displays the New Form dialog box, use the **Select A Table/Query** drop-down list to select **Contractors**, the "one table" of your relational database. Then select the **FormWizards** button.

2. In the next dialog box, select **Main/Subform** as the Wizard you want and select **OK**.

3. The next dialog box lets you select the table or query used as the basis of the subform. Notice that it mentions that Contractors is the main form. As the subform, select **Billing**, and then select **Next >**.

4. As the fields to include on the main form, select **First Name**, **Middle Initial**, **Last Name**, **Address 1**, **Address 2**, **City**, **State**, and **Zip**. After adding these to the Fields on main form list, select **Next >**.

5. As the fields to include on the subform, select **Date Billed**, **Hours Worked**, and **Hourly Pay**. After adding these to the Fields on subform list, select **Next >**.

6. In the next dialog box, to keep the default look, simply select **Next >**. In the final dialog box, enter the title, **Contractors with Hours Worked by Each**. Click the **Finish** button.

7. When Access prompts you, select **OK** to save the subform. Access displays the Save As dialog box. Enter **Subform With Billing Data** and select **OK**.

8. When Access displays the new form, select **Save** from the File menu. Enter the name **Contractors with Hours Worked by Each** in the Save As dialog box and select **OK**. Select the **Maximize** button so you can see all the features of the form, as shown in Figure 6.25.

9. Try using this form, and close it when you are done.

Notice that this form has two sets of arrow tools and two record numbers displayed at once: one for the main form and one for the subform. Try using the arrow tools to scroll through the records of the Contractors table, and notice that the related records from the Billing table (or a blank record, if there are no records entered yet in the billing table) are displayed in the subform.

If there are too many records to display in the subform, a scroll bar is added to it so you can scroll through all its records.

It is very easy to work with this new form. Use the main form to work with the data in the Contractor table, just as you would with its quick form or most other forms you create for it. The subform is tabular, and you can use it to work with the data for a given contractor in the Billing table just if you were working with any datasheet.

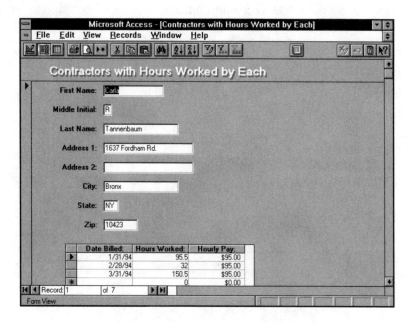

FIGURE 6.25   THE FORM AND SUBFORM.

To Sum Up

In this chapter, you learned simple methods of normalizing data, breaking up complex data into multiple tables. You learned to look for many-to-one, one-to-many, and many-to-many relationships, to use a primary key and a foreign key to relate two tables that are in a many-to-one relationship, and to break down a many-to-many relationship into two many-to-one relationships.

After looking at how to analyze data, you learned to work with multi-table databases in Access. You saw that it is best to begin by creating a default relationship that enforces referential integrity. You also learned to create queries based on multi-table databases, to use the ReportWizards to create reports on multi-table databases, and to use the Main/SubForm Wizard to create a form for a multi-table database.

Now you have learned all the basic features of Access that you need to manage your own data in most business applications. Part II of this book covers power features of Access. You can go on and read it now, or you can begin doing practical work with Access and come back to this book and work with *Power Features* whenever you find it useful.

Part II

Power Features

Designing
Custom Forms

*T*his chapter covers form design in general, but it focuses on the basic techniques that you will find most helpful in your own work, and it concludes with an exercise that uses these basic techniques to modify the design of a form. You may also want to try out some of the more advanced techniques of form design on your own. In this chapter, you learn:

❑ to select, resize, add and delete bands (sections) of the form

❑ to select, resize, and move individual or multiple controls of the form

❑ to use layout tools such as the Ruler, the Grid, Automatic Alignment, and Automatic Sizing to help place controls properly

❑ to edit and change the typeface and style of text in the form

❑ to use the palette to change the colors and special effects used in the form

❑ to use a field list to add fields to the form

205

❑ to use the toolbox to add objects such as labels, text boxes, lines, and rectangles

❑ to use the toolbox to add objects such as check boxes, radio buttons, and combo boxes, which can replace fields in order to ease data entry

❑ to specify default properties of the objects you add

❑ to display and make some changes in the Property sheets of objects

In Chapters 5 and 6, you created forms using FormWizards. Though these are adequate for many purposes, it is often useful to customize the forms that the Wizards create. For example, you will find that if a table has many fields, the forms you create for the table using the Wizards do not fit all the table's fields on a single screen. The table would be easier to work with if you rearranged the fields so you could see them all at once.

In this chapter, as you learn to design customs forms, you will see that Access' Form window in Design View gives you tremendous power. For example, you can rearrange the fields in the forms created by Wizards simply by clicking and dragging them to the location where you want them.

The Basics

Chapter 5 covered the basic mechanics of creating, modifying, and using a form. As with other objects, you select the **Form** button of the Database window to display the forms list and then select its **New**, **Open**, and **Design** buttons to create New Forms and work with existing ones.

You can also create a new form by selecting a table or query in the Database window and then clicking the **AutoForm** or the **New Form** tool on the toolbar.

Once you have created a form, you can use the toolbar to display it in Design View, Form View, or Datasheet View using the tools shown in Figure 7.1. Chapter 5 discussed how to use Form View and Datasheet View: in this chapter, you learn how to work with forms in Design View.

In general, it is best to begin by using a FormWizard or creating an AutoForm, even when you are creating a custom form. As you know, when you create a new form, the New Form dialog box gives you the option of using the FormWizards or creating a new form. If you select the **New Form** button,

Access displays a blank form. You can add fields of the table or query that it is based on to the form design using the methods you will learn below.

Datasheet View

Form View

Design View

FIGURE 7.1 DESIGN VIEW, FORM VIEW, AND DATASHEET VIEW TOOLS.

However, it is easier to use a Wizard to select fields, so you have all the fields that you need placed in the Form window when you begin. The last dialog box of every FormWizard has a button that lets you display the form you defined in Design View, so you can customize it. To create a form with all the fields, it is often easiest to start with an AutoForm.

Figure 7.2 shows the Form window in Design View. We look at all its features in the following sections.

You should open this form yourself and save it under a different name, so you can try the techniques of form design on it as you read about them in this chapter:

1. If necessary, open the **TEACHSLF** database. Click the **Form** button of the Database window to display the list of forms. **Contractors: AutoForm** should already be selected. Select the **Design** button to display it in Design View.

2. Select the **Maximize** button of the Form window so you have more room to work in.

3. Choose **Save as** from the File menu. When Access displays the Save As dialog box, Edit the Form Name so it reads **Contractors: Custom Form** and select **OK**.

Your screen should display the form shown in Figure 7.2.

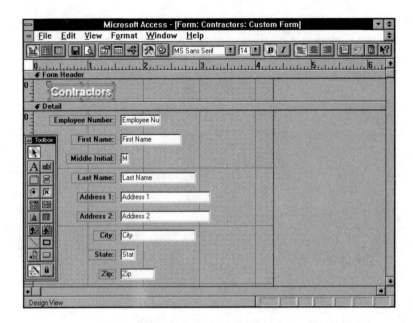

FIGURE 7.2   THE FORM WINDOW IN DESIGN VIEW.

Getting Oriented

All the items included in a form, such as fields, labels (text objects) and check boxes, are called *controls*. In Access, there are three fundamentally different types of control:

❏ *Bound controls* are associated with data in the table. All the fields displayed in the AutoForm are bound controls. This name is used because the information displayed in them depends on the data in the table. They are connected (or bound) to the table.

❏ *Unbound controls* are independent of the data in the table. The word Contractors in the header of the AutoForm is an unbound control. It always remains the same, regardless of the data in the table.

❏ *Calculated controls* are created using expressions. For example, you can create a calculated control that displays the sum of the values in a number of numeric fields. Because calculated controls require expressions, they are described Chapter 8, *Working with Expressions*.

There are a number of features of the Form window in Design View that you can display or hide by using the View menu. All of these are shown in Figure 7.3, but only a few are displayed by default. Beginners should not select **Code** from the View menu, but should use the other features.

FIGURE 7.3   THE VIEW MENU AND FEATURES IT CONTROLS.

After a feature is displayed, you can choose the menu option or click the tool again to close it, or close it using its control menu.

Take a quick look at the features controlled by the View menu to get an overview of how you design forms:

❑   The first three menu options, Form Design, Form, and Datasheet (like the first three tools on the toolbar) let you toggle among views of the form. As you learned in Chapter 5, you can display forms in Design

View, in Form View as a form with data, or in Datasheet View as a table with data

❏ Choose **Properties** from the View menu or click the **Properties** 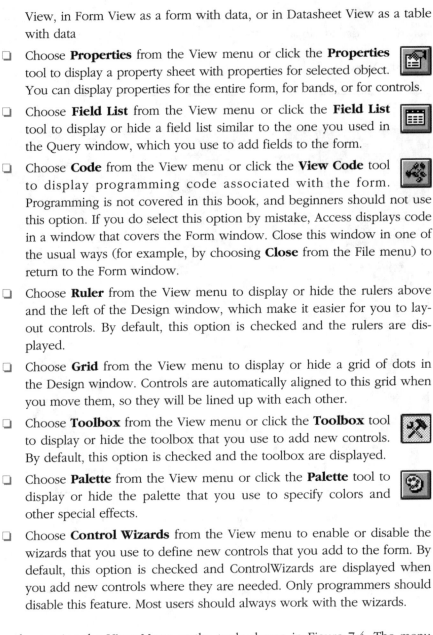 tool to display a property sheet with properties for selected object. You can display properties for the entire form, for bands, or for controls.

❏ Choose **Field List** from the View menu or click the **Field List** tool to display or hide a field list similar to the one you used in the Query window, which you use to add fields to the form.

❏ Choose **Code** from the View menu or click the **View Code** tool to display programming code associated with the form. Programming is not covered in this book, and beginners should not use this option. If you do select this option by mistake, Access displays code in a window that covers the Form window. Close this window in one of the usual ways (for example, by choosing **Close** from the File menu) to return to the Form window.

❏ Choose **Ruler** from the View menu to display or hide the rulers above and the left of the Design window, which make it easier for you to lay-out controls. By default, this option is checked and the rulers are displayed.

❏ Choose **Grid** from the View menu to display or hide a grid of dots in the Design window. Controls are automatically aligned to this grid when you move them, so they will be lined up with each other.

❏ Choose **Toolbox** from the View menu or click the **Toolbox** tool to display or hide the toolbox that you use to add new controls. By default, this option is checked and the toolbox are displayed.

❏ Choose **Palette** from the View menu or click the **Palette** tool to display or hide the palette that you use to specify colors and other special effects.

❏ Choose **Control Wizards** from the View menu to enable or disable the wizards that you use to define new controls that you add to the form. By default, this option is checked and ControlWizards are displayed when you add new controls where they are needed. Only programmers should disable this feature. Most users should always work with the wizards.

Open these using the View Menu or the tools shown in Figure 7.4. The menu option will be checked and the tool button will seem to be depressed to show they are in use. Access remembers which are open and closed when you stop designing the form. It displays the same ones the next time you open the Form window in Design View.

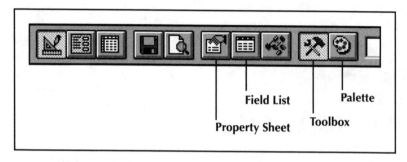

Field List

Palette

Property Sheet

Toolbox

FIGURE 7.4   TOOLS THAT LET YOU USE FORM DESIGN FEATURES.

NOTE

Although the toolbox is displayed by default, other important features of the Form window, such as the Field List and Palette, are not automatically displayed the first time you begin to design a form. Always keep the View menu and these tools in mind when you are designing a form, so you can open and use all of the features needed for designing forms.

You learn more about all these features of form design in the course of this chapter.

Working with the Form

In the next few sections, you see how to select and work with the form as a whole, with *bands* (or sections) of the form and with individual controls on the form. First, let's look at how to work with the entire form

Selecting the Form

To select the form, choose **Select Form** from the Edit menu. As you will see near the end of this chapter, you can display a property sheet for the whole form, as you can for other objects that you select, but this is useful primarily for programmers. After selecting the form, you cannot manipulate it in many of the simple ways that you can bands and controls.

Resizing the Form

Most users work with the entire form only by resizing it. To resize the form, simply place the pointer on its right edge, where it is displayed as a vertical line with arrows pointing in both directions. Then drag left or right to make the form narrower or wider. To change the height of the form, you must resize its individual bands, as described below.

Working with Bands

The Form design window is divided into bands or sections, as shown in Figure 7.5. Which band you place a control in determines how that control is used when you print the form or report or display it on the screen

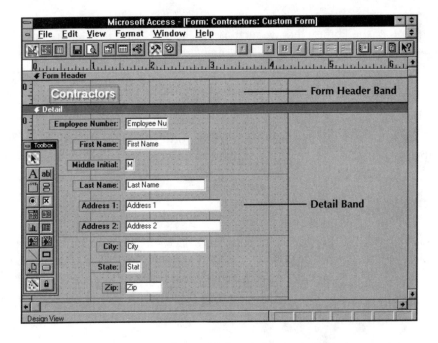

FIGURE 7.5 **Two sections (bands) of the form are visible.**

The AutoForm or any form that you create using a wizard, has three sections:

❏ *Form Header* is displayed at the top of the screen when you view the form on the screen and remains in that location when you scroll through a record. When you print the form, it is printed once at the beginning of the printout. In an AutoForm, the header has the title of the form, based on the name of the table—the word Contractors in the sample form.

❏ *Detail* scrolls when you scroll through the forms on the screen and is repeated for each record when you print the form. In an AutoForm, the Detail band includes all the fields of the table.

❏ *Form Footer* is displayed at the bottom of the screen, if space permits. When you print the form, it is printed once at the end of the printout. In an AutoForm, the Form Footer band has nothing in it by default, but you can add text or other features to it using the methods described later in this chapter.

Figure 7.6 shows the AutoForm in the Print Preview window. The header is displayed once and the fields in the Detail band are repeated underneath it.

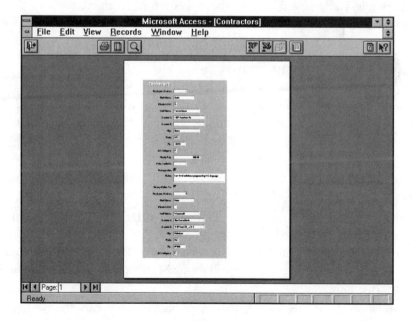

FIGURE 7.6 **THE FORM IN PREVIEW MODE.**

Selecting a Band

You can select a band simply by clicking it. You can also press **Tab** or **Shift-Tab** to select the bands in turn.

The bar with the band's name on it is shaded when it is selected. After you have selected it, you can change the color or other properties of the band using methods described later in this chapter.

Resizing Bands

You will often have occasion to change the size of bands when you are designing custom forms—for example, to make the Header band larger so it can hold a company logo.

You resize a band by clicking and dragging its lower border. When the mouse pointer is in the location where it can be used to resize the band, it is displayed as a horizontal line, with arrow heads pointing up and down. Then you can click and drag downward to make the band larger or upward to make it smaller. While you resize the band, the rulers are highlighted, to show the size of the band.

Adding and Deleting Bands

A form must have a Detail band, but you can delete the Form Header and Form Footer bands. In addition, you can add a Page Header and Page Footer bands to a form. These bands are not displayed on the screen, but they are printed at the top and bottom of every page if you print the form.

Use the Format menu to add or remove bands. The two final options on this menu are Page Header/Footer and Form Header/Footer.

When you first create the AutoForm, the **Form Header/Footer** option from the Format menu is checked, as you can see in Figure 7.7, to show that the form includes a form header and footer. Choose **Page Header/Footer** from the Format menu to add a page header and footer. This option will also be checked after they are added.

These options are toggles. If they are checked, you can choose either of them to remove the form or page header and footer. Choose them again to add the form or page header and footer.

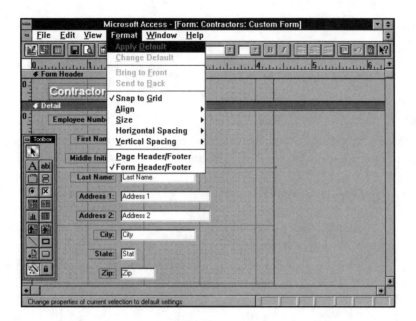

FIGURE 7.7 USE THE FORMAT MENU TO ADD OR REMOVE BANDS.

WARNING

If you remove form or page header and footers, Access also removes all the controls in them, so that you lose all previous work you did in designing them. Access displays a warning telling you this before removing headers and footers. Because Access cannot undo this change, it is best to save your work before removing a header and footer. Then you can undo the change after seeing its effect by closing the Form window without saving changes.

Working with Controls

As you know, all the individual items included in a form, such as fields, text boxes, and checkboxes—are called *controls*. This chapter covers Bound controls (such as the fields in the AutoForm), which are associated with data in the table, and Unbound controls (such as the word Contractors in the header of the AutoForm), which are independent of the data in the table. (Calculated controls, which are created using expressions, are covered in Chapter 8.)

There are many different types of controls that fall within these basic divisions. The AutoForm includes only three types of controls:

❑ *Labels*, which hold text. The word Contractors is an unbound label
❑ *Fields*, which where the user enters data.
❑ *Check Box*, which is used to enter and display data in its Yes/No field.

The Fields and the check box also have the field name attached to them as a label.

Later in this chapter, you learn to use the toolbox to add many other types of controls, such as list boxes, option buttons, and OLE objects.

Selecting Controls

To select a control, simply click it. To deselect a control, click anywhere in the Form window outside of that control.

Once a control is selected, you can press **Tab** or **Shift-Tab** to deselect it and select the next or previous control in turn.

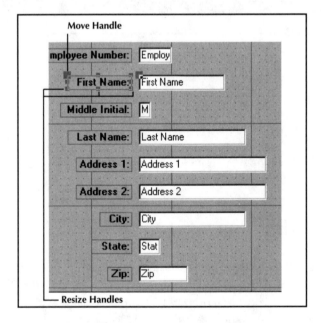

FIGURE 7.8   THE SELECTED CONTROL HAS TWO TYPES OF HANDLES.

When a control is selected, it has two types of handle, the *Resize handle* and the *Move handle*, as shown in Figure 7.8. In this section, you learn to resize and move selected controls. Later in this chapter, you learn to change many properties of controls after selecting them.

Notice that in the illustration, the First Name field's label is selected and has both the Resize handles and Move handle. The box where the field's data is entered has only the Move handle. Whenever you select a control or its label, the other one has just the move handle added in this way. As you will see in a moment, this lets you move the two controls independently or together.

Note, though, that a control must have Resize handles to be selected. The control with just a Move handle is not selected.

DELETING A CONTROL

Press **Del** to delete the selected control. Access does not display a warning before deleting it. In case of an error, you can select **Undo Delete** from the Edit menu.

If you delete a control, its label is automatically deleted, but you can delete a label without deleting the control

RESIZING A CONTROL

Click and drag the Resize handles to change the size of the control. When you put the pointer on one of these handles, it is displayed as a two headed arrow, indicating the directions you can drag that handle.

❏ Click and drag the top or bottom handle up or down to change the height of the control.

❏ Click and drag the side handles left or right to make the control wider or narrower.

❏ Click and drag the corner handles diagonally to change both the height and width of the control.

After resizing, you can choose **Undo Sizing** from the Edit menu to get rid of the change.

MOVING A CONTROL

To move a control, you can simply click and drag its Move Handle in any direction. When it is on the Move Handle, the pointer is displayed as a hand with its index finger extended.

Use this method to move a field's name or text box. Only the control whose Move box you drag will be moved, and the other will remain in place.

You can also move a control by placing the pointer anywhere on its edges except on the handles. The pointer is displayed as a hand with all its fingers extended when you can click and drag to move the control.

Use this method to move a field name and text box together. You must move the one that is selected—the one that has both Move and Resize Handles—but the other one, which has just a Move Handle, will move along with it so that it always remains the same distance from it.

After moving a control, you can choose **Undo Move** from the Edit menu to get rid of the change.

SPECIAL TECHNIQUES FOR WORKING WITH CONTROLS

In addition to these basic methods of selecting, moving and resizing controls, there are a few special techniques that make your work easier.

Selecting Multiple Controls

In general, a control is deselected when you select another control (or click anywhere in the Form window). There are times, however, when you want to select multiple controls—for example, to change the color of a group of controls.

You can also move or resize a group of controls simultaneously by selecting them all, and it is necessary to do this when you move or resize controls that are actually made of two controls to create a special effect, such as a shadowed look.

There are several ways to select multiple controls:

❑ To select adjacent controls, click and drag to form a square around the entire group of the controls you want selected. Click somewhere outside of any control, beyond one corner of the group, hold down the mouse button, and drag to the opposite corner of the group. Access displays a dotted line, as shown in Figure 7.9, to indicate the area you are dragging around. When you release the mouse button, all of the controls within the line are selected.

❑ To select controls that are not adjacent, hold down the **Shift** key as you click them. When you **Shift-click** a control, other controls are not deselected, so you can select an indefinite number of controls in this way.

❑ To select all the controls in all the bands of the form, choose **Select All** from the Edit menu.

You can press **Del** to delete all the selected controls and you can also resize or move them in tandem.

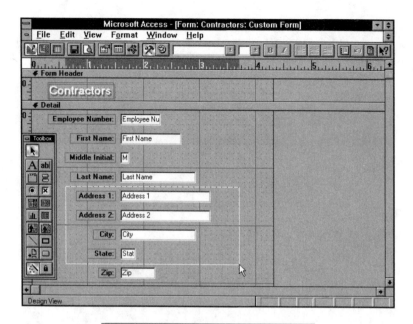

FIGURE 7.9 SELECTING ADJACENT CONTROLS.

Resizing Multiple Controls

When multiple controls are selected, if you resize one of them, all the others will be resized—as if you had clicked and dragged the same Resize handle of each of them in the same way.

Moving Multiple Controls

If you place the pointer on any one of the selected controls, it will be displayed as a hand, and you can click and drag the control to move it and move all the other selected controls the same distance in the same direction. You can also move just one of the selected controls and leave the others in place by using its Move handle.

Working with Controls that Use Special Effects

If you use the wizards to create controls with a Chiseled, Shadowed, or Boxed style, Access creates these effects by using two controls one behind another. In the AutoForm, the word Contractors in the Heading band has a shadowed look and is actually made up of two controls.

If you simply click and drag this sort of control, you will only move one and the other will be left in place, as in Figure 7.10.

NOTE

The way to move or resize this sort of control is to click and drag around it to select both of the controls it is actually made of. Then both will be moved or resized in tandem.

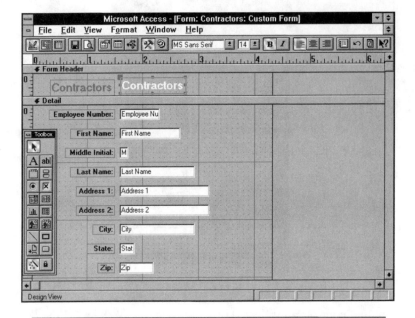

FIGURE 7.10   A SHADOWED CONTROL IS ACTUALLY MADE OF TWO CONTROLS.

Moving Controls in One Direction

To make it easier for you to keep controls in proper alignment, Access gives you the option of moving a control (or all selected controls) in only a horizontal or vertical direction. Hold down the **Shift** key when you begin to click and drag the control and it will only move horizontally or vertically, depending on which direction you move it in first.

Layout Tools

There are a few special layout tools that may make it easier for you to work with controls.

THE RULER

The ruler above or to the left of the grid is highlighted when you move an object to help you align it.

Choose **Ruler** from the View menu to display or hide these rulers. By default, this option is checked and the rulers are displayed.

THE GRID

As you learned earlier, a grid of dots is displayed in the Design window by default and controls are automatically aligned with this grid to make it easier to align them with each other.

Choose **Grid** from the View menu to display or hide this grid. If you hide it, controls are still aligned to it. Hiding it simply makes it easier to see some effects in the Form design. By default, this option is checked and the grid is displayed.

Choose **Snap to Grid** from the Format menu to turn this automatic alignment on and off. By default, this option is checked and controls are aligned to the grid. You might want to turn this feature off when you move one or two controls to make them stand out by not being aligned with the others.

You can change the fineness of the grid by using its property sheet, covered later in this Chapter.

AUTOMATIC ALIGNMENT

You can also select a number of controls and align them with each other automatically. When you choose **Align** from the Format menu, Access displays a submenu with additional options.

Choose **Left** to align the left edge of all the selected controls with the left edge of the leftmost one. Likewise, select **Right**, **Top**, or **Bottom** to align all the controls with the rightmost, highest, or lowest edge of any selected control.

Choose **To Grid** to align upper-left corners of the selected controls to the nearest grid points. This is useful if you had turned Snap to Grid off when you placed them.

AUTOMATIC SIZING

You can select controls and have Access automatically size them by choosing the **Size** from the Format menu and one of the following options from its submenu:

❑ Select one or more controls and choose **to Fit** to adjust the size of the control to fit the font of the text it contains.

❑ Select one or more controls and choose **to Grid** to adjust the size of the control so all of its edges fit the grid. This is useful if you have changed the fineness of the grid, so that controls that you placed earlier do not fit exactly into the new grid.

❑ You can also use this command to make a number of controls the same width or height. Select several controls and choose **to Tallest**, **to Shortest**, **to Widest**, or **to Narrowest**, in order to make them all as high as the tallest or shortest or to make them all as wide as the widest or narrowest.

SPACING

You can adjust the spacing of controls by choosing **Horizontal Spacing** or **Vertical Spacing** from the Format menu. Both of these have a submenu with the options Make Equal, Increase, and Decrease, which you can use to space all the controls evenly or to increase or decrease the spacing between them uniformly.

Changing Stacking Order

When you place objects in the form, the ones that you place later appear to be above ones that you placed earlier. If two objects overlap, the one that was placed later will hide the one that was placed earlier. The order in which objects cover one another is sometimes called their *stacking order.*

To change this order, select an object and then:

❑ Choose **Bring to Front** from the Format menu to make that object appear to be in front of all other objects.

❑ Choose **Send to Back** from the Format menu to make that object appear to be behind all other objects.

These options are only needed if objects overlap.

Changing Tab Order

You can also specify the tab order of controls in the form—that is, the order in which the user can access them by pressing **Tab** and **Shift-Tab** (rather than clicking them with the mouse). This is useful if you have moved controls or added new controls, so that the order in which the user accesses them by pressing **Tab** is not the same as the order in which they are displayed on the screen.

To do this, choose **Tab Order** from the Edit menu to display the Tab Order dialog box, shown in Figure 7.11. Use the Section radio buttons to specify which band's controls are displayed in the Custom Order list.

FIGURE 7.11   **THE TAB ORDER DIALOG BOX.**

SHORTCUT

In general, it is easiest to click the **Auto Order** button. Access automatically sets the tab order based on the location of the controls in the form, so the user tabs through from top to bottom and from left to right. The order of controls in the Custom Order list is changed to reflect this order when you select this button.

To set tab order by hand, move the rows in this list as you move the rows in a table. Use the selection boxes on their left to select one or more rows, and then click and drag the selection box to move the rows to specify tab order.

Working with Text

You can edit the text in a label or change the typeface and style of any text in the form in much the same way that you do using most Windows word processors.

Editing Text

You can edit the text in a label directly in the Form Design window. The text in some controls, such as fields, depends on what you enter in the table. You can edit the text on some other controls, such as push buttons that you add to the form. You can also edit the label that is attached to any type of control.

To edit text, first click the label (or other control) to select it. You must select only the control that you want to edit, and not select multiple controls.

Once the Label (or other control) is selected, the mouse pointer is displayed as an insertion bar when you move it over the label, as it is in any Windows word processor or editor. You can click in any location in the label to place an insertion point there, or click and drag to select text. Edit as you do with any Windows editor, using the methods described at the beginning of the section on "The Access Editor" in Chapter 3.

Changing Typeface, Style, and Alignment

Though you can only edit the text in a label, you can specify the typeface, style, and alignment of most controls that contains text. For example, you can change the typeface, style, and alignment of the data that is displayed in fields. You can also change the typeface of text on push buttons that you add to the form, but not its alignment, as it is always centered.

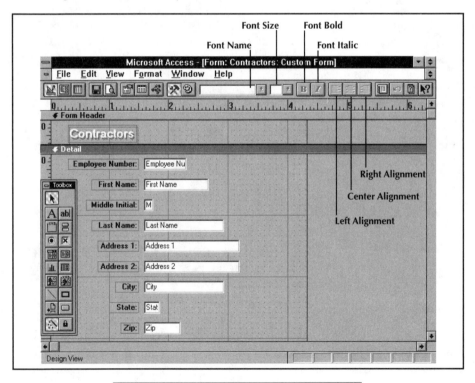

FIGURE 7.12   TOOLS USED FOR WORKING WITH TEXT.

When you select one or more controls that contain text, the tools on the toolbar that are used for working with text are enabled, as shown in Figure 7.12. You can work with them as you do with similar controls in Windows word processors:

❑ Use the Font Name drop-down list to select a font, such as Arial, Courier, or Times Roman. The fonts that are available in this list depend on the fonts you have installed under Windows.

❑ Use the Font Size drop-down list to specify the size of the type, in points. You may have to resize a control to hold a larger font size.

❑ Use the Font Bold and Font Italic buttons to display the text in boldface and/or italic type. The button appears to be pressed when it is selected, and you can click it again to deselect it, so the text is no longer bold or italic.

❑ Use the Left Alignment, Center Alignment, or Right Alignment buttons to determine how the text is aligned within its control. For example, data is ordinarily aligned to the left of the field it is displayed in, but you can use these buttons to center or right-justify it within the field.

All these features must be applied to an entire control. They are not enabled when you are editing text in a control, and so you cannot (for example) use a different typeface for some of the letters in a label. They can be applied to many controls at once simply by selecting all of the controls before applying them.

Working with Colors and Effects

You use the Palette, shown in Figure 7.13, to specify the colors of objects, to specify the type of border they have, and to create special effects, such as raised or lowered look.

Displaying the Palette

The palette is not displayed when you first open a form in Design View. You can display it at any time by clicking the **Palette** tool or by choosing **Palette** from the View menu.

The Palette tool appears to be pressed, and the Palette menu option has a check next to is when the palette is displayed.

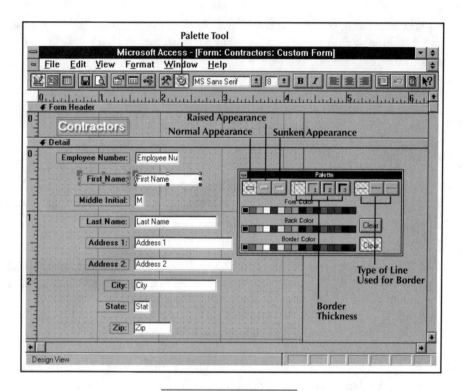

FIGURE 7.13   THE PALETTE.

Once it is displayed, you can remove the palette by selecting the **Palette** tool or choosing **Palette** from the View menu again.

Using the Palette

Before using the palette, you must select a band of the form or one or more controls, using the methods described earlier in this chapter. The palette's buttons are dimmed and its color bands are displayed in black and white if you have not selected an object to which they apply. Not all options on the palette are available if you select a band.

Most controls have three elements whose color you can specify:

❑   the *foreground*, for example, the text displayed in a label

❑   the *background*, for example, the area within the label around the text

❑   the *border*, for example, the box displayed around the label

You can specify colors for all of these and you can also specify the type of line used and special effects used in the border.

Use the three color bands of the palette to select the foreground, background, or border color. Simply click a color to apply it to the selected objects.

Notice that the Back Color and Border color bands both have clear buttons next to them. If one of these buttons is selected and appears to be pressed, the background or border will be transparent. That is, you will be able to see other objects through the background of the control or the control will appear not to have any border. As long as these buttons are selected, any colors that you apply to the object background and border will not be visible. You must click a **Clear** button to deselect it in order to see the colors you apply.

The buttons at the top of the palette let you control the appearance of controls' borders.

The first three buttons shade the border to create a lowered or raised effect, or leave it unshaded to create a boxed effect. By default, in an AutoForm, the title is boxed and the fields appear to be lowered. If you want one of the fields to appear to be raised instead, to make it stand out, you can select it and click the **Raised Appearance** button.

The next three buttons let you specify the thickness of the border. You can select a hairline, 1-point, 2-point, or 3-point thick border.

The final three buttons let you specify the type of line used for the border. You can use a solid, dashed, or dotted line.

Adding Controls

Even if you begin by creating a form with a Wizard, which places all the fields you want on it, you may well want to add extra controls to it. Most obviously, you might add rectangles, lines, or OLE objects as graphic enhancements; you might add new labels with help text or other descriptive text; or you might replace fields with controls such as list boxes to make data entry easier.

Adding a Field

You may need to add fields to a form design if you are starting with a blank form, if you forgot to include a field when you first defined the form, or if you deleted a field by mistake.

To add a field, first display the field list, if necessary, by choosing **Field List** from the View menu or selecting the **Field List** tool. This field list, shown in Figure 7.14, is used just like field lists in queries, except that it does not have an asterisk representing all fields.

FIGURE 7.14   THE FIELD LIST.

To add a single field to the form, simply click and drag it from the field list to the form.

After you have selected multiple fields in the field list, you can click and drag any of them to the form, and all of the others will be dragged along with it. To select multiple fields:

❑ Click a field to select it. Then hold down the **Shift** key and click another field to select all the fields between it and the first field.

❑ Hold down the **Ctrl** key as you click fields, to select additional fields without deselecting ones that are already selected.

❑ Double-click the title bar of the Field List to select all fields.

Fields that you add in this way are made up of a label and a text box for data entry, like the fields that Access places in the form initially. When you select the label or text box, a Move handle is automatically added to the other, and you can move them in tandem or separately, as described earlier in this chapter.

Using the Toolbox

You can add many other types of control using the toolbox. The tools available in the toolbox are shown in Figure 7.15.

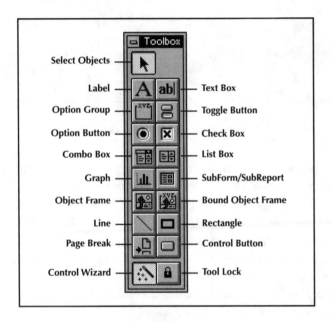

Select Objects	
Label	Text Box
Option Group	Toggle Button
Option Button	Check Box
Combo Box	List Box
Graph	SubForm/SubReport
Object Frame	Bound Object Frame
Line	Rectangle
Page Break	Control Button
Control Wizard	Tool Lock

FIGURE 7.15 TOOLS IN THE TOOLBOX.

In general, you add a new control to the form by clicking a tool in the toolbox and then clicking and dragging on the form to define the size and location of the control.

After you click one of these tools, the pointer changes its form to indicate that it is being used to add a control. In general, the pointer changes to crosshairs and an icon that indicates the type of control that you are adding. For example, the appearance of the pointer when you are adding a rectangle button is shown in Figure 7.16. It is made up of crosshairs and a rectangle icon.

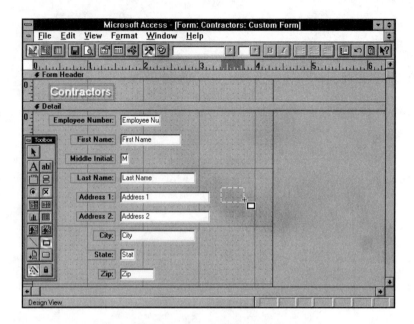

FIGURE 7.16   THE POINTER FOR ADDING AN RECTANGLE BUTTON.

Place the crosshairs the location where you want one corner of the new control to be. Then click and drag to the opposite corner to specify the location and the size of the control. (At any time after the control is placed, you can select it, and then resize or move it using the methods earlier in this chapter.)

When you release the mouse button after clicking and dragging to place a new control, Access may display a Wizard to let you define the control. No Wizard is displayed when you add a rectangle, for example, because no information beyond its size and location is needed to define it. However, if you are adding a checkbox, Access displays a Wizard to let you specify which field it represents.

All the tools in the toolbox are described below, along with details on placing each type of control. Remember that you can use the methods described earlier to move, resize, delete, and, when applicable, to specify the colors and fonts of these new controls.

SELECT OBJECTS

The Select Objects tool returns the pointer to its usual form, an arrow.

It can be used to cancel the operation of adding a new control. After you click the tool, the pointer changes to the form that lets you add that control.

Click the Select Objects tool to return the pointer to its usual form, so you are no longer adding that new control.

Label

To add new text to the form, you can click the **Label** tool, and click and drag to create a label box. After you release the mouse button, you can simply type text and it will be displayed in the box.

If the box is large enough for several lines of text, the text automatically wraps to the next line when you fill a line. It also automatically wraps to fit in it if you resize the text box later. To start a new paragraph, press **Ctrl-Enter** rather than Enter.

If you type too much text to fit in the box, it automatically expands to accommodate your entry. If your entry is on one line, the box gets wider. If your entry is already on multiple lines, it the box expands vertically to add extra lines. Remember that you can always resize the box after you have finished typing and the text is automatically rejustified to fit in it.

When you are done entering text, press **Enter** or click anywhere outside of the label box to continue designing the form. You can still edit the text at a later time, as you do any text, by selecting it and then clicking it to put an insertion bar in it.

You can also specify the font and style of the text by selecting it, as you do any label and then using the methods described in the section "Working with Text." You cannot specify font or style when you begin entering the text.

Automatically Sizing the Label

Rather than clicking and dragging to define the label box, you can automatically size it to fit the text you type.

Simply click the **Label** tool, click anywhere in the form, and begin typing. The box gets wider as you type to accommodate the text.

If you press **Ctrl-Enter** to add a new line, the box keeps that width and adds new lines to accommodate the text you type.

Attaching a Label to a Control

If a Bound control does not already have a label attached to it—for example, if you deleted the label for a field—you can use the Text tool to create a label and attach it to the control using the Cut and Paste options.

Create the label as usual. When you are done, select it and choose **Cut** from the Edit menu. Then select the control you want to attach it to and choose **Paste** from the Edit menu. Finally, use its Move handle to adjust its location.

The label is attached to the control in the same way that fields' labels are attached to them. When you select the label or control, a Move handle is automatically added to the other, and you can move them together or separately, as you learned to do in the section "Moving Controls," earlier in this chapter.

Text Box

To add a text box to the form, click the **Text Box** tool and then click and drag to place the text box. When you release the mouse button, Access displays a text box like the one you use to enter data in a field. The word Unbound is in the text box to indicate that it is not attached to a field. It has an arbitrary name made up of the word Field followed by a number, as shown in Figure 7.17.

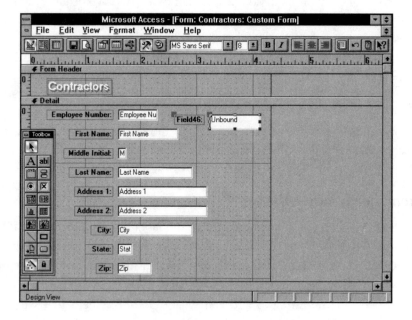

Figure 7.17   Adding a text box to a form.

You can use a text box to display a calculated value. For example, you could display value that is the sum or product of numbers in other fields.

After placing the text box, click inside of it to remove the word Unbound and place an insertion point in it. You can also select it and then click in it at any time to place an insertion point in it, as you to with labels. Type an Access expression in it and the result of that expression will be displayed in the form. (See Chapter 8 for more information about expressions.) Click anywhere outside of the text box to finish typing in it.

The value it displays is read-only. The user cannot edit it.

OPTION GROUP

The Option Group tool is used to create a group of controls that work together to give the user let the user enter data in a field that has only a few possible entries.

Types of Option Group

The most common type of Option Group is made up of radio buttons (option buttons), but this tool also lets you create a group of checkboxes or a group of toggle buttons (which can appear to be raised or pushed down). In any case, if the user selects one of the options, the others are automatically deselected. The Wizard lets you assign values to each option, which you can store in the field of a table or use later in a program.

If the Option Group replaces one of the fields on the form, you should delete that field from the design, if it was initially included in it.

N O T E

The main limitation of the Option Group is that the values assigned to the options must be numbers. If you are working with a numeric field with several possible values, you can use this type of control to enter these values in it. Developers can use these numbers to control other actions of an application. Beginners who want to use a control to enter data in a field should use a Combo box rather than an Option Group, as it is easy to use a Combo box to enter values of various data types.

Adding an Option Group

To add an Option Group, click the **Option Group** tool, and click and drag to place the box that will be the border around all the option buttons in the group. When you release the mouse button, Access displays the Option Group Wizard, which lets you enter the following data:

❏ Enter names of all the options in the first dialog box. You can add and edit these in the same way that you add and edit records in a table. Each name that you add will be displayed next to one of the buttons, so enter names that help the user decide which button to choose.

❏ Use the radio buttons in second dialog box to specify whether or not there will be a default value. If you do create a default value, you must use the drop-down list to select the name that you gave to one of the buttons. This button will be selected by default when the form is displayed.

❏ The third dialog box lists all the names that you entered and has a text box next to each where you can enter the value associated with it. This is the value that will actually be entered in the field if the user selects that button.

❏ Use the radio buttons in the fourth dialog box to decide whether or not to bind the option group to a field. Only developers should use the Don't Bind option. Non-programmers should select the **Bind To** radio button and use the drop-down list to its right to select one of the fields in the table or query that the form is based on. The value that the user selects will automatically be entered in this field. This value must be an integer.

❏ The fifth dialog box lets you choose whether the option buttons will be radio buttons, checkboxes, or toggle buttons, and whether the group will have a normal boxed appearance or a raised or sunken look. It displays the final appearance of the option group.

❏ The final dialog box lets you enter a label for the entire option group.

Which Control to Use

In general, it is best to use radio buttons in option groups, because users are accustomed to selecting options in this way.

Groups of toggle buttons can be used to create special effects, though you should be careful to use them in ways that do not confuse users, who expect push buttons to initiate actions.

WARNING

Option groups made of checkboxes can confuse users and should be avoided unless there is a special reason for using them. A checkbox is conventionally used to enter data in a field that can have only two values, most often a Yes/No field. They are not conventionally associated in groups, where one is deselected when others are selected.

Because they use only integers as their values, Option Groups are useful primarily for developers, who control later actions of an application on the basis of the selection in the option group.

Toggle Buttons, Option Buttons, and Checkboxes

In addition to associating them in groups to let the user choose among several values, you can place a single toggle button, option button, or checkbox to let the user enter a value into a Yes/No field.

If the control is selected, Yes is entered in the field, and if it is not, No is entered in the field.

Adding these Controls

To create one of these controls, first display the Field List. Then click the **Toggle Button**, **Radio Button**, or **Checkbox** tool in the Toolbox. As always, the pointer will be displayed as a crosshair with an icon next to it representing the type of control you are adding. Use this pointer to click and drag a Yes/No field from the Field List to the form. Access creates a toggle button, radio button, or checkbox that is bound to that field.

You can also click the appropriate tool and click and drag on the form to create an unbound toggle button, radio button, or checkbox. This is useful for developers who want to control some later action of an application on the basis of the option selected in one of these controls, but this is not advisable for non-programmers.

Which Control to Use

For non-programmers, it is best to use these controls to enter values in a Yes/No field.

A checkbox is best for this use, since this is the conventional method of selecting Yes or No in Windows applications, and users are accustomed to it. Use a toggle button for special effects.

WARNING

You can confuse users by using a radio button for this purpose, because radio buttons are conventionally used in groups to let users select one of several options. Be particularly careful not to use several radio buttons that are near each other to enter values in several Yes/No fields. Users expect to be able to select only one of them at a time.

Combo Boxes and List Boxes

In Access and other Windows applications, you often choose items from lists. Access lets you add two of these types of lists to forms, Combo boxes and List boxes.

The Difference between Combo Boxes and List Boxes

A Combo box is a combination of a drop-down list and a text box. The user can enter a value in the text box or select a value from the drop-down to display it in the text box. This is the same way that drop-down lists generally work in Windows applications, but Access calls this control a Combo box to emphasize the fact that, by default, users can enter a value in the textbox that is not on the list. (You can change this default by using the property sheet of the Combo box and selecting Yes as the Limit to List property, but this property is No by default.)

A List box displays choices and lets the user select one, but unlike a drop-down list, the options in the List box are always displayed. If there are more choices in the list than can be displayed in the area you define for the box, Access adds a scroll bar to its right edge to let the user display all the options. Unlike a Combo box, a List box does not let the user type in a value. Only the values in the list may be chosen.

Combo boxes and List boxes are very similar, then. Combo boxes are useful when you do not have much room on a form, because the options are not always displayed; they can also let users type in values that are not available on the list. However, the mechanics of defining a list of options to be displayed in a Combo box or List box are the same and the Wizards that you use to create them are identical.

Multiple Column Combo and List Boxes

Access lets you create Combo boxes or List boxes with multiple columns. In a Combo box, the value in the first column is displayed in the text box when the drop-down list is closed. In either case, you can select the column whose value will be entered in the table.

For example, you can create a Combo box with the full names of all the states in its first column and the two-letter abbreviation for each state in a second column next to the name. The full name of the state will be displayed in the text box. When the drop-down list is displayed, it will have a two-column list of state names and their abbreviations. You can define the Combo box so the abbreviation is entered in the table.

Two Ways of Adding These Controls

To add one of these controls, click the **Combo Box** tool or **List Box** tool, and click and drag to define its size and location the form.

When you release the mouse button, Access displays the Combo Box Wizard or List Box Wizard, which are used in the same way. The first dialog box of both lets you choose among two fundamentally different ways of defining the values in the list. You can type values in the Wizard when you define the control or you can have the control display the values in a table or query.

In general, you type in the values if there are a small number of them that will not change. You could do this to let the user enter a title such as Mr., Ms., Mrs., Dr., and so on. There are a limited number of these titles, and it is not difficult to type them in the Wizard when you are defining the control.

Use the values in a table or query when there are a larger number of values to choose among and when the available values may change. This is particularly useful in a relational database.

For example, in the relational database that you worked with in Chapter 6, you could create a data-entry form for the Billing table that includes a List box with three columns. It would display the last name, first name, and employee number from all the records of the Contractor table. The user could select the contractor by name, and the form could enter the employee number in the Billing table.

N O T E

You could also create special tables to be used as the basis of Combo boxes or List boxes. For example, you could create a table with the names and abbreviations of all the states, which you use as the basis of a two-column Combo box. It would display the state name in its text box, include both state name and abbreviation in its drop-down list, and enter the abbreviation in the table. If you create this special table once, you can import it into any database you are working on, and then you can add this extra touch with very little effort. Chapter 12 discusses importing tables.

Entering Values in the Wizard

If you indicate in the first dialog box of the Combo Box Wizard or List Box Wizard that you are typing in the values to be displayed, then you use the remaining dialog boxes to:

❏ Enter the values to be displayed in the same way that you enter data in a table, as shown in Figure 7.18. The figure uses just one column. You can also enter any number up to 40 in the # of columns box and define values for all the columns. After entering a number, press **Tab** or click to move the cursor to the table, in it will display the number of columns you indicated. Remember that the values you enter in the first column will be displayed in the text box, but you can enter values from any of the columns in the table.

FIGURE 7.18   ENTERING VALUES TO BE DISPLAYED.

❏ Use the same dialog box to specify the width of the columns displayed in the Combo box or List box by clicking and dragging the right edge of the column headings, as you do when you are resizing the columns of a table.

❏ If you are working with multiple columns, select which column of the Combo box has the value you want to store in the table. (If you are working with one column, the Wizard skips this dialog box.)

❏ Select the **Store that value in this field** radio button of the next dialog box, and use the drop-down list to its right to select a field of the table that the Combo box will be bound to. The option that the user selects in the control is automatically entered in this field. (Nonprogrammers should always select this button and select a field in this dialog box. Only developers should select the **Remember the value for later use** button.)

❏ Enter a label for the Combo box and select the **Create** button to place it in the form.

Creating a List box or Combo box in this way is very straight-forward.

Using Values from a Table or Query

It is a bit more complicated to create a List box or Combo box based on a table or query.

To make it clearer, examples are included in the steps that follow which you could use to create a three-column List box in the data-entry form for the Billing table. This List box displays the last name, first name, and employee number from all the records of the Contractor table, and enters the appropriate selected employee number in the Billing table.

Rather than basing this list on the Contractors table itself, you could begin by creating a query that sorts the records in alphabetical order by name and includes the Last Name, First Name, and Employee Number fields, so it will be easier for the user to look up the names in an alphabetical list.

After indicating in the first dialog box that you want to use values looked up in a table, you use the remaining dialog boxes to:

❏ Select a table or query in the database which the values will be taken from. For example, if you were creating a form for the Billing table, the query with an alphabetical listing of contractors table would be displayed in this list, because it is in the same database, and you would select it.

❏ Use a field picker dialog box to choose the fields that will be displayed in the columns of the Combo box or List box. The number of fields you select is the same as the number of columns. For example, select the **Last Name**, **First Name**, and **Employee Number** fields.

❏ Specify the width of the columns displayed in the Combo box or List box by clicking and dragging the right edge of the column headings, as you do when you are resizing the columns of a table.

❏ If you are working with multiple columns, select which column of the Combo box or List box has the value you want to store in the table. (If you are working with one column, the Wizard skips this dialog box.) For example, select the **Employee Number** field

❏ Select a field of the table that the Combo box or List box is bound to. In the example, the Wizard would display a list of all the fields in the Billing table, and select the **Employee Number** field. (Nonprogrammers should always select the **Bound** radio button and select a field in this dialog box. Only programmers should create an unbound control.)

❑ Enter a label for the Combo box or List box and select the **Create** button to place it in the form.

GRAPH

To add a graph to the form, click the **Graph** tool, and click and drag to define the size and location of the graph.

When you release the mouse button, Access displays the GraphWizard, which you use to define the graph. First select a table or query to serve as the basis for the graph. Then select at least one numeric field which holds the values to be graphed and a field to use for labels, as described in Chapter 5, in the section on using the FormWizards to create graphs.

Before closing the GraphWizard, Access gives you the option of linking the graph to the form, as shown in Figure 7.19.

FIGURE 7.19   YOU HAVE THE OPTION OF LINKING A GRAPH TO THE FORM.

If you do not link the graph, its values remain the same as you page through the form. If you link the graph, its values will change as you page through the form. This can be appropriate when you are working with a main form and a subform of a relational database. For example, in your sample database, you could add a graph of the hours worked each month by each contractor. It would reflect the values in the Billing table, displayed in the subform and it would change depending on which Contractor is displayed in the main form.

After you place the graph in this way, Access displays the ChartWizard to let you customize the graph. The ChartWizard, which is a feature of the Microsoft Graph mini-application that is embedded in Access, was discussed briefly in the section on FormWizards in Chapter 5. Its more advanced features are beyond the scope of this book.

SUBFORM/SUBREPORT

You learned about subforms in Chapter 6, when you created a form using the Main/Subform Wizard. As you know, if a form is used to display records from a table on the one side of a one-to-many relationship, it can include a subform with all the related fields from the table on the many side of the relationship—for example, all the bills from each contractor.

NOTE

In general, if you want to include a subform in a graph, it is best to use this Wizard to create it. You then can move and resize the subform as you do any other object in Design View.

To add a subform in Design View, you must use the property sheets of objects in fairly advanced ways.

If you are working with a relational database, you can use the Subform tool to add a frame for a subform to a form, simply by clicking and dragging. Attaching to the subform to the frame requires more advanced techniques. You must use the property sheet for the subform/subreport and select an existing form as its source object. That previously defined form will be displayed in the frame. You must also use the LinkChildFields and LinkMasterFields properties to link the forms, so the right records of the subform are displayed when you change the record displayed in the main form.

You can also add a subform to a form by dragging a form's name from the Database window to the Form Design window. Again, you must set the LinkChildFields and LinkMasterFields properties to link the forms.

Though these properties will be filled in automatically if you set up the database properly, it is generally easier for beginners to begin by using the Main/Subform Wizard and then to customize the form if necessary.

For more information on more advanced methods of creating a subform, search for the topic Creating a Subform in Access Help.

OBJECT AND BOUND OBJECT FRAMES

You can add OLE objects to the form by selecting the **Object Frame** or **Bound Object Frame** tool and clicking and dragging to define the size and location of the frame that will hold the OLE object.

A *bound OLE Object frame* displays the contents of an OLE object field of your database and changes as you move through records.

An *unbound OLE Object frame* displays an OLE object that remains the same as you move through the records. It is most commonly used to add a business's logo to its data entry forms.

Both of these tools are discussed in Chapter 12, which covers OLE Objects.

LINE

To add a line to the form, simply click the **Line** tool and click and drag on the form. Access adds a straight line connecting the places where you begin and end dragging. It may be horizontal, vertical or diagonal.

Lines are useful to underline or emphasize parts of the form or to divide the form visually into several parts.

You can use the palette, as described earlier in this chapter, to define the thickness, color, and type (solid, dotted, or dashed) of the line.

RECTANGLE

To add a rectangle to the form, simply click the **Rectangle** tool and click and drag on the form. Access adds a rectangle with opposite corners in the locations where you begin and end dragging. The edges of the rectangle are always horizontal and vertical.

Rectangles are useful to emphasize parts of the form or for visually grouping several controls by adding a box around them.

By default, rectangles have a hairline border, white background color, and sunken look, as shown in Figure 7.20, like the areas where you enter data in fields. You can use the palette, as described earlier in this chapter, to define the thickness, color, and type (solid, dotted, or dashed) of the line.

NOTE

The most common use of a rectangle is to place a box around an area of the form. To do this, use the palette to give it a clear back color, a boxed rather than an sunken look, and a thicker line as its border. You can also use Send to Back, rather than giving it a clear back color.

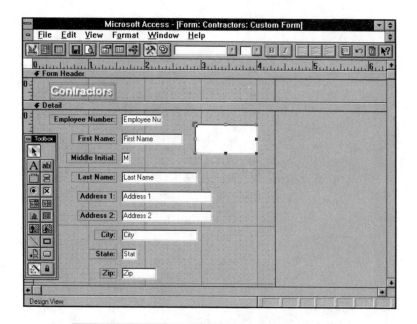

FIGURE 7.20 **THE DEFAULT APPEARANCE OF A RECTANGLE.**

PAGE BREAK

Use the Page Break tool to add a page break to the form. The page break is significant only when you print the form.

For example, if you want to print the form with each record on a separate page, add a page break in the Detail band, below the form's last field. When Access prints the form or displays it in Print Preview, it begins a new page whenever it reaches the page break.

The page break is displayed as a short, dark dotted line, at the left margin of the Form Design window, as shown in Figure 7.21. You can select it and move it as you do other controls. To remove the page break, select and delete it.

COMMAND BUTTON

A Command Button or Push Button actually executes some action.

The Command Button Wizard makes it easy to create buttons that perform many standard actions. For example, you can easily add buttons to the form that let you move to the first, previous, next, and last records, like the controls at the bottom of the Form window. You can also add buttons that let you search for a record, like the Search tool on the toolbar. Many of these are useful primarily for developers, who are creating applications that do not have the usual toolbar or other features of the Access interface.

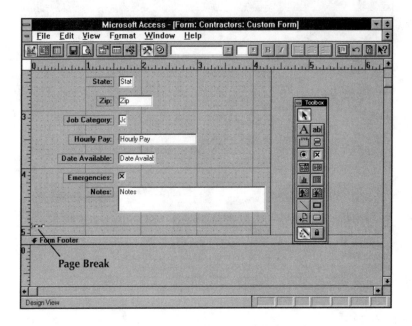

FIGURE 7.21   A PAGE BREAK IN FORM DESIGN WINDOW.

You can also use command buttons to perform custom actions that you cannot perform in one step using the Access interface. The easiest way to do this is to use a button to run a macro. Macros are covered in Chapter 11.

To add a Command button to a form. click the **Command Button** tool and click and drag to define the location and size of the Command button. When you release the mouse button, Access displays the Command Button Wizard, shown in Figure 7.22.

As you can see, the first dialog box of this Wizard lets you select categories (types of action) the button can perform. For each category, it displays a different list of actions. As you can see in Figure 7.22, the actions it allows for record navigation are all similar to things you can do from the Access Interface and they are easy to understand. The same is true of actions in most other categories. Only custom actions are difficult to create and require you to write an Access macro or a program.

FIGURE 7.22   THE COMMAND BUTTON WIZARD.

The first dialog box displays a picture of the push button with the standard icon representing that action—binoculars representing a Find in the illustration.

The second dialog box lets you replace this picture in several ways:

❑ *Standard Pictures* lets you choose from the standard icons that come with the Command Button Wizard. The Show All Pictures checkbox lets you display all available standard pictures or display only the pictures that are suggested for that control.

❑ *Pictures in Bitmap Files* lets you choose the Browse push button to display a dialog box that lets you select any bitmap (BMP) file to use as the picture on the button.

❑ *Text:* The Picture radio button is selected by default. You can use text rather than a picture on the push button by selecting the text radio button and entering the text in the box to its right.

The final dialog box lets you name and create the Command button.

CONTROL WIZARDS

All of the instructions in this section assume that the Wizards are available when you create new controls. The Control Wizards tool lets you turn these Wizards on and off. It is selected by default so that the Wizards are available. Only programmers should try to work without the Wizards.

TOOL LOCK

By default, you must click a tool each time you add a control to the form. After you add the control, the pointer returns to its usual form.

If you select the Tool Lock tool, however, you can add the same type of control as many times as you want without clicking the toolbox for each one. Click the **Tool Lock** tool, and then click the tool for the control you want to add. The pointer remains in the form used to create that control for an indefinite time, and you can keep clicking and dragging to add the control. To stop adding it, click the **Select Objects** (pointer) tool to return the pointer to its usual form. The Tool Lock tool is automatically deselected when you do this.

The Tool Lock tool can save you a significant amount of time, if you want to add a number of lines or other simple controls to a form.

Saving Time by Using Default Properties

As you can see, you can define many properties of a control. For a label, you can define foreground color, background color, border color, border width, font name, font size, and so on.

Rather than defining all of these for each new control you add, it is often easiest to create default properties for a control and then apply them to similar controls.

Defining Default Properties

To define the default properties for a type of control, simply select any control of that type that already has those properties, and choose **Change Default** from the Format menu.

For example, if you select a label with red letters, a green background, and a black border, and then choose **Change Default** from the Format menu, those colors will be the default colors for all labels. Other properties of that label, such as its font, will also be the default for all labels. You look at properties more generally in the section on property sheets.

Applying Default Properties

Any new control you add automatically has the default properties for that type of control. You can apply the default to existing controls by selecting them and choosing **Apply Default** from the Format menu.

For example, if you set the default colors and other properties for labels, as described previously, and then select an existing label in the form and choose **Apply Default** from the Format menu, the existing label will be red and green and have other properties of the default object.

A Look at Property Sheets

You can display a property sheet for an object, such as the entire form, a band of the form, or a control, by selecting it and choosing **Properties** from the View menu or clicking the **Properties** tool of the toolbar.

Once you display the property sheet, Access keeps it open and displays the properties of any object you select. Choose **Properties** from the View menu or click the **Properties** tool again, or use the property sheet's control menu, to hide the property sheet.

Typical Property Sheets

Some property sheets are useful primarily for programmers; others will be covered in later chapters of this book. For now, you should just glance at a few to get an idea of what sorts of properties objects have.

Figure 7.23 shows the property sheet for a label, which has relatively simple properties. Notice that it lists features such as the label's name, its caption, whether it is visible, its location and size; and its color code. You can change these features on the property sheet, but you can change most of them more easily using the methods described earlier in this chapter. This property sheet lets you create an invisible control, which you cannot do using the interface, but there is usually no reason for a nonprogrammer to want to do that.

Though labels do not have event properties, many object do. Event properties for a text box are shown in Figure 7.24. You can use a a macro or program as one of these properties to have it executed before or after the control is updated, when it is clicked or double-clicked, and so on. In general, only developers use these event properties.

FIGURE 7.23   THE PROPERTY SHEET FOR A LABEL.

Text Box: Field45

Event Properties

Before Update . . . .
After Update . . . . .
On Change . . . . . .
On Enter . . . .
On Exit . . . .
On Got Focus . . . .
On Lost Focus . . . .
On Click . . . .
On Dbl Click . . . . . .
On Mouse Down . .
On Mouse Move . . .
On Mouse Up . . . .
On Key Down . . . .

FIGURE 7.24   EVENT PROPERTIES FOR A TEXT BOX.

Since objects often have many properties, you can use the drop-down list at the top of the property sheet to limit the type of properties displayed. You can select All Properties, Data Properties, Layout Properties, Event Properties, or Other Properties.

Useful Properties for Beginners

As you can see, property sheets are meant to be used by developers, but there are also features of property sheets that the typical user may find useful. Some will be covered here and others in later chapters.

CHANGING THE FINENESS OF THE GRID

The property sheet for the form as a whole has Grid X and Grid Y as two of its layout properties, as shown in Figure 7.25. You can edit the values in them to change the fineness of the grid that Access automatically aligns controls to.

Form	
Layout Properties	
Caption	Contractors
Default View	Single Form
Scroll Bars	Both
Record Selectors . .	Yes
Navigation Buttons	Yes
Auto Resize	Yes
Auto Center	No
Control Box	Yes
Min Button	Yes
Max Button	Yes
Width	5.1 in
Grid X	10
Grid Y	12

FIGURE 7.25   LAYOUT PROPERTIES OF A FORM.

To use this property sheet, choose **Select Form** from the Edit menu and display the property sheet (if it is not already displayed).

LIMITING CHOICES IN A COMBO BOX

You learned earlier that the property sheet of the Combo box has a Limit to List property. You can select Yes as this property instead of the default No to prevent users from typing a value that is not on the list into the Combo box. This is one of its Data properties.

BINDING A CONTROL TO A FIELD

One useful Data property of many controls is the Control Source property, which lets you bind the control to a field. As you can see in Figure 7.26, you can display a drop-down list for this property and select any of the fields in the table or query that the form is based on to bind the control to that field. You can delete the value in the field and leave it blank to create an unbound field. This can be useful if you forget to bind a control to a field when you first place it in the form.

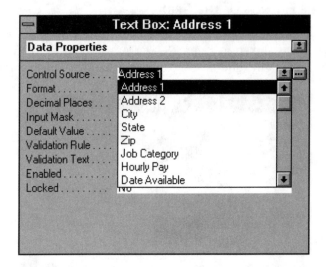

FIGURE 7.26 SETTING THE CONTROL SOURCE PROPERTY.

Property sheets have many features like this one, which may be useful on occasion, but are not generally needed by most people. You might want to look through the property sheets to get a general idea of what they contain. You can get context-sensitive help on any property by moving the cursor to it and pressing **F1**.

Designing a Sample Form

In this exercise, you display the AutoForm that you created in Chapter 5, save it under a different name, and modify it using the techniques you have learned in this chapter. The exercise will include a relatively small number of changes in the design of the form, but you might want to try others yourself.

1. Open the **TEACHSLF** database. Click the **Form** button of the Database window to display the list of forms. Be sure **Contractors: AutoForm** is selected, and select the **Design** button to display it in Design View. Select the **Maximize** button of the Form window so you have more room to work in.

2. Choose **Save As** from the File menu. When Access displays the Save As dialog box, edit the form name so it reads **Contractors: Custom Form** and select **OK**.

3. Click and drag the right edge of the form until it is five inches wide, as shown in Figure 7.27, so you can fit the name on a single line.

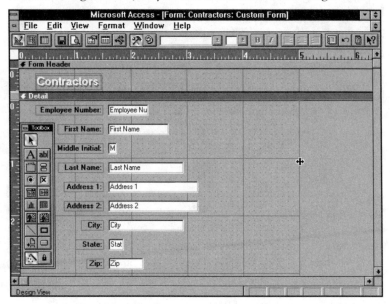

FIGURE 7.27   WIDENING THE FORM.

4. Click the **First Name** label to select it and click it again to place an insertion point in it. Edit it to read **Name**. Then click outside of it to stop editing, click it to select it, and choose **Size** and **to Fit** from the Format menu so the box is just large enough to fit the word Name.

5. Select the label **Middle Initial** and press **Del** to delete it. Likewise, select the label **Last Name** and press **Del** to delete it. Now, click and drag both of these fields on the same line as the First Name field, as shown in Figure 7.28.

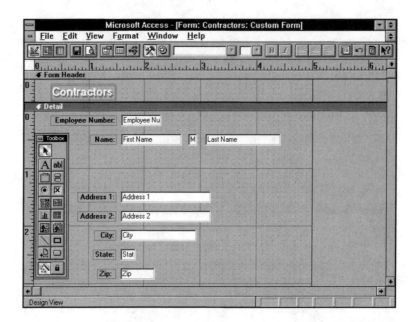

FIGURE 7.28   PLACING THE NAME ON ONE LINE.

6. Click and drag around the Address 1, Address 2, and City fields to select them all. Then drag them up so they are just under the Name field. Do not use the Move handle to drag just one; be sure to drag them all together. There should be just two lines of the grid between the Name and Address 1 fields, as there are between fields in the initial AutoForm.

7. Click outside the selected fields to deselect them. Then click the label of the State field and press **Del** to delete it. Likewise, select and delete the label of the Zip field. Then click and drag these fields so they are to the right of the City field. Finally, edit the label of the City field so it reads **City/State/Zip**, as shown in Figure 7.29.

8. Now, move the toolbox right, so it is out of the way. Then click the **Line** tool, and click and drag to place a line two gridlines below this basic data. Click the **Palette** tool to display the palette. Select **2-pt Border** as the thickness of this line, and close the palette. The form should look like Figure 7.30.

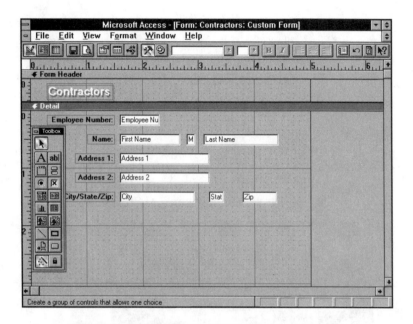

FIGURE 7.29 PLACING CITY, STATE, AND ZIP ON ONE LINE.

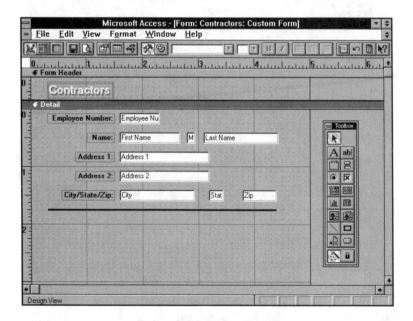

FIGURE 7.30 ADDING A LINE.

9. Now, you can add a drop-down list to make it easier to select Job Category. First, select the **Job Category** field and press **Del** to delete it and its label. Click the **Combo Box** tool in the toolbox, and click and drag to locate the list near the left edge of the form under the line you added. In the first dialog box of the Combo Box Wizard, select the radio button that lets you type in values; then click **Next>**.

10. In the next dialog box, keep **2** as the number of columns. On the first line, enter **Programmer** in Column 1 and **P** in Column 2. Likewise, on the next two lines, enter **Writer** and **W** and enter **Clerical** and **C**. Then narrow Column 1 a bit and narrow Column 2, so it is the right width to hold a single letter, as shown in Figure 7.31. Then click **Next>**.

FIGURE 7.31   DEFINING THE COMBO BOX.

11. In the next dialog box, as the value you want to store in your database, select **Column 2**; then click **Next>**.In the following dialog box, select the **Store the value in this field** radio button and select **Job Category** as the field to bind this control to; click **Next>**. As the label, type **Job Category** and select the **Finish** button to place the control.

12. Resize and move the control and its label as necessary to display their data and align them with the other controls, as shown in Figure 7.32. Finally, while this control is selected, click the **Property Sheet** tool, and select **Yes** as its Limit To List property in order to make invalid entries impossible. Close the property sheet.

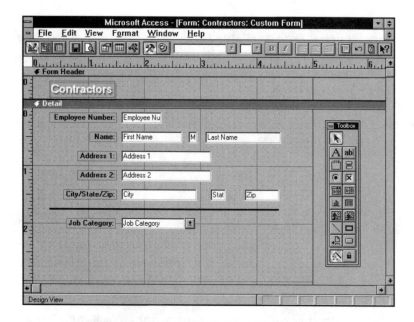

FIGURE 7.32 **PLACING THE LABEL AND COMBO BOX.**

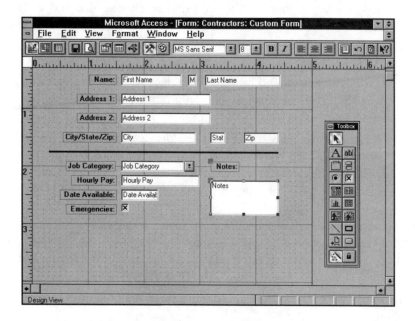

FIGURE 7.33 **LAYING OUT THE REMAINING FIELDS.**

13. Scroll down as necessary, and click and drag the **Hourly Pay**, **Emergencies**, **Date Available** fields. In addition, resize the Notes field and move its label independently of the field, as shown in Figure 7.33, to finish laying out the controls in the Detail band. Leave only one grid line between controls.

Using a drop-down list for the Job Category field (rather than a list box or radio buttons) makes it easier to fit all the fields in the window.

N O T E

14. Because you have laid out the fields in this way, you can make the title of the form larger. As is, it hardly stands out on the screen. Scroll upward to see the header. Then, increase the size of the Header band. Click and drag the bar with the name of the Detail band on it downward until the Form Header band is three-quarters of an inch wide.

15. Click and drag around the word **Contractors** to select both of the controls it is made of. (Remember that there is a second control for the shadow.) As the font size, select **24**. Then choose **Size** and **to Fit** from the Format menu to expand the box to hold the larger font. Click and drag to move both controls down a bit.

16. Finally, click elsewhere to deselect both these controls. Then click the word **Contractors** and be sure you select just the front control. Display the palette, select **Blue** as its foreground color. The final design is shown in Figure 7.34.

17. Click the **Form View** tool and Access displays the newly designed form. Click the **Restore** button of the Form window and resize the Form window to fit the new form, as shown in Figure 7.35. Select **Save** from the File menu to save the changes.

In an actual application, you might want to make the heading a bit more elaborate. For example, you might want to use an unbound OLE object to add a company logo to it and to use similar headings for all the forms used in each database.

Figure 7.35 shows how clear and easy to work with the custom form in our example is.

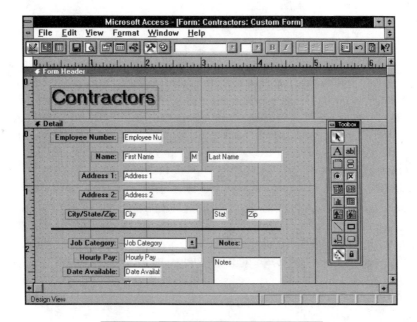

FIGURE 7.34 **THE FINAL DESIGN OF THE FORM.**

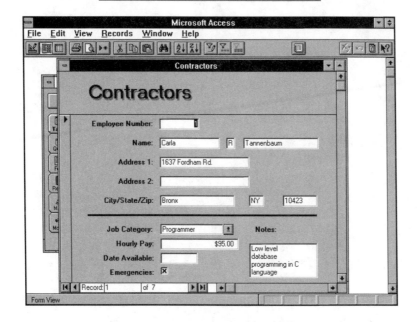

FIGURE 7.35 **USING THE FORM.**

To Sum Up

In this chapter, you learned to create custom forms. You learned to add, select, resize, move, and delete controls, to use layout tools such as the ruler and the grid to line up controls more precisely, and to use the palette to specify colors and effects for controls. You also learned special techniques for working with text controls. Finally, you learned to use the toolbox to add new controls, including simple controls, such as text boxes, lines, and rectangles, and also advanced controls, such as option groups, combo boxes and command buttons. You also looked briefly at the properties of controls, bands, and the form as a whole.

Report design is similar to Form design, and you will look at how to use these features in more powerful ways in Chapter 9, *Designing Custom Reports*. First, though, you will learn about Access expressions, which you must use to add advanced features, such as calculated fields, to forms and reports.

ACCESS

Chapter 8

Working with Expressions

*E*xpressions are a feature of virtually every programming language and of every database management system that is used by developers. They let you create many different types of results based on your data—calculations based on numeric data, transformations of text data, sums or averages of all the values in a field, and much more.

Expressions are one of the more complex features of Access that the ordinary user must work with. Programmers use them regularly. Users can gain extra power by using expressions to validate data, enter default values in fields, and create calculated fields in forms and reports. Access includes an Expression Builder that you can use in these situations to make it easier to create expressions.

This chapter gives you a basic overview of the elements that make up an expression. It also provides simple examples of the way that you use expressions as a nonprogrammer. Chapter 9, which covers report design, includes more complex examples of expressions used in calculated fields of reports. In this chapter, you learn the following:

259

❏ what elements are used in expressions

❏ how to use the Expression Builder to create expressions

❏ how expressions use identifiers to refer to objects or their properties

❏ how expressions use literals and constants

❏ how expressions use the arithmetic, comparison, logical, and assignment operators

❏ how expressions use functions

❏ what basic types of built-in functions are available in Access

❏ what are the common Access expressions, such as those used to add page numbers to reports

❏ how to use expressions to validate data as it is being entered

❏ how to use expressions to enter default values in fields

❏ how to use expressions in calculated fields in forms and reports

Understanding Expressions

An Access Expression is something like a calculation. Just as you perform a calculation in arithmetic and come up with a result, Access *evaluates* an expression and comes up with a result.

When you use expressions, Access displays the result rather than the expression. For example, later in this chapter you use an expression to create a calculated field that displays the total pay in a contractor's monthly bills. As the field's value, you use the following expression:

```
= [Hours Worked] * [Hourly Pay]
```

This expression calculates the total that is billed by multiplying the amount in the Hours Worked field by the amount in the Hourly Pay field. The calculated field based on this expression displays the result of this calculation, rather than displaying the expression itself.

Unlike calculations in arithmetic, Access expressions can evaluate to true or false, to dates, or to text, as well as to numbers. Expressions can also use many more elements than ordinary calculations, including the following:

❏ *Identifiers* let you refer to objects from the Access database, such as tables, forms, reports, controls, and their properties. You use identifiers primarily to refer to fields in the table you are working with.

❏ *Literals* are values that are used as they appear in the expression. For example, if you multiply the value in some field by the number 5, the field name is used to refer to the value in the field, but the number 5 is used literally.

❏ *Constants* are values that have constant, predefined values, such as Null.

❏ *Operators* are symbols that tell the expression what operations to perform on other values in it. For example, the + operator means that the other values are added.

❏ *Functions* are special calculations that you can use to give expressions more power. For example, there are functions that perform financial calculations such as Present Value and Future Value, and functions that return the current date and time. Access has a large number of built-in functions, and programmers can also create user-defined functions.

In the rest of this section, you look at all of these elements of expressions in more detail before you try using expressions practically.

The Expression Builder

Access generally lets you type in expressions or create them using the Expression Builder window, shown in Figure 8.1.

Cells that can have expressions in them have a button to their right with three dots on it, which you can click to display the Expression Builder. The expression you create here is entered in the cell when you select **OK**.

N O T E   The Expression Builder gives you hints about elements you leave out of the expression, does not display elements that are not appropriate in the current location, and even takes care of some details of syntax. It is best to use the Expression Builder to create expressions until you become familiar enough with them to be able to create them yourself.

How to Use the Expression Builder

You may type elements of the expression in the Expression Builder's text box, or you may enter them there by clicking the operator buttons (which represent the most commonly used operators). You can also add elements to the expression selecting them from the lists of Access objects, functions, constants, operators, and common expressions. Notice that there is no list of literals, since it is impossible to provide a list of *all* the words and numbers that you might want to use literally. You must type literals in the text box.

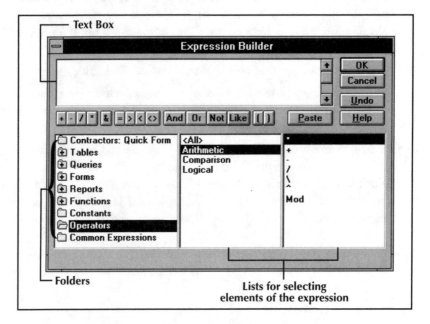

FIGURE 8.1   THE EXPRESSION BUILDER.

To copy elements of the expression from these lists, first click one of the folders on the left to display the type of element you want, such as operators or constants. Exactly which folders are included depends on what you were doing when you displayed the Expression Builder, and what types of elements are appropriate in expressions used there.

Some of these folders have a + sign on them to indicate that they have children folders, which you can display by double-clicking them. For example, the Functions folder has a child folder listing the built-in functions of Access, and may have other children folders. Click a folder with a + on it to display its children folders; when you do so, the + becomes a −, and you can click the folder to close its children.

Folders with + or − on them are used only to display children folders. When you click any other folder, though, a list of elements that you may use in the expression is displayed to its far right.

In some cases, the center panel also includes elements you can add to the expression. In general, however, it is used to limit the list displayed at the far right. For example, if you select the Operators folder, all operators are displayed by default. You can use the center panel, as seen in Figure 8.1, to display all the operators or only certain types of operators, such as the arithmetic operators that are displayed in the illustration.

To add an element from a list to the expression text box, simply double-click it or select it and click the **Paste** button.

To add commonly used operators, simply click one of the operator buttons above this list.

If there is an obvious gap in the expression you create, Access includes a word enclosed in angle brackets in the expression to tell you what type of element is missing. For example, if you add two fields to the expression text box one after another, Access adds **<<Oper>>** between them, as shown in Figure 8.2, to show you that an operator is needed between them. For example, it is the addition operator that is missing if the values in the two fields are to be added.

FIGURE 8.2   THE EXPRESSION BUILDER GIVES YOU
HINTS ABOUT MISSING ELEMENTS OF THE EXPRESSION.

You can edit the expression in the text box using the usual Windows editing techniques. Click to place an insertion bar in the expression and then edit it.

In general, double-clicking selects an entire element of the expression rather than just a single word as it usually does with Windows editors. For example, if a field name is made up of two words, double-clicking it will select the entire field name.

In addition, to make it easier for you to replace words such as **<<Oper>>** that Access adds, you can select them simply by clicking them. You cannot place an insertion bar in them and edit them, as you usually can in this text box.

After you select text in this text box, it can be replaced by a new element that you add as well as by text that you type. For example, if Access adds **<<Oper>>** between two fields, you can click that word to select it, and then click an operator button to replace it.

DISPLAYING THE EXPRESSION BUILDER

You should display the Expression Builder now because you can practice with it as you read the sections about the different elements of expressions.

The Expression Builder does not include elements that are not appropriate in the place where you invoked it. It is displayed in a complete version when you use it to enter the Control Source property of a field in a form. Remember that you learned in Chapter 7 that you can use the Control Source property of a control to bind it to a field. You can type it in or simply select the field from this property's drop-down list. You can also use an expression rather than just a field as the source of the data displayed in a control of a form: type it in or generate it using the Expression Builder.

Later in this chapter, you base a field on an expression in this way. For now, simply display the Expression Builder, as follows:

1. In the Database window, click the **Forms** button, select **Contractors: AutoForm**, and select the **Design** button.

2. Access displays the AutoForm in Design View. Click the **Properties** tool to display a Property List. Select **Data Properties** from the Property List drop-down list.

3. Click the text box where the First Name field is entered to select it. Click the **Control Source** property, which should be the first property listed in the property sheet. Click the **...** button to display the Expression Builder.

Now, you should use the Expression Builder to display the different types of elements used in an expression as they are discussed next.

Identifiers

Identifiers are the names of Access objects. They can be the following:

❑ the name of any field in the current object

❑ the name of any control in the current object

❑ the name of any control in any object in the database

❑ the name of a table or query

❑ the name of the property of an object

As a nonprogrammer, you use identifiers almost exclusively to refer to fields in the current object—that is, fields in the current table, query, form, or report.

How to Read an Identifier

To refer to fields or other controls in the current object, you can simply use their names. To use any other identifiers, you must write out their names in full. Generally, you do not need to do this as a nonprogrammer, except occasionally when you are working with multitable databases. Even then, you can generate the identifiers easily with the expression builder. This section describes how identifiers are named so you can read full names when you come across them.

When you write it out in full length, an identifier may consist of an object type (such as forms or reports), the name of an object of that type, the name of a control in the object, the name of a property, and the symbols summarized in Table 8.1.

Table 8.1   Symbols used in identifiers.

Symbol	Use	Example
[ ]	Encloses an object name longer than one word	[First Name]
!	Separates object names	[Contractors: AutoForm]![First Name]
.	Separates object names from a property	[Contractors: AutoForm]! [First Name].OnClick

For example, to refer to the OnClick property of the First Name field of the Contractors AutoForm, you would use the identifier:

```
Forms![Contractors: AutoForm]![First Name].OnClick
```

The example shows the two identifier operators. The **!** (exclamation point) operator is generally used before the name of an object such as a table, form, or control. The **.** (dot) operator is generally used before the name of a property.

The example also shows how identifiers use square brackets to enclose object names that are more than one word long. These brackets may be omitted for objects with single-word names. However, it is generally best, as a matter of style, to include them so the object name is obvious when you look at the expression that this identifier is used in.

SHORTCUT

The square brackets are the only symbols that nonprogrammers need to use in most identifiers. If you leave out the rest of the identifier, Access assumes that the object is a control in the current object, or for a form or report, a control in the table or query that it is based on.

When you use the Expression Builder to create identifiers, it uses the shortest form possible. Most of the identifiers that you generate in the Expression Builder will simply be field names enclosed in square brackets.

PAGE NUMBERS

The only properties you use frequently in expressions are the ones that refer to page numbers. The Expression Builder makes it easy for you to use these by listing them under the Common Expressions folder.

Access forms and reports have the following two properties:

❏ *Page* refers to the current page number, as the form or report is being printed.

❏ *Pages* refers to the total number of pages in the form or report.

These are obviously useful for numbering pages when you print a report, and are discussed in more detail, in the section "Common Expressions" later in this chapter.

USING THE EXPRESSION BUILDER TO CREATE IDENTIFIERS

The first five folders in the Expression Builder are all used to select identifiers (see Figure 8.2).

The first folder represents the current object (in this case, the AutoForm for the Contractors table). The folders that follow represent all the other tables, queries, forms and reports in the database. Their children are the names of individual tables, queries, forms, and reports.

Select any object to display its fields and other controls in the center panel. Select one of these controls to display its properties in the right panel.

If the current object is a form or report, it also has a Record Source option in the center panel. You can select the option to display the names of controls in the table or query that the form or report is based on in the right panel.

For example, Figure 8.3 shows an identifier for the BorderColor property of Field4 of the 5095 Mailing Labels report. To generate this, double-click the **Reports** folder to display its two children, double-click the folder for the child named **All Reports** to display a list of report names, and click the folder **5095 Mailing Labels** to display its fields in the center panel. Then click **Field4** to display its properties, and double-click the **BorderColor** property (or select it and select **Paste**) to place the identifier in the expression text box.

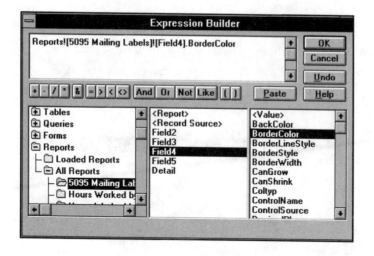

FIGURE 8.3   A COMPLEX IDENTIFIER.

This example is meant to let you look at a complex identifier, but in reality, beginners generally use fields from the current object or the table or query it is based on. In general, you either select a field from the center panel, or select **Record Source** from the center panel, so you can use the right panel to select a field from the table or query it is based on.

Literals and Constants

You simply type literals into the Expression Builder text box. As you learned in Chapter 4, when you used them in queries, you must use delimiters around a literal that depends on its data type:

❏   Text literals must be surrounded by the " delimiter.

❏   Date literals must be surrounded by the **#** delimiter.

❏   Number literals do not need delimiters and must not include the thousands separator or number sign.

In queries, you used literals such as **"NY"** and **#1/31/94#**.

Access expressions also let you use *constants*. These are like literals because they do not change depending on the content of the table. As you can see in Figure 8.4, the Expression Builder includes the following constants:

❏   *"" Empty String* matches a text expression with nothing in it.

❏   *Null* matches any expression with nothing in it.

❏   *False* matches a logical expression that evaluates to false.

❏   *True* matches a logical expression that evaluates to true.

FIGURE 8.4   DISPLAYING CONSTANTS IN THE EXPRESSION BUILDER.

You also used constants in queries, but notice that here they match any expression, not just the content of a field. For example, you could have a function that returns **Null** as well as a field with no value entered in it.

Operators

You also used operators in queries, but you may be confused by the way that operators are used in expressions unless you remember that queries use abbreviated expressions. Queries let you leave out the identifier and enter the rest of the expression in a column under a field name. The field name is assumed as the identifier before the rest of the expression.

For example, if you enter **>=#1/1/94#** under the Date Available field in the QBE grid, that is equivalent to using the expression **[Date Available] >=#1/1/94#**.

Many of the operators were covered in Chapter 4, but they are summarized here for reference, and details are included that were left out of the earlier chapter. Of course, the examples that are given are full expressions, rather than the abbreviated expressions used in queries.

If you select the Operators folder in the Expression Builder, all the expressions are displayed in the right panel, as shown in Figure 8.5. However, you can use one of the options in the center panel to display only one of the operator types described next.

FIGURE 8.5 DISPLAYING OPERATORS IN THE EXPRESSION BUILDER.

ARITHMETIC OPERATORS

The Arithmetic Operators, shown in Table 8.2, are used for ordinary mathematical calculations.

TABLE 8.2 THE ARITHMETIC OPERATORS.

OPERATOR	MEANING
+	addition
–	subtraction (or negation of a single number)
*	multiplication
/	division
^	exponentiation (raising a number to a power)
\	division with an integer result (decimal places are truncated)
Mod	modulo division (returns only the remainder)
( )	used for grouping

When they are used with numeric data, the data type of the result is generally the same as that of the most precise operand. For example, if you multiple an integer by a double, the result will be a double.

All of these operators require two operands except for the – (minus) operator. This operator can be used with two operands to indicate subtraction—for example, **[Date Available] – 30**. It can also be used with a single operand to negate its value—for example, **– [Hours Worked]**, which returns the value in the Hours Worked field as a negative number.

Order of Precedence

In arithmetic calculations, by default, multiplication and division are performed before addition and subtraction. However, you can change this default order of precedence by using parentheses, just as you do in ordinary mathematics.

For example, let's say that you give a contractor a $100 bonus for a month. You could use the expression **[Hours Worked] * [Hourly Pay] + 100** to calculate the total earned for a month. Because there are no parentheses, this expression uses the default order of precedence. First it multiplies hours worked by hourly pay to get the total earned for that month. Then it adds the $100 bonus to the total.

You could include parentheses and write the expression as **([Hours Worked] * [Hourly Pay]) + 100**, but it would not make any difference in the result.

On the other hand, lets say that you give an employee a $1 per hour bonus for a month. You would use the expression **[Hours Worked] * ([Hourly Pay] + 1)** to calculate the total earned. Here, you must use the parentheses to make Access add 1 to the hourly pay before multiplying it by hours worked. This is not the same as the default order of precedence so the result would be different if you left out the parentheses.

For example, if someone worked 10 hours and earned $50 per hour, then **[Hours Worked] * ([Hourly Pay] + 1)** would have the result **510**—first add 50 + 1, and then multiply the result by 10. On the other hand, **[Hours Worked] * [Hourly Pay] + 1** would have the result **501**—first multiply 50 times 10, and then add 1 to the result.

Date Arithmetic

The addition and subtraction operators can also be used to perform calculations on dates, to add or subtract a number of days to a date.

String Concatenation

The arithmetic operator **+** can also be used to combine, or *concatenate*, two text strings.

Access also provides a special operator **&**, which can be used only for string concatenation. It is generally considered the best style to use **&** for concatenation for the sake of clarity.

COMPARISON

The *comparison operators* are shown in Table 8.3. Expressions based on these operators return a value of true or false

TABLE 8.3 THE COMPARISON OPERATORS.

OPERATOR	MEANING
=	is equal to
>	is greater than
>=	is greater than or equal to

continued

OPERATOR	MEANING
<	is less than
<=	is less than or equal to
<>	is not equal to
Between...And	is within the range indicated

These operators can be used with numbers, text, and dates, but both operands must be the same data type. For example, it makes sense to use the expression **[Date Available] >=#1/1/94#** or the expression **[Last Name] < "M"**, but it obviously does not make sense to use the expression **[Last Name] < #12/1/94#**.

The **Between...And** operator lets you find a range of values. For example, the expression **[Date Available] Between #1/1/94# And #12/31/94#** evaluates to true for all records with the Date Available field that has a value in 1994. Notice that the range includes the two values you enter. In the example, it would include the dates 1/1/94 and 12/31/94.

The comparison operators listed in the table are all included in the Expression Builder. There are also a few special comparison operators, which are described below.

The Like Operator

The Like operator lets you create expressions with literals that use the wildcard characters:

❑ * represents any group characters.

❑ ? represents any single character.

For example, if the expression **[Last Name] Like "A*"** is evaluated as true for any record with a value in the Last Name field that begins with A.

In Operator

You can use the operator In to find values in a list that you specify. The list must be in parentheses following the word **In**, with its items separated by commas. For example, **[State] In ("NY", "NJ", "CT")** would be evaluated as true if the value in the State field is included in this list of three states.

The Is and Is Not Operators

The Is and Is Not Operators are used only in comparisons that use the constant Null. For example, the **[First Name] Is Null** would evaluate as true for records that have no entry in the First Name field.

THE LOGICAL OPERATORS

You use the logical operators, listed in Table 8.4 to combine two expressions that evaluate to true or false into a single expression.

TABLE 8.4   THE LOGICAL OPERATORS.

OPERATOR	MEANING
And	Both expressions must be true for the combined expression to be true.
Or	Either expression may be true for the combined expression to be true.
Xor	One of the expressions, but not both, must be true for the combined expression to be true.
Not	The following expression must be false to evaluate as true or true to evaluate to false.
Eqv	Equivalence is a bitwise operation used in programming.
Imp	Implication is a bitwise operation used in programming.
( )	Parenthesis are used for grouping.

All of these logical operators require two operands, except for **Not**, which has a single operand that follows it.

You can create more complex logical expressions by using these operators with operands that are already complex logical statements.

For example, the expression **[Job Category] = "P" Or [Job Category] = "W"** would evaluate as true for anyone who is a programmer or writer. Notice that it is made up of two expressions that can evaluate to true or false—the expression **[Job Category] = "P"** and the expression **[Job Category] = "W"**. Because they are connected using *Or,* the entire expression evaluates as true if either of these evaluates as true.

Now, suppose that you want this expression to find only programmers and writers who earn $80 per hour or more. You would use this expression:

```
( [Job Category] = "P" Or [Job Category] = "W" ) And
Hourly Pay >= 80
```

Notice how important the order of precedence is with logical expressions. The expression above would give you a different result from this expression:

```
[Job Category] = "P" Or ( [Job Category] = "W" And
Hourly Pay >= 80 )
```

If a programmer earned less than $80 per hour, the first expression would evaluate as false, but the second would be true.

NOTE

In general, when you create logical expressions of this sort, it is best to use parentheses to indicate precedence, rather than trying to rely on default precedence. Create one expression at a time, and enclose it in parentheses before you relate it to other expressions in order to see the more complex expression as a combination of two expressions. This is not necessary when you relate a string of expressions using Or between them all. It is clear that the entire expression is true if any one of them is true.

THE ASSIGNMENT OPERATOR

The = operator assigns a value to a control.

If you want a text box to display the first and last name, you can use the expression **= [First Name] & [Last Name]**. The **&** operator concatenates the values in the First Name and Last Name fields, and the = operator assigns that value to the control.

Access supplies the assignment operator for you when you are using the Expression Builder. For example, if you use the Expression Builder to select a field name as the control source of a control, Access will supply the = before it when you place the expression.

Do not confuse this *assignment operator* with the = *comparison operator.* The comparison operator compares two existing values, and the assignment operator gives an object a new value. The assignment operator = is always *unary*—used with only one operand, which follows it. The comparison operator

= is used with two operands, one before and one after it. However, in the QBE grid, it may be used with only the second of these operands because the first one is understood to be the field name at the top of the column.

Functions

In Chapter 5, you learned the function Date( ), which returns the current date. All functions must include the open and close parentheses after them, like Date( ). In most functions, these parentheses contain *arguments* that the function acts on. For example, if you use a function to capitalize text, you would include the text that is to be capitalized in the parentheses as the argument of the function. If a function has multiple arguments, they are all included in the parentheses, separated by commas. Even if a function does not take an argument, however, you must include the parentheses after it, so Access knows that it is a function.

These are a couple of other functions that are used almost as commonly as Date( ):

❑ *Now( )* returns the current date and time.

❑ *CurrentUser( )* returns the name of the person who is currently using Access.

It is obvious how you could use these three functions on forms, by adding text boxes to the form that display the date or date and time, and (if you are working on a network) the name of the person using the form.

N O T E   Now( ) is invaluable when you are designing printed reports. You usually must print them out several times to get them exactly the way you want them, and you can avoid confusion by being able to see at a glance which report was printed most recently. In the final report, where you want to include only the date, you can either replace Now( ) with Date( ) or format Now( ) so it displays only the date. In Chapter 9, you learn to use its property sheet to format it in the same way that you do a Date/Time field.

Access includes two type of functions. In addition to its built-in functions, it allows developers to create *user-defined functions*. This advanced feature of Access is not covered in this book. When beginners are working with the Expression Builder, they should always use the Built-In Functions folder under the Functions folder.

Access has over 100 built-in functions, many of which are useful primarily for programmers. Here, we summarize the different types of functions included in Access to give you a general idea of the program's capabilities. We also describe some of the important functions.

You can learn about functions by looking through the Expression Builder to see which are available and by using the help system to search for function by name or type.

To display functions in the Expression Builder, first double-click the **Functions** folder and then double-click the **Built-In Functions** folder. As you can see in Figure 8.6, the Expression Builder begins by displaying all the functions in the right panel, but you can use options in the center panel to display only one type of function.

FIGURE 8.6   DISPLAYING FUNCTIONS IN THE EXPRESSION BUILDER.

Notice also that when you highlight a function in the right panel, the function and the types of argument it takes are displayed in the lower left of the Expression Builder. In the illustration, the Abs( ) function, which returns the absolute value of a number, is selected, and Abs(number) is displayed below to show that it requires a number as an argument. When you add functions to the expression text box, they include words indicating the arguments they need, which you must replace with the actual arguments.

MATH FUNCTIONS

In addition to the arithmetic operators, which perform the basic mathematical operations, Access has a complete set of math functions that perform more advanced mathematical operations:

- ❑ *Sqr( )* returns the square root of the argument.
- ❑ *Abs( )* returns the absolute value of the argument.
- ❑ *Log( )* returns the natural logarithm of the argument.
- ❑ *Cos( )*, *Sin( )* and *Tan( )* are trigonometric functions that return the cosine, sine, and tangent of the argument.

For complete information, search in the help system for the topic "Math Functions."

FINANCIAL FUNCTIONS

Access includes a complete set of functions used in financial analysis:

- ❑ *PV( )* returns the present value of a series of payments.
- ❑ *FV( )* returns the future value of a series of payments.
- ❑ *IRR( )* and *MIRR( )* return the internal rate of return and the modified internal rate of return.
- ❑ *SLN( )* returns straight-line depreciation; *DDB( )* uses the double-declining balance method, and *SYD( )* uses the sum of years' digits method to calculate depreciation.

For complete information, search in the help system for the topic "Financial Functions."

STRING HANDLING FUNCTIONS

Access has a complete set of string handling functions similar to those used in most programming languages:

- ❑ *LCase( )* converts all the alphabetic characters in the argument to lower case.
- ❑ *UCase( )* converts all the alphabetic characters in the argument to upper case.

❏ *Left( )*, *Right( )*, and *Mid( )* isolate a number of characters from the beginning, ending, and middle of the text string use as their argument.

❏ *LTrim( )*, *RTrim( )*, and *Trim( )* remove unnecessary blank leading spaces, trailing spaces, and both leading and trailing spaces from the string used as their argument.

N O T E When you concatenate strings in Access, however, it generally removes unnecessary trailing blanks automatically, and so you do not need to use the functions that do this as you do in other database management programs. For example, if you use the expression **[First Name]** & " " & **[Last Name]**, Access prints the names with only one blank space between them. It automatically trims any trailing blank spaces that follow the first name in the first name field.

For more information on string functions, search in the help system for the topic "String Handling."

DATE AND TIME FUNCTIONS

Apart from Date( ) and Now( ), which were covered earlier, Access's most useful date and time function is DateDiff( ), which returns the time interval between two dates. For more information on this complex function, search in the help system for the topic "DateDiff."

AGGREGATE FUNCTIONS

The *aggregate functions* are sometimes called the SQL aggregate functions, as they are based on Structured Query Language (SQL). SQL is a query language used by many database management systems. They are very useful for creating controls that display summary calculations in reports, and they include the following:

❏ *Avg( )* returns the average (arithmetic mean) value in the specified field.

❏ *Count( )* returns the total number of records.

❏ *Max( )* and *Min( )* return the highest and lowest value in the specified field.

❏ *Sum( )* returns the total of all the values in the specified fields.

There are also functions for standard deviation and variance.

Access also includes a set of *domain aggregate functions* that can be used in some situations where the aggregate functions cannot. These are similar to the aggregate functions but begin with a **D**—for example, DAvg( ), DCount( ), and so on.

The SQL aggregate functions are adequate for most users, and can be used in calculated controls on forms or reports (except in controls added to the page header or footer band).

For complete information, search in the help system for the topic "Aggregate Functions."

OTHER FUNCTIONS

Access also includes equivalents for virtually all of the other functions that you might be familiar with from using other database or spreadsheet programs, for example:

- ❑ *Asc( )* returns the ASCII value of the first character of a string argument

- ❑ *CCur( )* converts the argument to the Currency type; *CInt( )* converts the argument to the Int type; and *CStr( )* converts the argument to the text (string) type. These are not needed as often as they are in other database programs, however, because Access generally lets you concatenate values of different data types without conversion.

- ❑ *IIF( )* is the Immediate If (or Inline If), which takes three arguments, and returns the second argument if the first evaluates to true, or returns the third argument if the first evaluates to false.

- ❑ *Format ( )* lets you control the format of the data that is returned. For example, Format ([Date], "mmmm") returns the month of the data field as a word. See the Help system for the codes for all the available formats.

This section has given you a brief description of the functions available in Access. You use some functions in the exercises later in this chapter and in Chapter 9. If you want to become a more advanced user, you should browse through the Expression Builder and the help system to learn more functions. Start by searching for the topic "Functions Reference" in the Help system.

Common Expressions

If you open the Common Expressions folder, the Expression Builder displays the meaning of commonly used expressions in the center panel, as shown in Figure

8.7. If you select one of these, the expression itself is displayed in the right panel, and you may add it to the expression in the usual ways.

FIGURE 8.7 DISPLAYING COMMON EXPRESSIONS.

The list includes the following common expressions:

❑ *Page Number* uses the expression **"Page " & Page**, which is made up of the text literal for the word *page*, followed by the concatenation operator, followed by the identifier *Page*, which specifies the current page in a form or report as it is being printed.

❑ *Total Pages* uses the expression **Pages,** an identifier that specifies the total number of pages in a form or report.

❑ *Page N of M* uses the expression **"Page " & Page & " of " & Pages**. The text literals **Page** and **of** are concatenated with the identifiers that represent the current page of a form or report being printed and the total number of pages in the report.

❑ *Current Date* uses the Date( ) function.

❑ *Current Date/Time* uses the Now( ) function.

❑ *Current User* uses the CurrentUser( ) function.

All of these common expressions are particularly useful in printed reports and you look at them again in Chapter 9.

Using Expressions

Now that you have a general overview of expressions, you can look at some practical uses of expressions. There are many uses of expressions that are only appropriate in programming, but the following sections look at the most common uses of expressions among users, such as validating data, creating a default value, and creating a calculated field. All of these features of Access were mentioned in earlier chapters of this book. Now you have the background to work with them.

The first few examples use simple expressions that are the easiest for you to type in. Then you will use a slightly more complex expressions that it is easiest to enter by using the Expression Builder.

You have the opportunity to use many more complex expressions in Chapter 9, where you work with custom reports.

Validating Data

One common use of expressions is *validation of data*. In Chapter 2, you learned that fields have validation rule and validation text properties, which let you test the data that is entered. The *validation rule* is an expression that is evaluated whenever data is entered or edited in the field. You must use an expression that evaluates to true or false. The *validation text* is displayed if the entry does not conform to the validation rule.

When you enter a validation rule, however, you do not use the entire expression. The name of the field that you are validating is assumed as the identifier, as it is when you enter criteria in the QBE grid.

One field in your sample application that should be validated is the Job Category field. Currently, a user can enter any letter in this field (except in the custom form, where the entry is made using a drop-down list), though it should allow only a P, W, or C to be entered. The easiest way to do this is by entering the validation rule **In("P", "W", "C")**. This is such a simple expression that it is easier to type this criterion into the Validation Rule cell than to use the Epression Builder:

1. In the Database window, click the **Table** button to display the Tables list, select **Contractors**, and select the **Design** button, to display this table in Design View.

2. Click the **Job Category** field to display its properties. Click the Validation Rule cell. Type **In("P", "W", "C")**.

3. Click the **Validation Text** cell and type **You must enter a P, W, or C in this field**, as shown in Figure 8.8

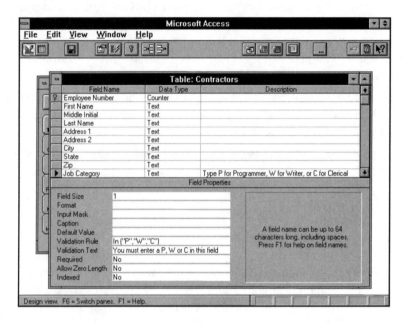

FIGURE 8.8   THE NEW PROPERTIES OF THE JOB CATEGORY FIELD.

4. Make an entry to test the new properties. Click the **Datasheet View** tool. When Access prompts you to save changes in the table, select **OK**. When Access displays the next dialog box, click **No** to skip checking existing data.

5. Click the **Job Category** field of the new record (marked by an asterisk). Type **X**, and press **Tab** to move the cursor to the next field. Access displays the message box, shown in Figure 8.9.

6. Select **OK** to return to the table. Delete the **X** from the Job Category field, and type **P** instead. Press **Tab** and Access lets you move the cursor to the next field. Now that you are done testing, press **Esc** to eliminate the new record.

FIGURE 8.9 ACCESS WILL NOT LET YOU ENTER INVALID DATA IN THE FIELD.

Default Values

You will also find expressions useful as a way of entering a default value in a field. To do this, use the Default Value property of the field, and enter an expression in it that begins with the = (assignment) operator to assign a value to the field. If you use the Expression Builder to create this expression, Access supplies the = operator.

In some cases, the = can be omitted when you assign a default value, but it is best to use it to make it clear that you are assigning a value.

Try a simple example of a default value. Let's say that you realize that most of your contractors are from New York state and want to enter this by default in the State field. You can edit this value if a contractor is from another state, and you can save time by using it for contractors from New York. Since this value is a literal, you can simply type it in as the property, rather than using the Expression Builder.

1. Click the **Table** button of the Database window to display the Tables list; then select the **Contractors** table and select the **Design** button. If

you are already using the Contractors table, simply click the **Design View** tool.

2. Click the **State** field. Click the **Default Value** property. As the default value, type **="NY"**, as shown in Figure 8.10.

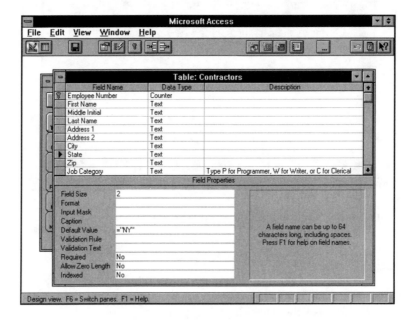

FIGURE 8.10   ASSIGNING A DEFAULT VALUE.

3. Click the **Datasheet** tool. Select **OK** to save the change in the table design. Notice that NY is displayed as the default value in the State field of the new record, as shown in Figure 8.11.

When you create a default value in a table in this way, it is also used in all the objects based on this table. For example, all the forms that include this field will also use **NY** as its default value when you add a new record. On the other hand, if you create a default value for a field in another object, such as a form, it only applies to the field when you are using that object to add new records.

Emp	First Nar	Mi	Last Name	Address 1	Address 2	City	Sta	Zip	Job	F
1	Carla	R	Tannenbaum	1637 Fordham Rd.		Bronx	NY	10423	P	
2	Peter		Woodworth	Star Consultants	4152 Front St., #31	Hoboken	NJ	07030	P	
3	Kevin	M	Smith	42 Elm Circle		Greenwich	CT	06830	W	
4	Samuel		Smalz	1701 Albemarle Rd		Brooklyn	NY	11226	C	
5	Jessica		Smythe	WordSmiths	910 University Ave.	Berkeley	CA	94709	W	
6	Josephine	B	Estevis	47 Bleeker St.		New York	NY	10010	P	
7	Sidney		Smithson	Computer Tool Wor	7943-2301 Techno	Provo	UT	84601	P	
▶	inter)						NY			

FIGURE 8.11   THE DEFAULT VALUE IS DISPLAYED IN THE NEW RECORD.

Calculated Fields

One of the most important use of expressions is to create calculated fields in forms and reports. You learned in Chapter 7 that the three basic types of fields in forms are bound, unbound, and calculated. You created the other two types of field in that chapter, and now you can create a calculated field.

To create a calculated field, simply add a text box to the form and use the appropriate expression as its Control Source property. You learned in Chapter 7 that you can use the Control Source property to select the field that a control is bound to. You can also use this property to base the control on an expression.

A SAMPLE CALCULATED FIELD

Here, you can create a field that uses a simple numeric calculation. Your Billing table includes fields for Hourly Pay and Hours Worked for each bill. You can multiply the values in these fields to display the total billed.

If you use the Expression Builder to generate this expression, Access automatically adds the = (assignment) operator, because you are assigning this value to the text box:

1. Close any open windows except for the Database window. In the Database window, select the **Table** button to display the Tables list, and select the **Billing** table. Then click the **AutoForm** tool.

2. After Access displays the AutoForm, select the **Design View** button so you can customize the form. Click and drag the lower border of the Detail band of this form to add room for a new field below the ones already included.

3. If necessary, display the toolbox. Click the **Text Box** tool in the toolbox. Then click and drag to add a text box below the Hourly Pay field that is the same size and uses the same spacing as the Hourly Pay and Hours Worked field, as shown in Figure 8.12.

FIGURE 8.12   ADDING A TEXT BOX.

4. Be sure the new text box is still selected. If necessary, display the property sheet and select **All Properties** from its drop-down list. Click the **Control Source** property. Then click the **...** button to display the Expression Builder.

5. Scroll through the center panel and double-click the **Hours Worked** field in it to add that field to the expression. Then click the button with

the * operator on it. Finally, double-click the **Hourly Pay** field to finish generating the expression, as shown in Figure 8.13. Select **OK**. Access places the expression in the property sheet, with the assignment operator added before it.

FIGURE 8.13 CREATING THE EXPRESSION USED IN THE CALCULATED FIELD.

6. This value is a dollar amount, and you want it displayed accordingly, so select the **Format** property in the property sheet, and use the drop-down list to select **Currency**.

7. Close the property sheet. Click the label of this calculated field to select it, and click it again to place an insertion bar in it. Edit it so it reads **Total Pay**. The final design is shown in Figure 8.14.

8. Click the **Form View** tool to display data in this form. Click the value in the **Total Pay** text box, and press the **Del** key to try to edit it. Access displays a message in the status bar, as shown in Figure 8.15.

9. Close the Form window. Select **Yes** to save the form. In the Save As dialog box, enter the name **Billing Form With Total** and select **OK**.

You can see that calculated fields in forms cannot be edited because they are based on the value of the expression. This sort of arithmetic calculation is even more useful in reports than in forms, and you look at it again in Chapter 9.

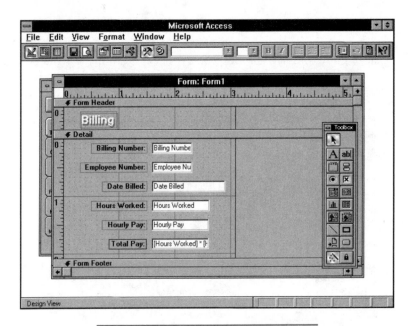

FIGURE 8.14   THE FINAL DESIGN OF THE FORM.

FIGURE 8.15   USING THE FORM.

OTHER TYPES OF CALCULATED FIELDS

Remember that calculated fields can contain any expression, not just an arithmetic calculation. In Chapter 9, when you design reports, you will work with calculated fields that:

❏ display the date and time, using the Now( ) function

❏ display the page number, using the Page property

❏ display text concatenated with field contents in a text box

❏ display summary calculations using the Sum( ) function

All of these are calculated fields are created by entering expressions in text boxes.

To Sum Up

Expressions can be made up of identifiers, literals and constants, operators—including arithmetic, comparison, logical, and assignment operators—and a wide variety of functions. The Expression Builder makes it easier to create expressions by letting you select their elements using push buttons and lists.

After learning how to create expressions, you learned to use them as the default value and validation rule properties of a field when you are designing a table, in order to make data entry faster and more accurate. You also looked at how to use expressions to create calculated fields. You will look at some other uses of expressions in Chapter 9, where you learn to design custom reports with calculated fields, and in Chapter 10, where you use them in queries.

Designing Custom Reports

*T*his chapter includes a brief summary of the features that report design has in common with form design, but it concentrates on special features of reports. Because you have now learned about expressions, this chapter also looks at how they are used in report design. What you learn about expressions in reports also applies to forms. In this chapter, you learn the following:

- ❏ the basics of report design, quickly reviewing the points that are similar to form design and emphasizing the points that are different
- ❏ to create sorted and grouped reports
- ❏ to create reports that are grouped on a range of values
- ❏ to create subgroups within grouped reports
- ❏ to control how groups are printed
- ❏ to set up the printer to print a report or form
- ❏ to set margins for the printed report or form

291

❑   to print only the data of a report or form, without graphic elements

❑   to create reports that use a repeated item

❑   to create form letters

As you read this chapter, you will see that report design is *similar* to form design in many ways. However, reports are also *different* from forms in a few important ways because they are meant to be printed rather than viewed on the screen. Because they are used to view a large number of printed records, rather than a single record displayed on the screen, reports let you group records and add headers and footers with summary data on the groups. For example, you can design a report that groups contractors by job category and includes a group footer with the average wage for contractors in each category. Because reports are meant to be printed, you must also know how to set margins and set up the page in other ways to take full advantage of them.

The Basics of Report Design

Figures 9.1 and 9.2 show a simple report in Design View and in the Print Preview window. You should be able to see, simply by looking at them and comparing them with what you learned about forms in Chapter 7, how similar report design is to form design. However, you should also notice a few differences.

FIGURE 9.1   A REPORT IN DESIGN VIEW.

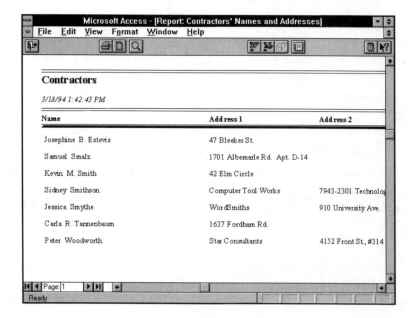

FIGURE 9.2   PREVIEWING THE REPORT.

You should review the features of the report design window, and particularly its differences from the form design window, before creating a sample report.

Changing Views

As you learned in Chapter 5, reports are displayed in Print Preview rather than in Datasheet View, because they are meant to be printed rather than edited. When you display the Reports list in the Database window, it has the following buttons instead of the New, Open, and Design buttons that other objects have:

❑   The *New* button creates a new report.

❑   The *Preview* button displays a report in the Print Preview window.

❑   The *Design* button displays a report in Design View.

When you create a new report in this way, you must select the table or query it is based on in the New Report dialog box. You can also create a report by selecting a table or query in the Database window and selecting the New Report or AutoReport tool.

The Toolbar

The toolbar that is displayed when you design a report is shown in Figure 9.3. It is similar to the toolbar displayed when you design a form, with a few exceptions.

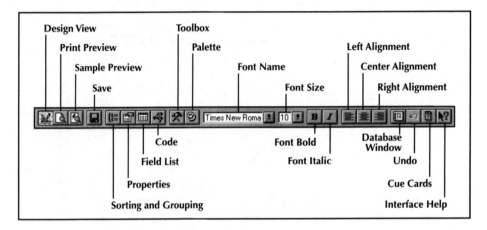

FIGURE 9.3   THE TOOLBAR FOR REPORT DESIGN.

SWITCHING VIEWS

The report toolbar does not include a Datasheet View tool. Instead, the following are its first three tools:

- ❏ *Design View* lets you change the design of the report
- ❏ *Print Preview* displays the report in the Print Preview window
- ❏ *Sample Preview* displays the report in the Print Preview window, with only a small amount of sample data available

SHORTCUT

If your report is based on a table or query that has a large amount of data in it, Access can be slow at displaying the Print Preview, and you can save time by using Sample Preview instead.

OTHER FEATURES OF THE TOOLBAR

The only other feature of the toolbar that is different in Report View is the Sorting and Grouping tool, which is covered later in this chapter. Other features of the toolbar are described in Chapter 7.

Working with Objects

When you are designing reports, you select objects as you do when you are designing forms:

- ❏ To select the report, choose **Select Report** from the Edit menu.
- ❏ To select a band, simply click it, or press **Tab** or **Shift-Tab** to select the bands in turn. The bar with the band's name on it is shaded when it is selected.
- ❏ To select a control, simply click it. To deselect a control, click any place in the Form window outside of that control. You can also select multiple controls, using the methods described in "Special Techniques for Working with Controls" in Chapter 7.

WORKING WITH BANDS

You add and remove Page and Report Header/Footer bands for reports as you do for forms. Choose the Format menu then **Page Header/Footer** and **Report Header/Footer**. Both these options are toggles. They are checked if the header and footer is displayed, and you can choose them again to remove the header and footer.

Report headers and footers appear once at the beginning and end of the report, and Page headers and footers appear at the top and bottom of each page. You can add page numbers to the page header or footer by using the Page property, which is in the Common Expressions folder of the Expression Builder. Refer to Chapter 8 for more information on the Page property.

Reports also have group headers and footers, which are not available in forms. These are not added and removed using the Format menu. Instead, they are controlled using the Sorting and Grouping dialog box described later in this chapter.

Resizing Bands

To resize a band, simply click and drag its lower border up or down.

Displaying Just a Header or Footer

Page headers and footers must be added to the report design in pairs. You can display just a header or just a footer by using the Format menu to add both and then resizing the one you do not want so its size is zero.

Group headers and footers can be added individually.

WORKING WITH CONTROLS

When a control is selected, it has two types of handle, the Resize Handles and the Move Handle, as shown in Figure 9.4.

FIGURE 9.4   SELECTING A CONTROL.

You work with controls in reports as you do in forms:

❑   To resize a control, click and drag one of the resize handles.

❑   To move a control, click and drag on the move handle or anywhere on the control where the pointer is displayed as a hand.

❑   To delete a control, select it and press **Del**.

To edit text, first select the control and then click to place an insertion point in it.

Notice that it is much less common to have labels attached to fields in reports than in forms. This is because the label with the field's name is usually in the Page Header band, and the field itself is usually in the Detail band.

OTHER FEATURES OF REPORT DESIGN

The Report Design window has the same features controlled by the View menu and the equivalent tools as found in the Form Design window (see Figure 9.5).

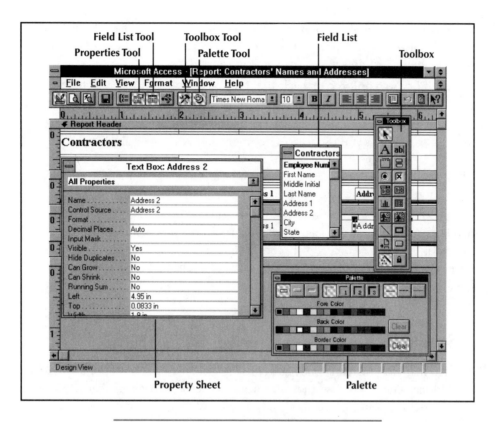

FIGURE 9.5   FEATURES OF THE REPORT DESIGN WINDOW.

These are the options you can choose from the View menu:

❏ Choose **Field List** or click the **Field List** tool to display or hide a field list, which you can use to add fields to the report.

❏ Choose **Properties** or click the **Properties** tool to display a property sheet with properties for selected objects, either for the entire form, bands, or controls.

❏ Choose **Ruler** to display or hide the rulers above and to the left of the window.

❏ Choose **Grid** to display or hide a grid in the design window. Controls are automatically aligned to this grid when you move them, so they will be lined up with each other. Choose **Snap to Grid** from the Format menu to turn this automatic alignment on and off. Use the property sheet of the entire report to change the fineness of the grid. In reports, horizontal and vertical lines one inch apart are displayed in addition to the grid of dots.

❑ Choose **Toolbox** or click the **Toolbox** tool to display or hide the toolbox that you use to add new controls.

❑ Choose **Palette** or click the **Palette** tool to display or hide the palette that you use to specify colors and other special effects.

All of these features work in the same way in report design as in form design. See Chapter 7 for more information on these features.

The toolbox is the same in reports as it is in forms, though you will never need to use some of its tools in reports. There is no reason to use the Combo Box tool to create a drop-down control in a report, as you did in the sample form you created in Chapter 7, for quicker data entry. Access keeps these features consistent in form and report design in order to make it easier for you to learn to use these two windows.

A Sample Report

Though many of the techniques used are the same, you create reports differently than forms, simply because they are meant to be printed rather than viewed on screen. Before going on to more advanced features of report design, such as grouped reports, you should try creating a sample report. The sample report will help you solidify your understanding of the basics and get some sense of the design elements involved in laying out reports. In addition, it gives you an opportunity to use expressions, which you had not yet learned when you laid out forms.

Let's suppose that you want to produce a simple tabular report on names and addresses of contractors. To improve the report's appearance, you want the name to be listed in a single column, rather than having separate columns for first, middle, and last names.

You can place the First Name and Last Name fields in a single column by using a text box with the expression:

```
[First Name] & " " & [Last Name]
```

As you learned in Chapter 8, **&** is the concatenation operator used to combine text strings. This expression is made up of the value of the First Name and Last

Name fields with a blank space added as a text literal (enclosed in quotation marks) between them. If you did not add this literal, the two names would run into each other. Adding the middle initial requires a more complex expression, which is described later in this chapter.

GENERATING THE INITIAL REPORT

As always, it is easiest to begin by using a Wizard to place fields on the report, and then to use Design View to customize it.

If you only used the Wizard to add the address, city, state, and zip fields, you would have to move them all to the right to make room for the name. Instead, you begin by using the wizard to add the First Name and Last Name fields, which will hold a place for the new expression you are creating. Including them initially also lets you use them as the basis of the sort order.

1. Open the Database window and click the **Table** button to display the Tables list. Then select the **Contractors** table, then click the **New Reports** tool.

2. Access displays the New Report dialog box, with **Contractors** already selected in the drop-down list as the name of the table. Select the **ReportWizards** button. In the next dialog box, select **Tabular** as the wizard you want, and select **OK**.

3. The first dialog box of the wizard lets you select the fields to include. Double-click **First Name**, **Last Name**, **Address 1**, **Address 2**, **City**, **State**, and **Zip** to move them into the Field order on report list, as shown in Figure 9.6. Then select **Next >**.

4. In the next dialog box, select **Last Name** and **First Name** as the fields to be used to determine the Sort order of the records. Click **Next >**.

5. Click **Next >** in the following dialog box to accept the default style, line spacing, and pPage orientation (landscape). In the final dialog box, select the **Modify the report's design** radio button. Then select **Finish** to generate the report.

6. Access takes a moment to generate the report and then displays it in Design View. Choose **Save** from the File menu. In the Save As dialog box, enter **Contractors' Names and Addresses** as the report name, and select **OK**.

7. Click the **Maximize** button to maximize the window. The report design is shown in Figure 9.7. Click the **Print Preview** tool to display the

report in the Print Preview window, and zoom the window, as shown in
Figure 9.8. After you have looked at the initial report, select the **Close**
tool to return to Design View.

FIGURE 9.6   INCLUDING FIELDS IN THE REPORT.

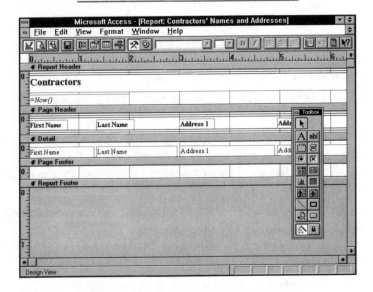

FIGURE 9.7   THE INITIAL DESIGN OF THE REPORT.

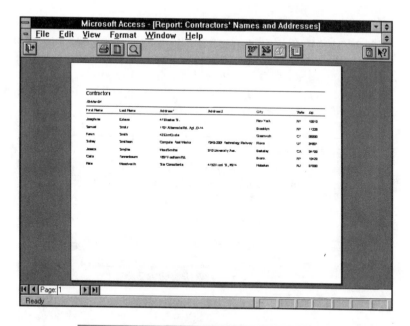

FIGURE 9.8 A PRINT PREVIEW OF THE INITIAL DESIGN.

WORKING WITH EXPRESSIONS

Now you can modify the initial report to get some practice working with expressions.

Notice that the Print Preview (see Figure 9.8) has the date in the report title band, but that the initial design (see Figure 9.7) has the expression **=Now( )** in the title band (the assignment operator followed by the Now( ) function). Though this function returns both the date and time, it is formatted to display only the date. Let's assume that you want to know the time that you print out sample copies as you design this report. You can change its format temporarily, assuming that you will change it back when you have the finished report.

You must also add a text box that includes the First and Last Name field to replace the actual fields. As you know, you do this by adding a text box to hold the expression and then entering the expression as its Control Source property. The easiest way to do this is move the First Name and Last Name fields out of the way, then add the text box, and finally delete the First Name and Last Name fields. As long as the fields are still in the report, you can select them in the Expression Builder. You will see later how to type in field names even if they are not in the expression builder, but for a beginner it is easier to select them.

1. Select the text box that contains the expression **=Now( )**. Click the **Property Sheet** tool to display its property sheet, and select **All Properties** from its drop-down list. The third property is Format, and it is currently Medium Date. Click this cell and then click to get its drop-down list. Scroll upward in the drop-down list, and select the first format in the list, **General Date**, as shown in Figure 9.9.

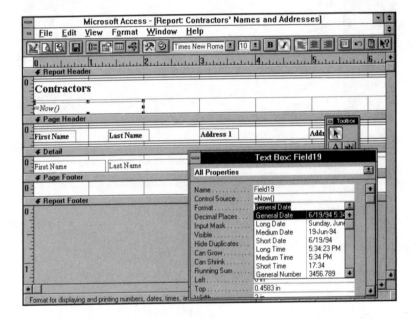

FIGURE 9.9   CHANGING THE FORMAT OF A DATE/TIME EXPRESSION.

2. Now that you have the property sheet displayed, you can also use it to add a text box with an expression that displays the name. First, click and drag the **First Name** field right, so it is on top of the Last Name field, simply to get it out of the way. Be sure you move the First Name field in the Detail band, *not* the words "First Name" in the Page Header band, which are a label.

3. Now, click the **Text Box** tool in the toolbox and click and drag to place a text box where the First Name field was originally located. Make it wide enough to hold both first and last names. It should overlap the First Name and Last Name fields to its right, as shown in Figure 9.10.

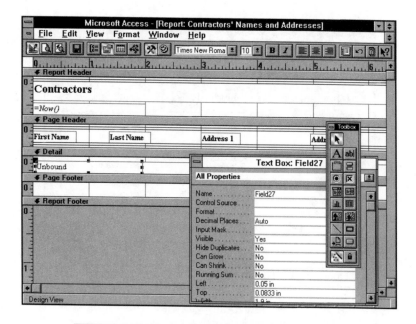

FIGURE 9.10 PLACING THE TEXT BOX TO HOLD THE NAME.

4. The text box is selected after you place it, and its Control Source property is the second property in the property sheet. Click the **Control Source** property and then click the **...** button to its right to display the Expression Builder.

5. The objects from the current report are displayed in the center panel. Scroll down to find **First Name**, and double-click it to add it to the expression. Then click the **&** button. Then you must enter the Literal **" "** by hand. Then click the **&** button again. Finally, double-click **Last Name** in the center panel to add it to the expression, as shown in Figure 9.11, and select **OK**. Click anywhere in the design window to place the expression in the text box, and then close the property sheet.

6. Now you must delete the original First Name and Last Name fields. Click the location of these fields, to the right of the new text box, to select the **First Name** field, and press **Del**. Click there again to select the **Last Name** field, and press **Del** again.

7. Finally, change the labels to fit the new fields. Select the **Last Name** label in the Page Header band, and press **Del**. Select the **First Name** label, then click it again to place an insertion point in it. Edit it so it just reads **Name**.

FIGURE 9.11   THE EXPRESSION USED TO DISPLAY THE NAME.

8. Click the **Print Preview** button to view the report as it is currently designed, as shown in Figure 9.12.

FIGURE 9.12   THE REPORT WITH THE NEW DATE/TIME AND NAME EXPRESSIONS.

The report includes both the date and the time in the header, and has the first and last names concatenated as a single name.

ADDING GRAPHIC ENHANCEMENTS

Looking at the report in Print Preview, you might want to add a few more graphic enhancements. Try making the line under the heading heavier and also adding a heavy line under the data, in order to make the detail lines of the report stand out.

1. Select the **Close** tool to return to design mode. Click the line that is near the bottom of the Page Header band to select it. Click the **Palette** tool to display the palette. If necessary, drag the palette to get it out of the way. Select the palette's **3-pt Border** button to create the heavy line as shown in Figure 9.13.

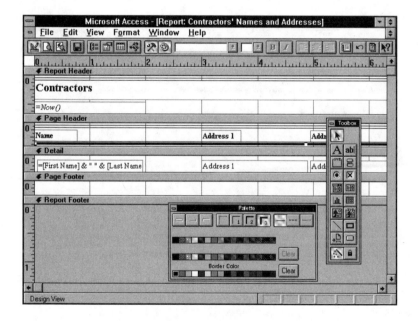

FIGURE 9.13   CHANGING THE STYLE OF A LINE.

2. Now you must add a similar line near the top of the Page Footer band to be displayed under the data. Click the **Line** tool in the toolbox. Click and drag beginning at the left margin next to the top of the Page Footer band. Continue dragging right beyond the right edge of the screen. The

report scrolls automatically to let you continue the line. Keep dragging right until the line goes as far as the line in the Report Header band.

3. After you have placed the line, select the palette's **3-pt Border** button, to create a second heavy line. Scroll left to make sure the line is placed properly, and select and move it if necessary to place it where it is shown in the final design.

4. The final design is shown in Figure 9.14. Click the **Print Preview** button to display the report shown in Figure 9.15.

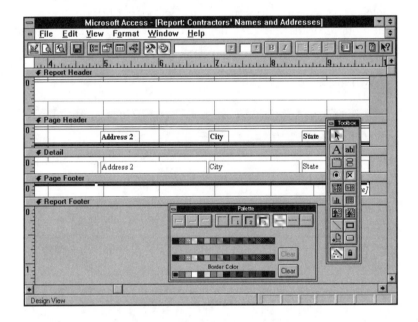

FIGURE 9.14   THE FINAL DESIGN.

In an actual presentation quality report, you would also want to adjust the spacing of the columns. Because the First and Last Name expression took the place of two fields, it has too much white space to its right. You should click and drag the other fields and labels left in order to even out the spacing, but this is so easy to do that there is no need to include it in an exercise.

USING A COMPLEX EXPRESSION

The next exercise adds the Middle Initial field to the expression that displays the name in this report—a much more difficult problem.

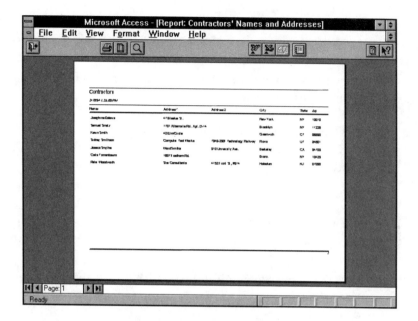

FIGURE 9.15   THE FINAL REPORT.

Your first impulse might be simply to use the concatenation operator to add the Middle Initial field, expanding the expression from the current

    [First Name] & " " & [Last Name]

to

    [First Name] & " " & [Middle Initial] & "." & [Last Name]

Here, you use both a period and a space as the text literal after the middle initial, rather than just a space, to display names in the form **Carla R. Tannenbaum**.

The problem is that some people do not have a middle initial entered in the table, and this expression would also include the extra period and space after the first name for them. What you need is an expression that displays nothing if there is no entry in the Middle Initial field, and displays the middle initial followed by a period and a space if there is an entry in the Middle Initial field.

To create this expression, you use the IIF( ) function, covered in Chapter 8. This function takes the form:

    IIF(expr, truepart, falsepart)

The initial expression must evaluate as true or false. If it evaluates as true, the function returns the "truepart" expression that follows. If it evaluates as false, the function returns the final "falsepart" expression.

To display the middle initial in the way you want, you can use the following expressions within the IIF( ) function:

❑ the *initial expression:* **[Middle Initial] Is Null**. This evaluates to true if there is no entry in the Middle Initial field. You can follow it with the two expressions that you want if there is no entry and if there is an entry.

❑ the *"truepart" expression:* **""**. Two quotation marks with nothing between them represent an empty string—in other words, nothing. If there is no entry in the Middle Initial field, the expression returns the empty string and nothing is displayed.

❑ the *"falsepart" expression:* **[Middle Initial] & ". "**. If there is an entry in the Middle Initial field, the expression returns that entry followed by a period and a space.

Now that you have looked at each element in the expression used to display the middle initial, you should be able to understand the function used to display the middle initial:

```
IIF( [Middle Initial] Is Null, " " , [Middle Initial]
& ". " )
```

This is a bit hard to read because the commas that are used as separators do not stand out as strongly as they should, but it becomes clear if you look individually at each of the three expressions used in the function.

Remember that this function just handles the display of the middle initial, and to display the entire name, you must concatenate it with the First Name and Last Name fields to form the expression:

```
[First Name] & " " IIF( {Middle Initial] Is Null, "",
[Middle Initial] & ". " ) & [Last Name]
```

Notice that there is always a space following the first name. If the middle initial is not included, the last name comes right after this space. If the middle initial is included, it is followed by a period and another space.

The exercise uses what is probably the easiest method of changing the expression that you now have in this text box. It uses the Expression Builder but types the three expressions within the function by hand, rather than generating them. You can try other methods if you want. Sometimes editing in the Expression Builder is tricky. If you delete something, you should make sure that extra elements of the expression were not deleted along with it.

1. Select the text box that holds the expression that displays the name. If necessary, select the **Properties** tool to display the property sheet and remove other features of the design window that are in the way.

2. Click the **Control Source** property and click the **...** button to display the Expression Builder.

3. Place the insertion point just before the initial square bracket of Last Name. Double-click the **Functions** folder, click **Built-In Functions** then scroll down in the right panel until **IIf** is displayed, and double-click it.

4. The Expression Builder adds the IIF( ) function and also indicates that there is an operator missing after it, as shown in Figure 9.16. The missing operator is the concatenation operator. To add it, click **<Oper>** to select it, and then click the **&** button.

FIGURE 9.16   ADDING THE IIF( ) FUNCTION.

5. Now, type in the initial logical expression of the IIF( ) function. Click **<expr>** to select it, and type **[Middle Initial] Is Null**.

6. Next, click **<truepart>** to select it, and type **""**, the empty string. Finally, click **<falsepart>** to select it, and type **[Middle Initial] & ". "** to create the final expression shown in Figure 9.17. Select **OK**.

FIGURE 9.17   THE FINAL EXPRESSION.

7. Click anywhere to place the expression. Then click the **Print Preview** tool to display the report, as shown in Figure 9.18. When you are done, close the Report window and save your changes.

FIGURE 9.18   THE REPORT USING THIS EXPRESSION.

Sorting and Grouping

So far in this chapter you have looked at ways of designing reports that are similar to the ways you design forms. In addition to the basics of report layout, you have used a few different types of calculated fields, which you were not able to use when you designed forms in Chapter 7, because you had not yet learned about expressions. In the future, you can apply what you learned about calculated fields to forms also.

Now, you will look at the one major feature of reports that does not apply to forms—sorting and grouping.

When you are designing printed reports, you often want to group records and to include a header and footer for each group. For example, you might want to do a report on your Contractor table that is grouped by job category, so the programmers, writers, and clerical help are listed separately. You could include a header for each group that says something like **Contractors in Job Category "P"**, and a footer for each group that says something like **The average wage for this Category is ... per hour**. You also could use just a header.

You can include summary data for the group, such as the average wage, by creating a calculated field that uses aggregate functions you learned about in Chapter 8, particularly:

❑ *Avg( )*, which is the average value in the specified field

❑ *Count( )*, which is the total number of records

❑ *Max( )* and *Min( )*, which are the highest and lowest value in the specified field

❑ *Sum( )*, which is the total of all the values in the specified field

After you look at how to create groups, you will look at how these functions are used.

The Sorting and Grouping Dialog Box

In Chapter 6, you used the Groups/Total ReportWizard to create groups for you. You can also create or modify groups from the Report design window by selecting the **Sorting** or **Grouping** tool or by choosing the View menu then **Sorting and Grouping** to display the Sorting and Grouping dialog box shown in Figure 9.19.

FIGURE 9.19   THE SORTING AND GROUPING DIALOG BOX.

Simply use the drop-down lists in the grid in the upper portion of this dialog box to select the field or fields that the report can be grouped on, and to specify whether they are sorted in ascending or descending order. You may select a field from the drop-down list or type an expression directly in the cell.

You must sort on the fields or expressions specified here in order to group on them. Any fields that you sorted using other methods are automatically included in this list. For example, primary key fields and fields that you sorted on in a query, if the report is based on a query, are listed in this dialog box the first time you open it.

Whether the data also is actually grouped on the fields or expressions that you sort them on depends on the Group Header and Group Footer properties that you specify below. By default, the Group Header and Group Footer properties are set to **No** when you add a new field or expression. The report is sorted on the field or expression but not grouped on it.

To create groups, select **Yes** for one or both of these properties. Access creates a header and/or footer for the group that separates it from the other groups.

For example, if you sorted by job category in ascending order, all the clerical help would be listed first, then the programmers, and then the writers, but the records would just follow one after another without being separated. If you also created a group footer for job category, then the footer after the records in each category would separate it from the records in the other categories. This example shows why you can sort without grouping but cannot group without sorting.

If you have defined a header or footer for the group, Access displays the Grouping symbol to its left, as was shown in Figure 9.19.

GROUPING BY RANGE

Use the Group On property to group on a range of values. For text or number values, it must be used in combination with the Group Interval property.

Normally the Group On property is set to **Each Value**, so Access creates a new group whenever the value in the field or expression changes—for example, a new group for each job category or a new group for each employee number.

There are also cases where you want similar values to be included in a single group. For example, if you are grouping records by date, you might want all the records in the same month to be grouped together. The month is the range of values that you want to group on.

Grouping Date/Time Data by Range

The drop-down list in the Group On cell, shown in Figure 9.20, lets you select different ranges of values to group on. If the group is based on a Date/Time field, it includes a selection of ranges of dates and times—Year, Qtr, Month, Week, Day, Hour, and Minute.

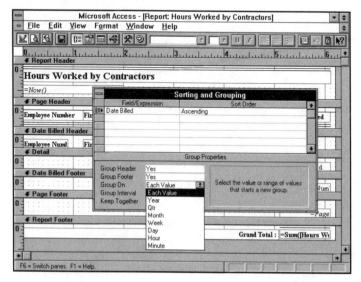

FIGURE 9.20   SELECTING A RANGE OF VALUES TO GROUP ON.

Grouping Text Data by Range

You can also group text data on a range of values by selecting **Prefix Characters** as the Group On property and using the Group Interval property to specify how many characters the group is based on.

For example, if you want to group records by the first letter of the last name, so all names beginning with A, B, and so on are listed together, you would select **Last Name** as the field to group on, **Prefix Character** as the Group On property, and **1** as the Group Interval, indicating that the group is based on one character at the beginning of the last name, as shown in Figure 9.21.

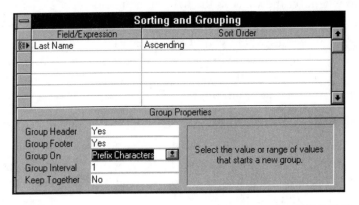

FIGURE 9.21 GROUPING TEXT DATA BY THE FIRST LETTER OF LAST NAME.

To group on the first two characters of the last name, do the same but enter **2** as the interval.

NOTE

Grouping Numeric Data by Range

To group numeric data (including Number, Currency, or Counter fields) by a range of values, select **Interval** as the Group On property and select the number that represents the range as the Group Interval property.

For example, you could group contractors by their hourly pay, with $10 as the range of values, so contractors who earn less than $10 per hour are included in one group, contractors who earn $10 or more but less than $20 are included in a second group, and so on. To do this, select **Hourly Pay** as the field to group on, select **Interval** as the Group On property, and select **10** as the Group Interval property, as shown in Figure 9.22.

Sorting and Grouping		
Field/Expression	Sort Order	
Hourly Pay	Ascending	

Group Properties		
Group Header	Yes	
Group Footer	Yes	Interval or number of characters to group on.
Group On	Interval	
Group Interval	10	
Keep Together	No	

FIGURE 9.22   GROUPING NUMERIC VALUES BY RANGE.

Sorting When You Group by Range

When you group by range, the sort also is based on the range. For example, Access might sort records by year but not by the date within the year, or might sort records by the first letter of the last name but not sort alphabetically by the entire last name.

> To sort properly, you can use the same field or expression a second time as the basis of a sort grouped on each value.

NOTE

For example, you could select the same Date field in two cells in the grid. In the first, use it just as the basis of a sort, with Each Value as the Group On property, so Access sorts all the records by date. In the second, set the Group Header and/or Footer property to **Yes**, and select a range such as Month as the Group On property, so Access groups by month.

KEEPING GROUPS TOGETHER

You can specify how groups are organized by page when the report is printed by using the Keep Together property, which lets you select among the following options:

❑ *No* prints the report without regard to page breaks. A group may run over onto a second page.

❑ *Whole Group* prints the entire group on a single page if it fits. If a new group will not fit on the remainder of the current page, it is printed beginning at the top of the following page.

❑ *With First Detail* prints at least one detail record on the same page as the group header. If there is no room for a record under it, the group header is printed at the top of the following page.

For presentation quality reports, it is always better to select **With First Detail** rather than **No**, at least for major groups. The header of a major group should not be printed at the bottom of a page with no records following it.

SHORTCUT

You can also control printing by adding page breaks at the top of a Group Header band or at the bottom of a Group Footer band, so the group always begins on a new page. As you learned in Chapter 7, you can add a page break to a form or report by clicking the **Page Break** tool of the toolbox and then clicking a location on the design. The page break is displayed as a heavy broken line next to the left margin.

CREATING COMPLEX SORTS AND SUBGROUPS

As you know, you cannot always sort on a single field. If you want to sort alphabetically by name, for example, you have to use the first name and middle initial as tiebreakers in cases where the last name is the same.

To create complex sorts like this, simply select all of the fields in the Field/Expression column, from the most important to the least important. For example, to sort alphabetically by name, use the sort order shown in Figure 9.23. The first field is the primary sort order, and the ones below are only used as tiebreakers.

Nested Groups

You create groups with subgroups in the same way. Simply create a complex sort and select **Yes** as the Group Header and/or Group Footer property for all the groups.

For example, you might want to group by state, and have all the records within each state grouped by city, and have all the records within each city grouped by zip code. You can do this by using the sort order shown in Figure 9.24. You can include Header and Footer bands for all the groups. For example, you might want to include footers for all groups, as shown in Figure 9.25. Then you could add footers for each of these groups: they might use the Count( ) function to display the total number of records from each zip code, from each city, and from each state.

Sorting and Grouping

Field/Expression	Sort Order
▶ Last Name	Ascending
First Name	Ascending
Middle Initial	Ascending

Group Properties

Group Header	No
Group Footer	No
Group On	Each Value
Group Interval	1
Keep Together	No

Select a field or type an expression to sort or group on

FIGURE 9.23   SORTING ALPHABETICALLY BY NAME.

Sorting and Grouping

Field/Expression	Sort Order
State	Ascending
City	Ascending
Zip	Ascending

Group Properties

Group Header	No
Group Footer	Yes
Group On	Each Value
Group Interval	1
Keep Together	No

Select a field or type an expression to sort or group on

FIGURE 9.24   CREATING GROUPS WITH SUBGROUPS.

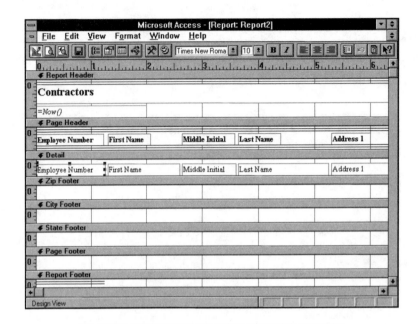

FIGURE 9.25 GROUPS AND SUBGROUPS IN DESIGN VIEW.

Changing the Definition of a Sort or Group

To change the definition of sorts and groups, you can edit them just as you do when you are changing the design of a table.

Edit text and make selections from drop-down lists in the usual ways.

The select boxes for the rows of the Sorting and Grouping dialog boxes are like the select boxes for the rows of tables, and are used in the same way. Click the select box to select a row. Then, to change sorting and grouping order, click and drag the select box to move the selected row. To remove a group or sort, press **Del** to delete the selected row.

WARNING

If you delete a row, you also lose any properties associated with it and any controls you added in that group's header and footer in Design View. You cannot undo this change. As a precaution, it is best to save the design before modifying a complex group or sort. Then you can close the design without saving changes if you made a mistake.

A Sample Grouped Report

To get some experience working with grouped reports, you should try redesigning the grouped report on contractors total work hours, which you created in Chapter 6.

This report was based on a query that joined the Hours table with the Contractors table, so the records had repetitive data on the contractors' employee numbers and names. The wizard let you group by Employee Number field and placed this field in the group header, but you had to leave repetitive values in the First Name and Last Name fields.

By now you should realize that you can correct this problem simply by dragging these field names from the Detail band to the Group Header band. While you are at it, you can add a bit more detail to the Group Footer and Report Footer bands.

1. In the Database window, select the **Report** button. In the Reports list, select **Hours Worked by Contractors**. Then select the **Design** button to display the report design shown in Figure 9.26.

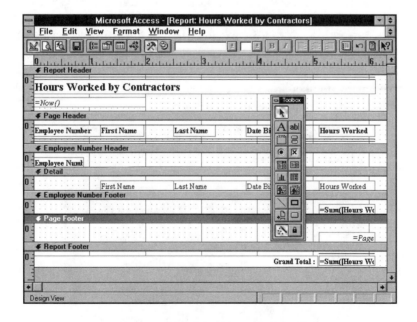

FIGURE 9.26   THE INITIAL REPORT DESIGN.

2. If you want to refresh your memory of what the report looks like, select the **Print Preview** button to display it with data, and then close the Print Preview window when you are done. You can see in Figure 9.26 that the Page Header band has field names, and the Page Footer band uses the Page property to display a page number. The Employee Number band has the Employee Number field, and all the other fields are in the Detail band. The Employee Number and Report Footer bands use the Sum( ) function to display the total number of hours worked for each contractor and for all the contractors included in the report.

3. Click and drag around the **First Name** and **Last Name** fields to select them both. Be careful not to select any other field. Then click and drag both fields from the Detail band to the Employee Number Header band. To move the fields across bands, you cannot use the Move handle. You must display the pointer as a hand. Since the fields are already selected, you can click the **Font Bold** tool to display them both in boldface, like the Employee Number field.

4. Next, click the text box in the Group Footer band, which includes the Sum( ) function. If necessary, select the **Properties** tool to display its property sheet. Click the **...** button to the right of its Control Source property to display the Expression Builder. Edit the expression so it reads **="Total Worked by Employee Number " & [Employee Number] & ": " & Sum([Hours worked]) & " Hours"** as shown in Figure 9.27. Leave several blank spaces after the colon to separate the summary number from the text that precedes it. Select **OK**, and then click anywhere to place the expression.

FIGURE 9.27 THE EXPRESSION FOR THE GROUP FOOTER.

5. Close the Expression Builder to get it out of the way. Click and drag the left Resize handle of this text box, to make it large enough to hold the new expression. The left edge of the text box should be at about 2.75 inches on the top ruler. Click the **Font Bold** tool so this expression is not displayed in boldface.

6. The final design of the report is shown in Figure 9.28. Select the **Print Preview** tool to display the data shown in Figure 9.29. Select **Save** from the File menu to save the changes and then close the Report window.

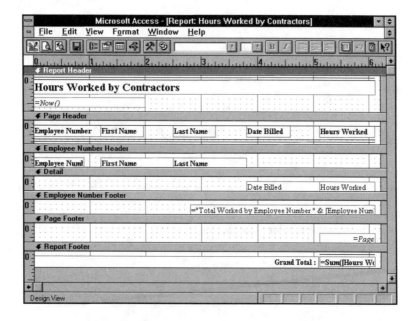

FIGURE 9.28 THE FINAL DESIGN OF THE REPORT.

This is obviously a much more attractive report than what was originally generated by the Wizard. You might want to try moving the fields and changing the size of the Group Header or Footer band to make it even more attractive.

Print Setup and Reports with Repeated Items

Now that you are designing custom reports, you may need to work with the Print Setup dialog box in either its initial or its expanded form. To display this dialog box, first select **Print Setup** from the File menu or click the **Print Setup** tool to display the Print Setup dialog box.

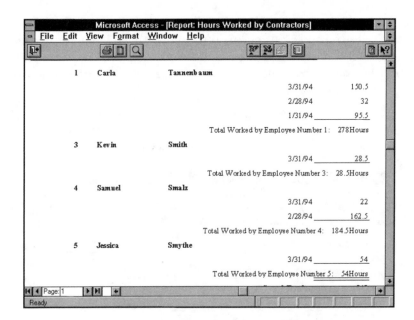

FIGURE 9.29 **THE DATA DISPLAYED BY THIS REPORT.**

In its initial form, shown in Figure 9.30, the Print Setup dialog box has features that let you control the printer, like the equivalent dialog boxes in other applications, and a couple of other options that most applications would treat as page formatting rather than as print setup features.

FIGURE 9.30 **THE PRINT SETUP DIALOG BOX.**

You can also display this dialog box in an expanded form by selecting its the **More >>** button. This button is available only in the Print Setup dialog box for forms and reports. It displays other important page formatting features that are used to work with reports that use repeated items, which are described below.

Print Setup for Conventional Reports

You use this dialog box set up the printer in the usual ways:

❏ To specify which printer the output will be sent to, select the **Default Printer** radio button or select the **Specific Printer** radio button and use the drop-down list below it to select a printer name.

❏ Use the **Portrait** or **Landscape** radio buttons to control the orientation of the items on the paper. You can switch from portrait to landscape to make room for more fields across the width of a page.

❏ Use the two **Paper** drop-down lists to specify the Size and Source of the paper you are printing on. The Source drop-down list applies only if your printer has multiple paper sources such as several paper trays, an envelope tray, or the like.

❏ Select the **Options** button to display an Options dialog box, which lets you do things such as control the darkness and fineness of the printing. The options in this dialog box depend on your printer.

Other options in the Print Setup dialog box actually control what is printed rather than how it is printed.

PRINTING DATA ONLY

Select the **Data Only** checkbox to print only the data in the report, leaving out graphics, borders, and the like.

You can use this feature to print a draft report (since graphics take longer to print) or to print the data on a preprinted form.

SETTING MARGINS

Use the four Margin text boxes to specify the size of the left, right, top, and bottom margin.

If a Wizard creates unusual settings for the left and right margin, they are probably necessary to fit the data within the width of the page. If you change these margins, make sure the data from each page does not run onto a second page.

Reports with Repeated Items

The remaining options in the Print Setup dialog box are used primarily for designing and printing reports with a repeated item such as a mailing label, which prints the same design many times on each page.

You will understand these reports better if you look at the design of the mailing labels you created with the ReportWizard in Chapter 5, shown in Figure 9.31, and the expanded Print Setup dialog box for these labels, shown in Figure 9.32.

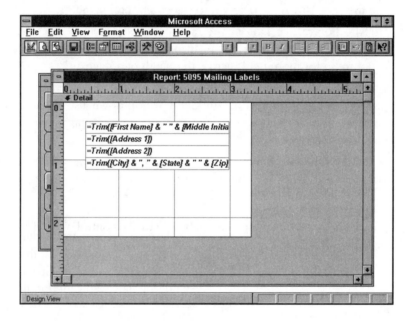

FIGURE 9.31   THE DESIGN FOR MAILING LABELS.

Unlike all the other reports you have worked with, the mailing label design takes up only a small part of the page—the area of a single label. The Print Setup dialog box lets you control how the item that you define in the design is laid out in multiple rows and columns on the page.

These features of the Print Setup dialog box are described below, and you have a chance to work with them in the next section when you create a sample form letter.

FIGURE 9.32   THE PRINT SETUP DIALOG BOX FOR THE MAILING LABELS.

CREATING MULTIPLE COLUMNS

To create a multicolumn report or to change the number of columns in a report, enter the number of columns you want in the Items Across text box.

N O T E

You also must be sure that the items are the right size to fit in the number of columns you specify. Take into account the width of the area of the page that is between the left and right margins, the width of the space between columns (specified in the Column Spacing text box discussed below), and the size of the items (specified in the Item Size area discussed below).

ROW AND COLUMN SPACING

To change the spacing between items, enter the measurement you want in the Row Spacing or Column Spacing text box.

Row spacing refers to the vertical spacing between items. Column spacing refers to the horizontal spacing between items, and it is disabled if you are working on single-column reports.

ITEM SIZE

Use the Item Size area to specify the size of the item. Usually you can select the checkbox to make the item the same size as the total detail area of the report. In some cases, you need a different item size. For example, if you are creating mailing labels, the item must be the right size to fit a single label, so that the item you design in the Report window is printed for each label. You learn how this works in the next section.

ITEM LAYOUT

Use the Item Layout radio buttons to determine if the items are printed across each row or down each column.

For example, when you use the ReportWizard to create mailing labels, **Horizontal** is selected so that the labels are printed across each line before going to the next line. Select **Vertical** if you want the labels to be printed down each column before beginning at the top of the next column.

Creating Form Letters

Though it has a Mail Merge Wizard that works with word processors, Access could also use a wizard to create its own form letters. A *form letter* is really just a report with the name, address, salutation, and body of the letter in the Detail band so that the entire letter is repeated for each record in the table or query that it is based on. It could have a letterhead in the Page Header band, or it could simply leave this band blank and print the form letters on paper with a preprinted letterhead.

You could create a form letter manually by adding expressions to the Detail band that are similar to the one you used earlier to concatenate the first and last name. Remember, though, that when you created mailing labels, the Mailing Label Wizard concatenated the fields for you.

It will be instructive for you to modify the mailing labels you created earlier to create a form letter. In addition to modifying the design in the design window, you change the settings in the Print Setup dialog box because the mailing labels that you begin with are a report that uses a repeated item.

When you are working with this report, notice that the wizard created the full name by using the expression **=Trim([First Name] & " " & [Middle Initial] & " " & [Last Name])**. When you were laying out the mailing labels, Access had no way of knowing that the Middle Initial field was an abbreviation with a period and that it would be missing in some records. As a result, the mailing labels do not have a period after the middle initial, and they skip two spaces between the first and last name for records that have no middle initial. If you want, you can edit this expression and change it to the more precise expression that you used to display the full name earlier in this chapter. This exercise leaves it as is for the sake of brevity.

1. In the Database window, select the **Report** button, select **5095 Mailing Labels** in the Reports List, and select the **Design** button. If necessary, press the **Maximize** button to maximize the Report window.

2. Choose **Save As** from the File menu. In the Save As dialog box, enter the name **Form Letters**, and select **OK**.

3. Now, change the Print Setup dialog box to print a single item rather than multiple items. Choose **Print Setup** from the File menu again,. Select the **More >>** button in the Print Setup dialog box. In the **Items Across** box, enter **1**. For **Row Spacing,** enter **0** inch. As Item Size, select **Same as Detail**. You should also use standard letter margins. Enter **1** inch in all the margin boxes. Select **OK**.

4. Now, make the report large enough to hold an entire page rather than a single item. Drag the right edge of the report design right until the ruler shows that it is 6.5 inches wide—enough to fit on an 8.5 inch wide paper with a 1-inch margin on each side. Then drag the bottom of the report down until the ruler shows that it is 8 inches high. In addition to the 1-inch top and bottom margins, this leaves an extra inch at the top for a preprinted letterhead.

5. To add space for the letterhead, select **Page Header/Footer** from the Format menu. Scrolling as necessary, click and drag the bottom edge of the footer so its size is **0**, and click and drag the bottom edge of the header so it is **1** inch high.

6. Finally, to make the name and address flush with the left margin, you can select all those text boxes and resize them by dragging their left edges left. Now that you have the basic page layout of the report, as shown in Figure 9.33, you might want to open the Print Preview window to see how the report looks, as shown in Figure 9.34. Then close the Print Preview window to return to Design View when you are done.

As you can see, you created a layout with the name and address where it would ordinarily be located on the page of a business letter with a preprinted letterhead. You might have to adjust the size of the header a bit to allow for the actual size of your letterhead.

FIGURE 9.33   THE BASIC PAGE LAYOUT FOR A FORM LETTER.

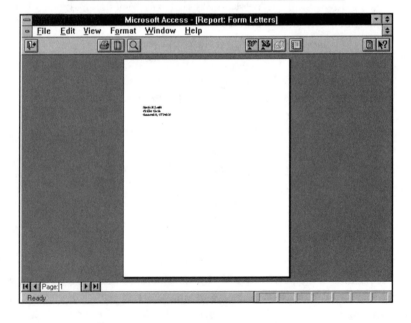

FIGURE 9.34   PREVIEWING THE PAGE LAYOUT.

All you need to do now to create a form letter is to add a date, salutation, and a text box where you can type the body of the letter. When you first planned the Contractors table, you decided that you would address people by first name in the salutation of letters.

If you wanted to address people by last name, you would have included a field in the table to hold a title such as Mr., Ms., Prof., Dr., and the like. You could have named this field Honorific, and used the expression **"Dear " & [Honorific] & " " & [Last Name]** as the salutation of the letter. For this exercise you simply use the expression **"Dear " & [First Name] & ","**.

1. To add a date, display the toolbox, then click the **Text Box** tool of the toolbox. Click and drag to place the text box in upper right of the Detail band beginning at 4.5 inches and extending to the right margin. This box should be entirely above the first line of the Name and Address fields. Click the **Property** tool to display its property sheet. Click the **Control Source** property, and type **=Date( )**. Use the drop-down list in for the Format property to select **Medium Date**.

2. Next, click and drag to place a text box under the Name and Address fields, with enough space for a skipped line between them. As its Control Source property, type **="Dear " & [First Name] & ","**. Click anywhere to place the expression, and then close the property sheet.

3. Finally, to create a space for the body of the letter, click the **Label** tool, and click and drag beginning at the left margin, with enough space below the salutation for a skipped line and ending at the right margin lower in the Detail band. Scroll back to the upper left of this text box, and begin typing **I am writing to let you know that** as the body of the letter.

4. Now, to set the font, first choose **Select All** from the Edit menu since you want all the controls to have the same typeface. Use the Font Name drop-down list on the toolbar to select a font such as **Times New Roman**. Use the Font Size drop-down list to select **12**. Click both the **Font Bold** and **Font Italic** buttons twice so none of the text is either bold or italic. Select **Save** from the File menu to save the layout. The final design is shown in Figure 9.35, and in the Print Preview window in Figure 9.36.

You may remember that the labels that you based this form letter on were sorted by zip code. It is best to keep this sort order for the form letters to make it easier to collate them with the mailing labels.

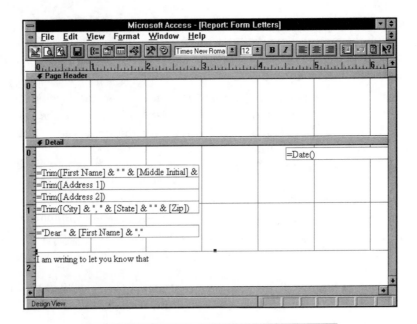

FIGURE 9.35 **THE FINAL DESIGN OF THE FORM LETTER.**

FIGURE 9.36 **PREVIEWING THE FORM LETTER.**

When you want to send a form letter, you can use this report in Design View, click the label box that holds the body of the letter to place an insertion bar in it, and type the letter as usual. The main difference between typing in a label box and in an ordinary word processor is that you must use **Crtl-Enter** rather than just **Enter** at the end of paragraphs. Since an Access label holds a maximum of 2,048 characters, you may have to add additional labels if you are writing a long letter.

N O T E

If you produce form letters with any frequency, it would make sense to save a dummy form letter layout like this, designed to fit your own letterhead or to print a letter head for you. Save form letters you create under different names, so that you always have this dummy letter to use as the basis of them.

To Sum Up

This chapter began with a review of the basics of report design, which are similar to the basics of form design, and then went on to cover more advanced features of Report design.

You learned to create sorted and grouped reports, including reports that have subgroups within groups. You learned to control how groups are printed, for example how to setup the printer and set margins for the report. You learned how to create reports that repeat the same item on the page, such as mailing labels. Finally, you learned how to use the report design screen to create form letters.

The next chapter covers advanced queries, including action queries, which let you use expressions to update groups of records in your table.

Using
Advanced Queries

*I*n Chapter 4 you learned to use basic Select queries to specify which records and fields are displayed and their sort order. Queries offer many more features than the basics you have already learned.

Select queries include more advanced features than you learned in the earlier chapter. There is also another category of queries, Action queries, which are entirely different from Select queries: they let you change the data in tables, rather than just specify what data is displayed.

This chapter covers advanced features of Select queries and Action queries. You learn to:

❏ use expressions rather than fields at the top of a column in the QBE grid.

❏ work with field properties and query properties

❏ rename fields or expressions to change column headings

❑ create Parameter queries

❑ create Make Table queries

❑ create Update queries

❑ create Append queries

❑ create Delete queries

❑ create Summary queries

❑ create Crosstab queries

❑ use the Query wizards and understand the queries they generate

Special Features of Query Design

Many special features of query design are accessible from the Access toolbar, as shown in Figure 10.1.

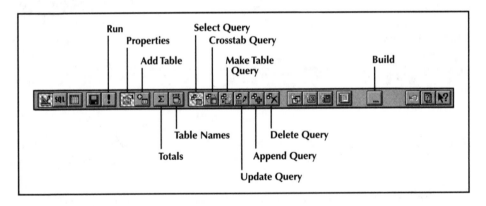

FIGURE 10.1 **THE TOOLBAR FOR DESIGNING QUERIES.**

Both the Query menu and the tools in the middle of the toolbar let you choose among the different types of queries. You create a query in the usual way and then select the tool or menu option for the type of query you want. The title of the Query window changes to reflect the type of query it is:

❑ *Select query* is the sort of query you have already learned about, which specifies which records and fields of the underlying table or query are displayed and their sort order. Use this tool or menu option if you have converted a query to another type and later want to convert it back to a Select query.

❑ *Crosstab query* cross-tabulates data in the underlying table or query to summarize its data by category.

❑ *Make Table query* makes a new table based on the underlying table or query.

❑ *Update query* changes the values in all the fields or in a set of fields in the underlying table or query.

❑ *Append query* adds data from the underlying table or query to an existing table.

❑ *Delete query* deletes groups of records in the underlying table or query.

❑ *Parameter query* lets you enter criteria each time you run the query. This type of query is accessible only from the Query menu, not from the toolbar.

Each of these types of queries are covered in detail in a later sections of this chapter.

The Totals tool uses features of the QBE grid similar to those used in Crosstab queries. Because these are among the most advanced features of query design, they are covered near the end of this chapter.

There are a few other features of query design accessible through the toolbar that you should look at briefly now.

Using Expressions in Queries

You can select the Build tool to display the Expression Builder, and use it to enter expressions in the current cell of the query. This tool is enabled only when you are in a cell that can hold an expression.

In Chapter 4, you looked at how expressions are used in Criteria cells to determine which records are displayed, though you had not yet learned to use the Expression Builder then.

You can also use expressions rather than field names in the Field cell of a column. For example, if you are doing a summary report on your employees and you want the result of the query to display only the year that someone was hired, rather than the exact day, you can use the expression **Year([Hire Date])** rather than the field name Hire Date in the Field cell.

You might use this expression if you wanted to sort the records by year, and sort the employees hired each year alphabetically. You could use the expression to sort even without displaying the year, by deselecting the **Show** cell in that column.

Expressions are covered in Chapter 8 of this book. The section on Crosstab queries later in this chapter, uses some more advanced expressions.

Using Properties in Queries

Select the **Properties** tool or choose **Properties** from the View menu to display a property sheet, which works in queries as it does in other objects. Property sheets were covered generally in Chapter 7.

FIELD PROPERTIES

If the cursor is in the QBE Grid, Access displays the Field Properties sheet for that field, as shown in Figure 10.2. As you can see, it displays properties similar to those displayed in the Properties panel when you design a table, which you learned about in Chapter 2. For example, you can specify the format in which the field is displayed or an input mask, as you do when you design a table.

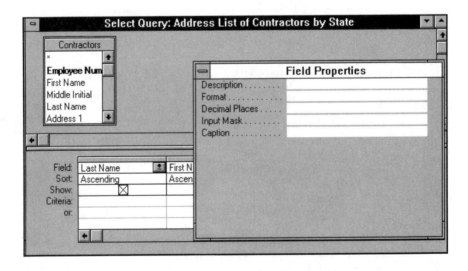

FIGURE 10.2   THE FIELD PROPERTIES SHEET.

QUERY PROPERTIES

If the Field Property sheet is open, you can select the entire query by clicking anywhere in the Query window except in the QBE grid or in a field list. Access displays the Query Properties sheet shown in Figure 10.3.

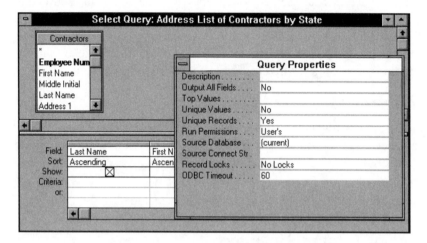

FIGURE 10.3 THE QUERY PROPERTIES SHEET.

If the Query Property sheet is not yet open, you can open it with the properties for the entire query simply by double-clicking in the same location.

SHORTCUT

You can display help on any of these properties by moving the cursor to a property name, and pressing **F1**. A few of the query and field properties are particularly useful and are covered next.

CREATING UNIQUE VALUE QUERIES

Select **Yes** for the Unique Records or Unique Values property to eliminate duplicate values in the result of the query:

❑ *Unique Records property* eliminates repetitive records. If a record has the same data in all of its fields as another record, it is not displayed in the result.

❑ *Unique Values property* eliminates repetitive data in any field. For a record to be displayed, the data in each of its fields must be unique.

You may only use one of these at a time. If you select **Yes** for one, Access automatically selects **No** for the other. By default, of course, both are No, and the result of the query includes a record for each record in the underlying table.

These properties are useful for summarizing data in the table. For example, if you want a list of all the states that your customers live in, you could do a query that includes just the State field, and set either the Unique Records or Unique Values property to **Yes**. If you did not use one of these properties, you would get a long list that repeated the names of some states many times, but if you use one, you get a list that includes each of the states just once.

Outputting All Fields

If you select **Yes** for the Output All Fields property, all the fields in the table or tables underlying the query will be displayed in the result, rather than just the fields whose Show box is selected in the QBE grid.

This is useful if you want to create a form or report based on the query, and you want to include fields that are not shown or included in the QBE grid.

Changing Column Headings

By default, the name of the field is displayed as the heading of the column that holds that field in the query result. This heading might be inappropriate, particularly if you use an expression rather than a field name. You can change the column heading in two ways:

❑   *Caption property:* display the Field Property sheet of the field or expression, and enter the heading you want as its Caption property. As you learned in Chapter 7, the Caption property controls the label displayed for a field in a report or form and the heading displayed at the top of the column in a table or query.

❑   *Renaming the Field or Expression:* enter the new name followed by a colon before the field name or expression in the QBE grid. Only the part of the name that is before the colon is used as the column heading.

If you use an expression in the Field cell of a query, Access assigns it an arbitrary name, followed by a colon, which it automatically adds to the expression. In this case, you must delete the arbitrary name and replace it with the name you want to use as the column heading. You look at an example of how to rename a field later in this chapter.

Displaying the Table Name in the QBE Grid

Select the **Table Names** tool to add an extra row to the QBE grid, under the Field row, that contains the name of the table the field is in, as shown in Figure 10.4. This is useful if you are working with complex relational databases with many tables.

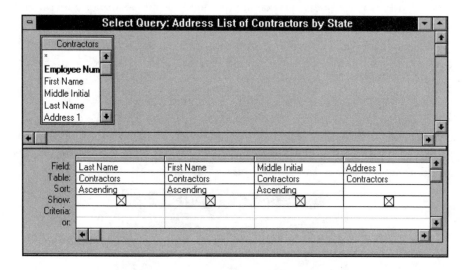

FIGURE 10.4 **DISPLAYING TABLE NAMES.**

The table name is automatically filled in when you drag and drop a field from the field list. You can add new fields by using the drop-down list in the table cell to select the name of a table that is included in the query, and then using the Field drop-down list to select its field. Drag-and-drop is generally easier.

Parameter Queries

All of the queries you have used so far have had unique criteria entered in the query form itself, but there are also times when you might want to use a query with criteria that vary.

For example, you created a query in Chapter 4 to isolate the names and addresses of contractors from New York. In reality, though, you would not want to have to create 50 different queries to isolate the contractors from all of the states.

A Parameter query lets you create a single query and enter the criterion in a dialog box that Access displays each time you run it. In this way, you could use *one* query to find contractors from any of the states.

Creating a Parameter Query

To create a Parameter query, you create the query design as usual, but you enter a parameter in one of the Criteria cells, rather than an actual value.

The parameter is displayed as a prompt in a dialog box when you run the query. It must be enclosed in square brackets, and it may not be the name of a field.

You must also choose **Parameters** from the Query menu to display the Query Parameters dialog box, shown in Figure 10.5. You use this dialog box to define the data type of the parameters. Enter the parameter in the left column, just as you typed it in the QBE grid (though you may omit the square brackets around it), and select its data type in the right column.

FIGURE 10.5   THE QUERY PARAMETERS DIALOG BOX.

The easiest way to enter the parameter in this dialog box is by copying and pasting. Select it in the QBE grid and choose **Copy** from the Edit menu (or use the shortcut keys, **Ctrl-C**), and then display the dialog box and press **Ctrl-V** to paste it. Though the menu is not accessible when you are using a dialog box, you can still paste using this shortcut key combination.

When you run the query, Access displays a small dialog box with the prompt you specified and lets you enter the value for the criterion.

You can use criteria entered as parameters in the same ways that you use values that you actually enter in the QBE grid. For example, you can use a parameter in a logical AND or a logical OR relationship with some other value that you entered in the QBE grid, just as you learned in Chapter 4.

You can also create a query with several parameters in a logical AND or a logical OR relationship with each other. When you run the query, Access displays a dialog box for each parameter, with the prompt you specified, and it uses all the values you enter as the basis of the query.

A Sample Parameter Query

Try creating a simple parameter query by changing the query that you created earlier to find names and addresses from New York so it finds names and addresses from any state:

1. Select the **Query** button of the Database window. In the Queries list, select **Address List of Contractors from New York**. Select **Rename** from the File menu. Edit the name in the Rename dialog box so it reads **Address List of Contractors by State**, and select **OK**. Then select the **Design** button.

2. Scroll right through the QBE grid until you can see the criterion under the State field. Delete the criterion that is now there, and instead type **[Enter the Name of the State]**, as shown in Figure 10.6. (The column has been widened in the illustration.)

3. Now, select (highlight) the parameter you just entered and choose **Copy** from the Edit menu, and then deselect the parameter. Choose **Parameters** from the Query menu. Access displays the Query Parameters dialog box, and you can press **Ctrl-V** to enter the parameter in it, and press **Tab** to move to the Data Type column, where **Text** is entered by default as shown in Figure 10.7. Select **OK**.

4. To run the query, click the **Datasheet View** tool. Access displays the Enter Parameter Value dialog box, and you can enter **CA**, as shown in Figure 10.8, and select **OK**. Access displays the query in Datasheet View with the one record from California, as shown in Figure 10.9.

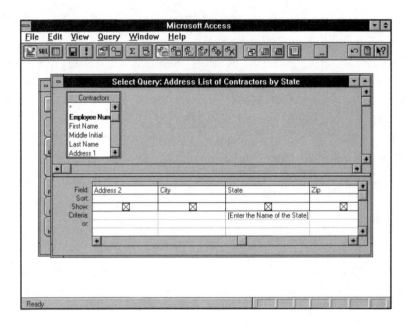

FIGURE 10.6   ENTERING THE PARAMETER.

FIGURE 10.7   DEFINING THE PARAMETER'S DATA TYPE.

FIGURE 10.8 **ENTERING THE PARAMETER VALUE.**

	Last Name	First Nar	Mi	Address 1	Address 2	City	Stal	Zip
▶	Smythe	Jessica		WordSmiths	910 University Ave.	Berkeley	CA	94709
＊							NY	

Select Query: Address List of Contractors by State

Record: 1   of 1

FIGURE 10.9 **A RESULT OF THIS QUERY.**

5. If you want, you can switch back to Design View and try the query with other values, or try entering a second parameter in a logical OR or a logical AND relationship. When you are done, close the Query window and save the changes.

Access also displays the Enter Parameter dialog box whenever you run this query by selecting it from the Database window and clicking the **Open** button.

Action Queries

Select queries, which you learned about in Chapter 4, are used to determine which records and fields are displayed and their sort order, but do not affect the contents of the fields. Access also lets you create Action queries, which change existing data or add new data to tables. You can use the following types of Action queries:

❏   *Make Table query* creates a new table that holds the data that is the result of the query.

❏   *Update query* changes the data in the table in ways that you specify.

❏   *Append query* adds the data in records in the current table to another table.

❏   *Delete query* deletes records that you specify.

WARNING

All of these Action queries work quickly and their results are not reversible. To avoid errors, you should always back up a table before performing an Action query on it.

In addition, to avoid losing data, it is always best to run an Action query as a Select query first. After you are sure that it isolates the records you want, convert it to an Action query and run it.

The Basics

Action queries are all created in a similar way. After displaying the Query window in Design View, you can select **Make Table**, **Update**, **Append**, or **Delete** from the Query menu or use the equivalent tool to convert the Select query to an Action query. The title bar changes, to indicate the type of Action query you are working on.

In some cases, Access displays a dialog box before creating the query, and in some, it changes the QBE grid to let you specify the action. These features are covered in later sections on the individual queries.

You can run the query from Design View by clicking the **Run** tool of the toolbar or choosing **Run** from the Query menu.

When you save an Action query, Access uses special icons in the Database window to show what type of query it is. Figure 10.10 shows the icons for the different Action queries.

When you open an Action query from the Database window, by double-clicking it, or by selecting it and selecting the **Open** button, Access runs the Action query and displays the data with the changes that the query made. Before opening the query, Access displays a dialog box that lets you cancel the action.

FIGURE 10.10   ICONS FOR ACTION QUERIES.

SHORTCUT

Remember that it is best to back up a table before running an Action query on it. The easiest way to do this from the Database window is to select the table and choose **Copy** and then **Paste** from the Edit menu. Access displays the Paste As dialog box, which lets you enter a new name for the copy of the table.

Using Make Table Queries

Use a Make Table query to create a new table that holds the result of the query, or to replace all the data in an existing table with the result of the query.

When you choose **Make Table** from the Query menu or click the **Make Table Query** tool, Access displays the Query Properties dialog box, shown in Figure 10.11. You can then specify the table that the data will be stored in.

The **Current Database** button is selected by default. If you want to store the data in a table in the current database, simply enter its name in the **Table Name** text box. If you enter the name of a new table, Access creates that table and stores the result of the query in it. If you enter the name of an existing table or use the drop-down list to select it, Access replaces the data in that table with the result of the query.

FIGURE 10.11   THE QUERY PROPERTIES DIALOG BOX.

If you want to store the data in a table in another database, select the **Another Database** button, and enter the full path name of the **.MDB** file in the File Name dialog box. Then enter or select the table name.

When you finish with the Query Properties dialog box, use the Query window exactly as you do for a Select query to specify the records, fields, and sort order of the new table.

If you want to change the table the results are stored in, you can do so by choosing **Make Table** from the Query menu at any time while you are designing the query to display the Query Properties dialog box again.

Using Update Queries

Update queries let you change the values in some or all of the records of a table.

When you choose **Update** from the Query menu or click the **Update Query** tool, Access displays the Query window in the form shown in Figure 10.12. Notice that the Show and Sort rows of the QBE grid have been removed because they do not apply when you are changing the data in a table. Instead, an Update To row is added, where you enter an expression that represents the new value for the field.

If you want only some of the records updated, enter criteria in the rows to specify the records you want changed, just as you do in a Select query.

Usually, you use an expression in the Update To row that is based on an existing value in the field. For example, to give all your contractors a raise of $5 per hour, you could use the Update query shown in Figure 10.12, with the expression **[Hourly Pay] + 5** as the Update To value for the Hourly Pay field.

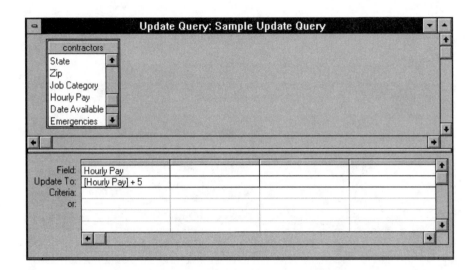

FIGURE 10.12   THE QUERY WINDOW FOR AN UPDATE QUERY.

It is also common to include criteria for other fields to specify which records are updated. For example, you could give a pay raise only to the contractors who are writers.

You can also use an expression that uses a values from other fields in the table or in other tables that are joined to it, as long as the expression produces a unique value for the field. Thus, you can use a field from a table that the current table is in a many-to-one relationship with, but not one that it is in a one-to-many relationship with.

There are also times when you would want to use a literal as the Update To value—for example, if you have a table that requires the same value in a field in all the records that meet a specific criterion.

Using Append Queries

Append queries are similar to Make Table queries except that the data is appended to an existing table, without affecting the data already in that table.

When you choose **Append** from the Query menu or click the **Append Query** tool, Access displays the Query Properties dialog box described earlier in the section on "Using Make Table Queries." This dialog box lets you specify the table that the data will be appended to. Use this dialog box in the same way you use it for Make Table queries.

For an Append query, Access displays the Query window shown in Figure 10.13. Notice that the QBE grid does not have the Show row that it does in Select queries.

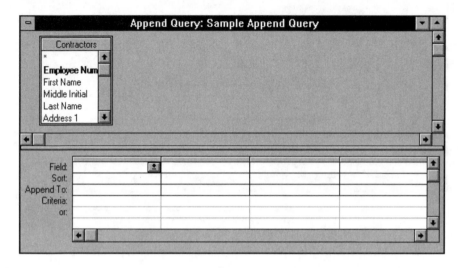

FIGURE 10.13 THE QUERY WINDOW FOR AN APPEND QUERY.

Instead, it has an Append To row, which you may use to select fields in the table you are appending the data to, in order to indicate which fields in the current table they correspond to. Click a cell in the Append To row to display a drop-down list that lets you choose among the fields in the table you are appending to.

If there are fields in the two tables that have the same name, they are displayed in these cells by default.

Use the Sort and Criteria cells as you do in Select queries to specify which records will be appended to the table and the order in which they will be added to the end of the table.

COUNTER FIELDS IN APPEND QUERIES

If you are using an Append query with tables that include counter fields, you can append the values in the counter fields in two ways.

If you do not include the counter field in the fields to be appended, it will be filled in automatically in sequence for all the records that are appended, just as it would be if you appended these new records by hand.

If you do this, the value in the counter field in the table that you appended to will have nothing to do with its value in the original table. Instead, it will just continue the sequence of entries that are already that field. For example, if you have a table of employees with employee numbers from 1 to 100, and you append new records to it in this way, they will begin with employee number 101.

If you include the counter field in the QBE grid as one of the fields to be appended, on the other hand, the values that it has in the original table will be kept in this field in the appended records. Note that this can create errors if the same value already exists in that field in the table you are appending records to, because a Counter field cannot have the same value in two records. This subject is discussed later in this chapter in "Correcting Errors in Action Queries."

N O T E

In general, it is best not to include the counter field in the QBE grid as one of the fields to be appended, unless you have some special reason to. If the counter is a key field, for example, it is usually best to give it arbitrary values in sequence when you append records, just as you would if you were entering new records by hand.

Using Delete Queries

It is easy to select individual records in a table and press **Del** to delete them, and it is easy to choose **Select All** from the Edit menu and then press **Del** to delete all the records in a table. If you have to delete records that meet some criterion, though, it is obviously easier to use a Delete query than to select the records individually.

When you select **Delete** from the Query menu or click the **Delete Query** tool, Access displays the Query window shown in Figure 10.14. It does not include the Sort or Show rows from a Select query. It includes only a Field row, Criteria row, and a Delete row.

To use a Delete query, first drag the **asterisk** from the field list to the QBE grid. As you learned in Chapter 4, the asterisk represents all of the fields in the table, and you obviously must delete all the fields to delete the record. In addition, drag the individual fields that you will use to enter criteria.

As you can see in Figure 10.14, the Delete row includes the word **From** below the table name, which was placed automatically when you dragged the asterisk, and **Where** below name of the individual fields. This is simply meant to remind you that you can enter criteria only under fields.

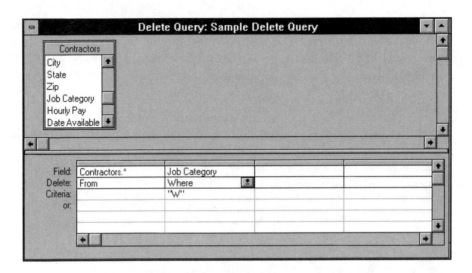

FIGURE 10.14   THE QUERY WINDOW FOR DELETE QUERIES.

Enter the criteria to specify which records are to be deleted just as you do for Select queries. For example, the query in Figure 10.14 would delete all writers from the Contractors table.

It is particularly important to run a Delete query as a Select query first to make sure it applies only to the records you want.

WARNING

Correcting Errors in Action Queries

The data that you can enter in a table using an Action query is limited in the same ways as the data you enter manually.

When you are entering data manually, Access displays a warning that prevents you from entering invalid data in each field. When you are entering data using an Action query, Access displays a single dialog box that summarizes all the errors.

This error message is displayed before the Action query is executed. If there is an error, it is generally best to select **Cancel** so the query is not executed until you correct it.

N O T E

If you select **OK**, the fields or records that contain errors will not be affected by the Action query in the way you intended. The most common error messages are:

❏ *Contents of fields were deleted*: the data is not valid for the field because of data type or because a validation rule. The field will be left blank if you run the query.

❏ *Records were lost due to key violations*: there is a duplicate value or no value in the data being added to a field used as the primary key of a table. Records cannot be added to the table without a valid primary key.

❏ *Records were locked and couldn't be modified*: someone else on a network is modifying records, and they cannot be changed until that person closes them.

Remember that, despite the phrasing of these error messages, the table has not yet been changed, and you can select Cancel to avoid performing an Action query that creates errors.

Sample Action Queries

Action queries can save you a considerable amount of work if you use them properly, and so you should try creating one.

There are times when it makes sense to use an Action query with the same criteria as a Select query that you are using, so you can modify the records that the Select query has isolated. For example, imagine you are doing a series of mailings to groups of people on a mailing list, and the mailings will depend on different types of criteria.

In practice, you would be likely to do this sort of mailing if you bought a list of prospects and you are sending them an initial letter. You might want to do mailings that depend on demographic data that comes with the list. For example, first you might send your offer to all the people who have bought a similar product previously, then to all with more than a certain income, and so on.

In the exercise, you use the Contractors table and start with a mailing to all contractors who have more than a certain hourly pay rate. Then you do a mailing to all contractors who are writers.

The question is how to avoid mailing duplicate letters to people who belong to more than one category—for example, to writers who earn more than that pay rate.

It is easy to do this by adding a Yes/No field named Already Mailed To to the table. Initially, No is placed in this field in every record by default. Every time you use a query with certain criteria to produce the mailing labels, you can use an Action query with the same criteria to add Yes to its Already Mailed To field. Then, when you do later mailings, you can use two criteria: as well as meeting the actual criterion for that mailing, the record must have No in its Already Mailed To field to be included among the records that mailing labels are produced for.

First, design the objects you need to use in this process:

1. First, add the new field to the table. Click the **Table** button of the Database window, select **Contractors** in the Tables list, and select the **Design** button. Scroll down to the bottom of the Field window, add a new field by entering the field name **Already Mailed To**, select the Data Type **Yes/No**, and enter the Description **Changed By an Action Query After Mailing Labels are Produced**, as shown in Figure 10.15. Close the Table window and select **Yes** to save the change.

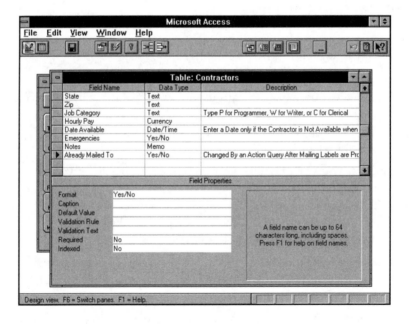

FIGURE 10.15   ADDING A NEW YES/NO FIELD.

2. Now, create the query to produce the mailing labels. Click the **Query** button to display the Queries List, and select the **New** button. In the New Query dialog box, select **New Query**. From the Add Table dialog box, select **Contractors**, select **Add**, and then select **Close**.

3. In the Query window, double-click the title bar of the Field list to select all the fields, and then click and drag them to the first column of the QBE window, to place them all in the QBE grid. Close the Query Window, select **Yes** to save the changes, and in the Save As dialog box, enter the name **Query Used for Targeted Mailings**.

4. Now, the easiest way of creating mailing labels for this query is by changing the Record Source property of the mailing labels you created earlier. Click the **Report** button, select **5095 Mailing Labels** in the Reports list, and select **Design**. Select the **Properties** tool to display the property sheet and select **Data Properties** from its drop-down list. The properties for the entire report should be displayed. If you inadvertently select some object in the report, choose **Select Report** from the Edit menu to select and display the property sheet for the entire report. Use the drop-down list for the Record Source property to select **Query Used for Targeted Mailings**. Then close the Report window and select **Yes** to save the change.

If you had to do mailings to the full list as well as targeted mailings, you could have choosen **Save As** from the File menu after changing the Report Source property for the mailing labels to produce two sets of mailing labels. One set would be based on the table to mail to the whole list, and the other would be based on this query.

Now that you have created the objects you need, you can try to produce a targeted mailing. First, do a mailing to the highest paid contractors on the list, and then do a mailing to all programmers (except those you already mailed to). Enter the criterion **No** in the **Already Mailed To** field from the beginning and save it for later use. It will not make any difference in the first mailing because all of the fields still have the value **No**.

1. Select the **Query** button, select **Query Used for Targeted Mailing** from the Queries list, and select **Design**. As the criterion for the Hourly Pay field, enter **>= 100**, and as the criterion for the Already Mailed To field, enter **No**, as shown in Figure 10.16. (Columns have been narrowed in the illustration to show both criteria.)

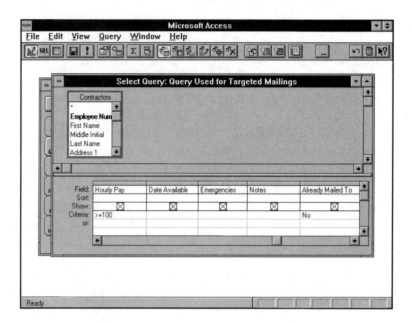

FIGURE 10.16 **CRITERIA FOR THE FIRST MAILING.**

2. Select the **Datasheet View** button to run the query. Note that only one person qualifies, and he is a programmer. Choose **Save** from the File menu to save the result of the query, and then, without closing the Query window, open the report **5095 Mailing Labels**. Notice that it has only that record in it. In a real case, you would print the labels now, but instead you can simply close the Report window.

3. Now, select the Query window, click the **Design** button to display it in Design View, and choose **Update** from the Query menu to change it to an Update query. Scroll right, noticing that the criteria you used for the Select query are still there. Enter **Yes** in the Update To cell of the Already Mailed column, as shown in Figure 10.17.

4. Select the **Run** button and select **OK** to update the data. Close the Query window. Since you will want to use this as a Select query rather than an Update query the next time you work with it, select **No** so the changes are not saved.

5. Now, open the table in Datasheet View, and scroll right so you can see that the data was changed. Notice that the Already Mailed To field for one record now has Yes in it. Close the Table window when you are done.

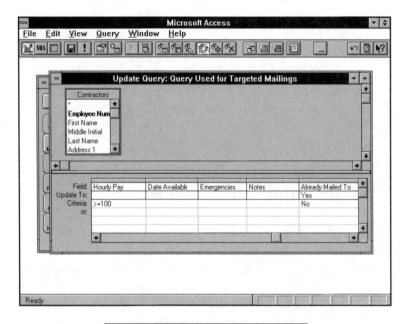

FIGURE 10.17   USING THE UPDATE QUERY.

6. It is time for the next mailing. Click the **Query** button of the Database window, select **Query Used for Targeted Mailings** from the Queries list, and select the **Design** button. Delete the criterion for the Hourly Pay field, and instead, enter **P** as the criterion in the Job Category column. Access adds the quotation mark delimiters around it when you move the highlight. The criterion No should still be entered in the Already Mailed To field.

7. Click the **Datasheet View** tool to display the result of the query. Notice that it includes the three programmers who earn less than $100 per hour, but not the programmer who earns more for whom you already prepared a label. If you would like, you could save the query and view the mailing labels, as you would do in a real case. However, it is not necessary for this exercise since you know that they would include the labels for these three records. Close the Report window when you are done.

8. Click the **Design View** tool to display the query in Design View. Choose **Update** from the Query menu to change it to an Update query. As you did last time, leave the criteria as is, and enter **Yes** in the Update To cell of the Already Mailed column. Select the **Run** tool and select **OK** to run the query. Then close the Query window without saving the changes.

9. You might want to look at the table in Datasheet View again, to confirm that Yes is entered for all the records that you have already prepared labels for.

NOTE Even though you tested it on just a small amount of data, you can imagine how useful this technique would be if you wanted to avoid duplication when doing a series of targeted mailings for a database with hundreds of thousands of records.

Queries with Totals and Groups

You can also use queries to produce summary data on a table, such as the average value in a field.

You can produce summary data for the entire table, but it is more common to want to group the data that you summarize. For example, you can find the average wage for all your contractors. However, you are more likely to want to know the average wage for programmers, writers, or clerical help, which involves grouping by job category.

To create a Summary query with totals, create a query as usual, and select the **Totals** tool to add an extra Total row to the QBE grid, as shown in Figure 10.18.

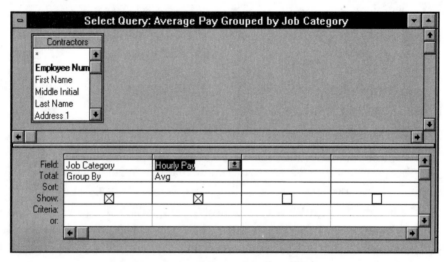

FIGURE 10.18   CREATING A QUERY WITH TOTALS.

Add the fields needed for the query to the QBE grid, and use the drop-down list in the Total cell to indicate the function of each field in the query.

The name of the Total row is a bit misleading. In addition to selecting a summary operation to perform on the field, you can use this row to indicate that the field is the basis of a grouping or that it is only used to enter criteria that specify which records are included in the query. The drop-down list in a Total cell includes the following options:

❑ *Group By* means the field is used as the basis of grouping. This is the default value.

❑ *Sum* displays the total of all the values in the field.

❑ *Avg* displays the average of all the values in the field.

❑ *Min* displays the minimum value in the field.

❑ *Max* displays the maximum value in the field.

❑ *Count* displays the total number of records that have a value in the field.

❑ *StDev* displays the statistical standard deviation of values in the field.

❑ *Var* displays the statistical variance of values in the field.

❑ *First* displays the value in the field in the first record.

❑ *Last* displays the value in the field in the last record.

❑ *Expression* lets you enter an expression instead of a field name in the Field cell.

❑ *Where* indicates that this field is used only to hold criteria that determine which records are included in the query. The field is not included in the result of the query.

Though the Total row lets you include calculations, a Summary query is a type of a Select query, and you can use its other features in the same way that you do in ordinary Select queries. For example, use the Show box to specify which fields are displayed in the result, and the Sort cell to specify sort order.

Sample Queries with Totals

Summary queries are easy enough to create that you can see how they work by creating a few sample queries. It should be easy for you to create queries to display the average hourly pay for all contractors, the average for each job category, and the average for each job category for contractors from a single state.

1. In the Database window, select the **Query** button, and select **New**. Select the **New Query** button in the New Query dialog box. Then add the **Contractors** table to the query, and close the Add Table dialog box.

2. Select the **Totals** tool. As the field in the first column, select **Hourly Pay**. In the Total cell, select **Avg**. The query is shown in Figure 10.19. Click the **Datasheet View** tool to display its result, as shown in Figure 10.20.

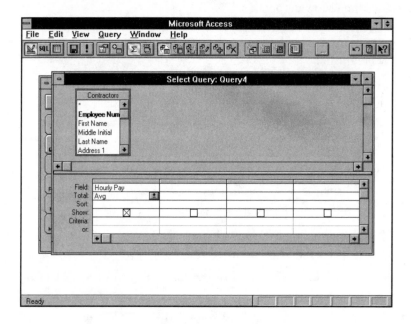

FIGURE 10.19   A QUERY TO FIND AVERAGE HOURLY PAY.

3. To find the average pay by job category, click the **Design View** tool. In the second column of the QBE grid, select **Job Category** as the field, and leave **Group By** in the Total cell. To display the columns in the correct order, click the selection box of the **Job Category** column to select it, and then click and drag the selection box left to make it the first column; then click anywhere to deselect it. This query was shown in Figure 10.18. Click the **Datasheet View** tool to display its result.

4. Finally, to restrict the query to contractors from New York state, click the **Design View** tool. In the third column of the QBE grid, select **State** as the field. In its Total cell, select **Where**. In its Criteria cell, enter **NY**; Access will add delimiters to the criterion. Click the **Datasheet View**

tool to display its result, and notice that it includes only programmers and clerical workers from New York state.

5. Choose **Save Query** from the File menu. As the query name, enter **Average Pay: Contractors from NY**, and select **OK**. Then close the Query window.

FIGURE 10.20 **THE RESULT OF THIS QUERY.**

Using Expressions to Group and Summarize

As with other queries, you may use expressions rather than field names in the Field cell of each column. Simply type in the expression rather than selecting a field.

You can use an expression either for grouping or to perform a calculation for the following reasons:

❏ Use an expression as the basis of a grouping to group on some value that is not the value of a field. For example, if you wanted a report that showed how much you paid your contractors each month, you could use the expression **Month([Date Billed])** in the Field cell of a column and select **Group By** in its Total cell.

❑ Use expressions to create summary calculations that are not available in the Total drop-down list. Enter an expression in the Field cell that uses functions, operators, and the field names to specify the calculation. Select **Expression** in the Total cell.

If you enter an expression in the Field cell, and select a calculation to perform on it in the Total cell, Access automatically changes the field expression to incorporate the calculation you selected, and enter **Expression** in the Total cell, if possible.

You use expressions in a Crosstab query in an exercise later in this chapter.

Grouping on Multiple Fields

You can base totals on groups that are made up of multiple fields. Simply include these fields in the QBE grid and select **Group By** for all of them. Access produces a separate summary calculation for each set of records that has the same values in all the fields you group by.

For example, Figure 10.21 shows the design of a query to display the average hourly pay for each job category in each state. Figure 10.22 shows the result of this query. Notice that the result has a row for every combination of job category and state in the table, but not for combinations of fields that have no value in the table.

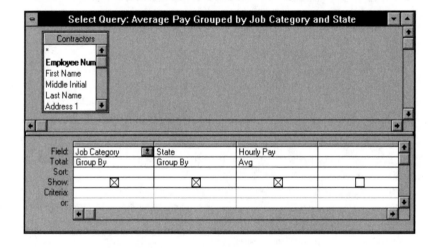

FIGURE 10.21   A QUERY GROUPED ON MULTIPLE FIELDS.

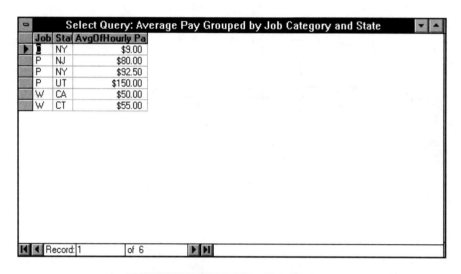

FIGURE 10.22   THE RESULT OF THIS QUERY.

Rather than grouping on multiple fields, you might prefer to display this sort of data using a Crosstab query, described in the next section.

Crosstab Queries

If you want to summarize data grouped on multiple fields, you can use a Crosstab query to arrange the summary data in rows and columns based on values in the fields.

For example, Figure 10.23 shows the result of a Crosstab query that displays average hourly pay grouped by job category and state. Each column represents a job category, and each row represents a state, and the cells represent average pay.

Unlike a Summary query based on multiple fields, a Crosstab query includes cells for all values, even if there are not entries in the table for them. For example, both the Summary query shown above and this Crosstab query show that the average pay for writers from California is $50. The Crosstab query also has cells showing there are no clerical workers or programmers from California.

You can see why this is called *cross-tabulation*. Compare the Summary query, which just lists the data in columns, with the Crosstab query, which uses one field as the basis of the row heading, one field as the basis of the column heading, and fills in the cells of the result table with summary information about all the records that fall under both the row and the column heading. Usually, a Crosstab query is much easier to understand than a ordinary columnar Summary query.

Stal	C	P	W
CA			$50.00
CT			$55.00
NJ		$80.00	
NY	$9.00	$92.50	
UT		$150.00	

Crosstab Query: Average Hourly Pay by Job Category and State

Record: 1 of 5

FIGURE 10.23   A CROSSTAB QUERY WITH HOURLY PAY BY JOB CATEGORY AND STATE.

When you are working with a large database, Crosstab queries can be very valuable. For example, if you are running a mail-order business that has tens of thousands of customers, you can do a Crosstab query that shows you at a glance the average order by the customers from each state or the total number of customers you have from each state. This is information that would be very valuable in future marketing efforts.

It would not make sense to edit the values in the result of a Crosstab query because the row headings, column headings, and values are all based on values in multiple records.

Working with Crosstab Queries

When you save a Crosstab query, Access uses the icon shown in Figure 10.24 in the Database window so you know it is a Crosstab query. You work with Crosstab queries from the Database window just as you do with other queries.

To create a Crosstab query, after creating a new query (or opening an existing one), choose **Crosstab** from the Query menu or click the **Crosstab Query** tool to convert it to a Crosstab query.

FIGURE 10.24   THE ICON FOR CROSSTAB QUERIES.

Figure 10.25 shows the Query window in Design View for the Crosstab query whose result was illustrated previously. As you can see, it has two extra rows in the QBE grid:

❏ *Total* is used just like the Total row in Summary queries, usually to indicate that you want to group on a row or to select the summary calculation you want to perform on it.

❏ *Crosstab* indicates the function of the field in the result of the query. If you group on a field, you may select **Row Heading** or **Column Heading** in this row. If you use it for a calculation, you must choose **Value** to indicate that the result of the calculation is displayed. You may also choose **Not Shown** in this cell, as the QBE grid does not have Show boxes.

In a Crosstab query, you must specify one field and only one to use as the column heading. Select **Column Heading** in its Crosstab cell and **Group By** in its Total cell.

You must specify at least one field to be used as row heading, with Row Heading in its Crosstab cell and Group By in its Total cell. You may use more than one field as row headings to create more complex groupings. This is just like grouping on multiple fields in a Summary query, as described previously.

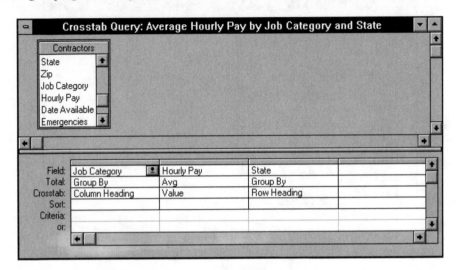

FIGURE 10.25   A CROSSTAB QUERY IN DESIGN VIEW.

You must specify one field that the summary values are taken from. Select **Value** in its Crosstab cell and specify the value as you do in a Summary query, by selecting a summary function in the Total cell, or by selecting **Expression** in the Total cell and entering an expression in the Field cell. See "Queries with Groups and Totals" for more details.

A Sample Crosstab Query

Crosstab queries are a relatively advanced feature of Access that many users will probably never need. If you want to get a feel for these queries, you can do this exercise. It creates a Crosstab query to summarize how much you paid for each category of contractor each month of a year, and illustrates a number of more advanced features of queries.

For this exercise, you have to include two tables in this query since the Job Category field is in the Contractors table and the fields you use to calculate the pay are in the Billing table. You calculate the pay using the expression **[Hours Worked] * [Billing].[Hourly Pay]**. Note that you must use the table name for the Hourly Pay field, because there are fields with this name in both tables. When you enter this expression and select **Sum** in the Total cell, Access converts the expression to **Sum([Hours Worked] * [Billing].[Hourly Pay])** and selects **Expression** in the Total field.

Apart from the value, this query has columns grouped by the Job Category field and rows grouped by the expression **Month([Date Billed])**. Note that you cannot simply group rows by the Date Billed field because there would be a different row for every date in the table.

The Month( ) function is workable because we are only displaying results for one year. To display data from many years, you would use a combination of **Year([Date Billed])** and **Month([Date Billed])**. In this case, it would make sense to have multiple row headings, one with each of these expressions.

However, the Month( ) function does not give you good row titles because it returns a number rather than the name of the month. After creating the query in a preliminary form, you alter it to change the row titles.

To restrict the query to one year, you have to use an additional column with Where in its Total cell, another feature that you may need in actual the Crosstab queries you do. The Field expression you use for the column is **Year([Date Billed])**, and the criterion is **1994**. This is not strictly necessary because your table has data only from 1994, but it is included in the exercise because you would normally need it in practical work.

Create the query as follows:

1. Select the **Query** button of the Database window, and then select the **New** button. In the New Query dialog box, select **New Query**. Use the Add Table dialog box to add both the Contractors and the Billing tables, and then close the dialog box. Access automatically creates the default relationship between the tables.

2. Choose **Crosstab** from the Query menu. Then, drag the Job Category field from the Contractors field list to the first column of the QBE grid. Leave Group By in the Total cell of this column, and select **Column Heading** in its Crosstab cell.

3. In the next column of the QBE grid, enter the expression used for the row heading, as explained previously. In its Field cell, type **Month([Date Billed])**. Leave Group By in its Total cell, and select **Row Heading** in its Crosstab cell.

4. In the next column, enter the value to be displayed. In its Field cell, type **[Hours Worked] * [Billing].[Hourly Pay]**. In the Total cell, select **Sum**. In the Crosstab cell, select **Value**. As mentioned earlier, Access

changes this sort of entry. It converts the entry in the Total cell to Expression, and the entry in the Field cell to **Expr2: Sum([Hours Worked] * [Billing].[Hourly Pay])**, which changes the expression to incorporate the calculation you selected and to give it an arbitrary name.

5. In the final column, enter the expression that limits the data to one year. In its Field cell, type **Year([Date Billed])**. In its Total cell, select **Where**. In its Criteria cell, type **1994**.

6. Choose **Save** from the File menu. As the Query Name, type **Monthly Cost by Job Category** and select **OK**. The design of the query is shown in Figure 10.26. Select the **Datasheet View** tool to display its result, as shown in Figure 10.27.

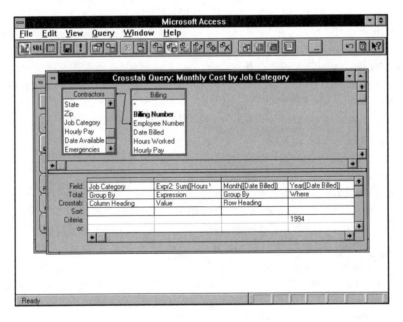

FIGURE 10.26   THE DESIGN OF THE CROSSTAB QUERY.

All that is left to do is to give the months their proper names rather than numbers, and to put the right heading at the top of the Month column.

Changing the heading is easy. Access gives the expression **Month([Date Billed])** the arbitrary name **Expr1**. You just have to change Expr1 to **Month** to display it at the top of the column.

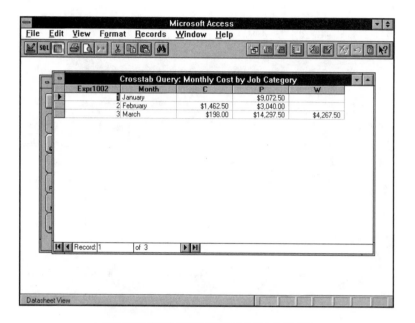

FIGURE 10.27 **THE RESULT OF THIS QUERY.**

It is a bit more difficult to display month names in the column. You can return the names of months by using the function **Format([Date Billed], "mmmm")** instead of **Month([Date Billed])**, but if you do, the months will be sorted in alphabetical order instead of in chronological order. The solution is to use two columns, one with the Format( ) function, which is displayed as the row heading, and the other with the Month( ) function, which is not displayed but is used as the sort order:

1. Select the **Design View** tool. Edit the function that displays the row heading so it reads **Month:Format([Date Billed], "mmmm")**. The names of months will be displayed with the title Name at the top of the column.

2. In the fifth column, which is now blank, type **Month([Date Billed])** in the Field cell, leave **Group By** selected in the Total field. In the Crosstab field, select **Not Shown** and in the Sort field, select **Ascending**. The final query design is shown in Figure 10.28 (with the Window maximized to show it all). Select the **Datasheet View** tool to display its result, as shown in Figure 10.29.

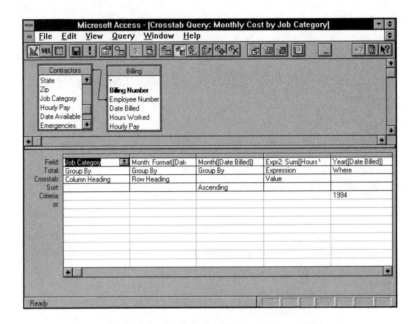

FIGURE 10.28   THE FINAL DESIGN OF THE QUERY.

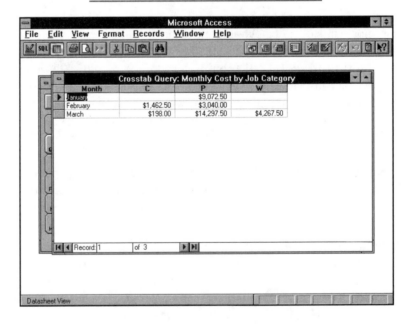

FIGURE 10.29   THE RESULT OF THIS QUERY.

The Query Wizards

The Query wizards give you easier ways of creating advanced queries. When you create a new query, you can select the **Query Wizards** button of the New Query dialog box to display the list of Query wizards shown in Figure 10.30.

FIGURE 10.30   AVAILABLE QUERY WIZARDS.

At this point, it should be easy for you to use these advanced queries. Because they are cleverly designed and some use advanced query features, however, you may find it instructive to use the wizards to create some of them and switch to Design View to look at them so you can see how they get their results.

The Crosstab Query Wizard

The Crosstab Query Wizard gives you a graphic method of creating Crosstab queries by illustrating the result of the query as you make your selection. It automatically includes row totals.

Its first dialog box lets you select the table or query the Crosstab query is based on.

The second dialog box lets you select the field or fields used for the row heading and displays a sample illustrating your selection.

The third dialog box lets you choose a field for the column heading and illustrates your selection.

The fourth dialog box lets you choose the field that the value will be based on and the type of summary calculation used, as shown in Figure 10.31.

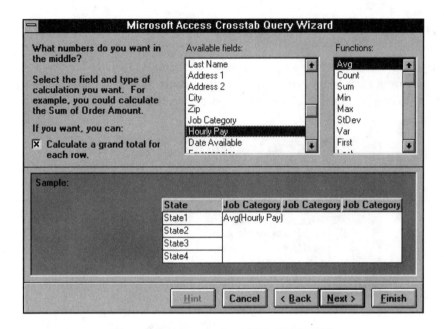

FIGURE 10.31   SPECIFYING THE VALUE DISPLAYED.

The final dialog box lets you name and create the query. Figure 10.31 creates a query to display the average pay of contractors in each job category by state, and its result is shown in Figure 10.32.

Sta	RowTotal	C	P	W
CA	$50.00			$50.00
CT	$55.00			$55.00
NJ	$80.00		$80.00	
NY	$101.50	$9.00	$92.50	
UT	$150.00		$150.00	

Record: 1   of 5

FIGURE 10.32   THE RESULT OF THIS CROSSTAB QUERY.

If you display this query in Design View, shown in Figure 10.33, you can see that it renames two fields to create the Row Total column.

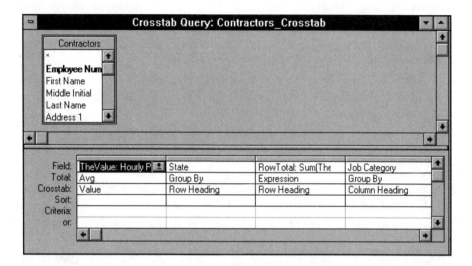

FIGURE 10.33 **THE DESIGN OF THIS QUERY.**

The field in its first column is **TheValue: Hourly Pay**. The value is based on the Hourly Pay field, but Access renames it TheValue as a convenience, to make it easy to refer to it in the expression that creates row totals.

The field with totals is an expression with **RowTotal: Sum(TheValue)** in its Field cell. **Sum(TheValue)** is the expression that calculates the total of all the values in the state. The expression is renamed **RowTotal** so that a word is displayed as its column heading. This is a perfect example of renaming a field because it is based on an expression that is not appropriate for a column heading.

WARNING

Notice that you would not usually want a column that sums a list of averages, as you have here. If the average programmer in New York earns $92.50, and the average clerical worker in New York earns $9.00, there is no reason to sum these to get a row total of $101.50 for New York. It would be best to customize this query by deleting the RowTotal column. There are limits to what a Wizard can do to generate a query as complex as a Crosstab, and you should examine any queries that you generate to make sure that they make sense.

The Find Duplicates Query Wizard

The Find Duplicates Query Wizard finds records that have the same data in one or more fields, and it is very simple to use.

❏ The first dialog box is the familiar field picker, which you use to select one or more fields to check for duplicate values.

❏ The second dialog box lets you display data from additional fields in the query's result.

❏ The third dialog box lets you name and create the query.

Figure 10.34 shows the result of the query that finds records with duplicate data in the state field and also displays last and first names. In other words, it shows you the names of any contractors who live in a state with more than one contractor living in it. In the sample table, that is true only of New York state.

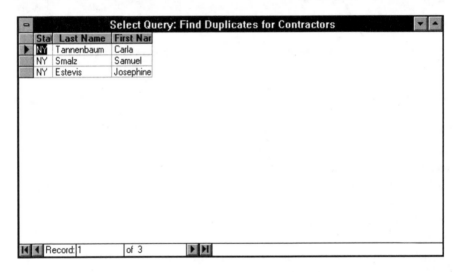

FIGURE 10.34 THE RESULT OF A FIND DUPLICATES QUERY.

Figure 10.35 shows the design of the query, which works in an ingenious way. It creates a temporary second table that includes only the field in which you are searching for duplicates, and stores only repeated values from the first table in the second table. It joins the two tables with the Join property shown in Figure 10.35, so a record is displayed only if both tables have that data in that field.

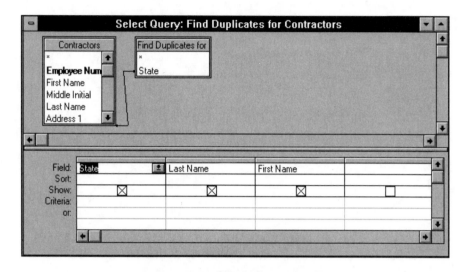

FIGURE 10.35 **THE DESIGN OF THIS QUERY.**

The Find Unmatched Query Wizard

The Find Unmatched Query Wizard is used with a relational database to display records in one table that have no related records in another table. It is very easy to use:

- ❏ In the first dialog box, select the table that has the records you want to see in the result.
- ❏ In the second dialog box, select the related table.
- ❏ In the third dialog box, specify the common key field that relates the two by selecting it in field lists for both tables.
- ❏ In the fourth dialog box, specify the fields you want to see in the result.
- ❏ In the fifth dialog box, name and create the query.

Figure 10.36 shows the result of a query to find contractors who do not have any data in the Billing table. Figure 10.37 shows the design of this query. It simply relates the two tables, and uses Is Null as the Criterion for the Foreign Key field of the second table to isolate only those records that do no have entries in that table.

FIGURE 10.36   THE RESULT OF A FIND UNMATCHED QUERY.

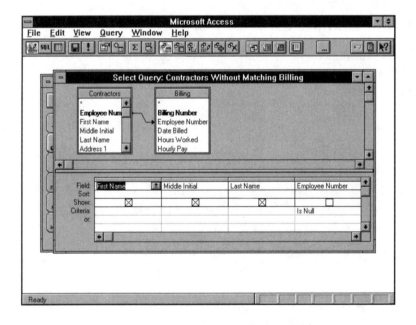

FIGURE 10.37   THE DESIGN OF THIS QUERY.

The Archive Query Wizard

The Archive Query Wizard copies the data from an existing table into a backup table. It also gives you the option of deleting the original table.

❑ In the first dialog box, select the table to back up.

❑ In the second dialog box, enter criteria to specify which records to copy. Create an expression by selecting a field name from the first drop-down list, an operator from the second drop-down list, and enter a value in the third drop-down list. You can also select the checkbox to copy all the records in the table.

❑ In the final dialog box, enter the name of the backup-table, and choose whether to delete the original table. Then run the query.

This wizard creates a Make Table query that uses the criteria you specified to isolate the records to be backed up.

To Sum Up

In this chapter, you learned about types of queries that are more advanced than the basic Select queries that were covered in Part I of this book.

You learned to create more powerful Select queries by using expressions rather than fields at the top of columns in the QBE grid, by using Field Properties and Query Properties, and by creating Parameter queries, where you enter different criteria each time you run the query. You also learned to create Action queries, including Make Table queries, Update queries, Append queries and Delete queries. Finally, you learned to create grouped queries with summary results and Crosstab queries.

Action queries let you automate your work by modifying an entire group of records at once. In the next chapter, you learn to automate your work even further by using macros.

ACCESS

Chapter 11

Saving Time
with Macros

*A*s you do practical work with Access, you will probably find yourself doing certain tasks over and over again. You can save yourself time by creating *macros* to perform this sort of repetitive task, particularly if it involves a long series of actions.

A macro is a group of actions that are combined so that you can execute them using a single command. You "play" the macro to perform the entire series of actions.

In many applications, you create macros by recording keystrokes. You turn on the macro recorder and actually go through the actions that you want the macro to perform. Access uses an entirely different method of creating macros—you enter the actions in a list. After you have created macros in Access, you can run them in many ways. For most users, it is most common to run them from the Macros list of the Database window or to attach them to push buttons.

Macros have many features that are useful primarily for developers. In this chapter, you learn the basics that are useful for the average user, and look at some more advanced features. This chapter covers the following:

❑ how to create a macro

❑ the components of macros: actions and their arguments

❑ adding actions using drag-and-drop

❑ adding actions using the drop-down list

❑ specifying the arguments of an action

❑ editing macros

❑ using a macro to combine a query with a report or form

❑ running macros from the menu, the macro window, a form or report, or a push button

❑ creating macro groups

❑ using conditional actions in macros

❑ running a macro a single step at a time to debug it

❑ creating a macro that runs automatically when you start Access

Creating Simple Macros

You work with macros from the Database window much as you do with other objects. Select the **Macro** button to display the Macros list. As you can see in Figure 11.1, the buttons that you use to work with macros are similar to the ones used to work with other objects:

❑ *New* creates a new macro.

❑ *Run* plays an existing macro. You select the macro name in the Macros list and then select the **Run** button.

❑ *Design* lets you change the design of an existing macro. Select the macro name from the Macros list and then select the **Design** button.

Only the Run button is different from the buttons used with other objects.

Other basic methods for managing macros are also the same as the methods used for other objects. For example, select **Save** from the File menu to save the macro and **Save As** to save it under another name.

FIGURE 11.1 DISPLAYING MACROS IN THE DATABASE WINDOW.

The Components of Macros

When you select the **New** button, Access displays the Macro window shown in Figure 11.2.

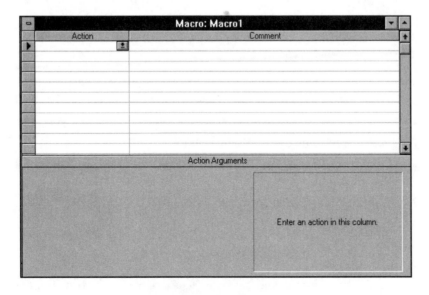

FIGURE 11.2 THE MACRO WINDOW.

In its initial form, which is all you need to use for most macros, this window is very simple:

❑ *Action:* list all the actions you want the macro to execute. The macro performs these actions in the order they are listed.

❑ *Comment:* add descriptions of the actions to make it easier to understand what the macro is doing. These comments are optional, but it can be difficult to understand and maintain older macros if they are left out.

❑ *Arguments* are displayed in the Action Arguments panel in the bottom half of the window. Most actions require arguments, which are options that control the way that actions are performed.

You can simply click and drag the line between these two columns to change their width, as you do with Access tables and other objects.

MACRO ACTIONS

There are many different types of actions that you can add to the Action list, including the following:

❑ *ApplyFilter* applies a filter or query to a form, which limits and determines the sort order of the records that the form is based on.

❑ *Beep* makes the computer beep to alert the user.

❑ *Close* closes an object.

❑ *DoMenuItem* performs any Access menu command. The command you specify must be appropriate in the situation where this action is executed.

❑ *FindRecord* finds a record that matches some criterion that you specify.

❑ *Maximize* maximizes the current window.

❑ *OpenForm, OpenQuery, OpenReport,* and *OpenTable* opens the object specified.

❑ *Print* prints the object that is currently selected.

❑ *Quit* quits Access.

❑ *RunMacro* runs the macro you specify from within the current macro.

❑ *SelectObject* selects an object that you specify. You then can perform actions that apply to the currently selected object, such as printing, to that object.

❑ *ShowAllRecords* removes all filters from the form that is currently selected, so all records in the table or query it is based on are displayed.

This is only a sample list of the actions that a macro can perform. However, it includes those actions that are most useful for beginners and it gives you an idea of some of the things macros can do.

ARGUMENTS OF AN ACTION

The arguments of an action specify the object that the action applies to and options that control the way the action is performed.

Most actions in macros require arguments. For example, if you use the OpenTable action, you must include an argument that specifies which table should be opened.

When you highlight an action in the Action list, its arguments appear in the Action Arguments panel in the bottom half of the screen—much as the properties of each field are displayed in the bottom half of the screen when you are designing a table.

Figure 11.3 shows the arguments of the OpenTable action. You obviously must specify the name of the table to be opened. You also can specify the view to open the table in (Datasheet, Design, or Print Preview) and specify a data mode of Add, Edit, or Read Only.

FIGURE 11.3   THE ARGUMENTS OF THE OPENTABLE ACTION.

HELP ON MACRO ACTIONS

This book does not list all the actions and arguments available in Access macros, but it is very easy to get help on them.

Select an action or any of its arguments and press **F1** to display context-sensitive help on that action and all of the arguments that can be used for it. Figure 11.4 shows the Help topic for the OpenTable action.

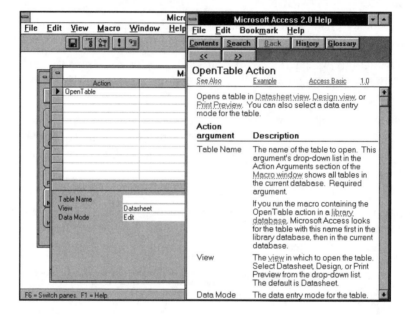

FIGURE 11.4   GETTING HELP ON AN ACTION.

Creating Macros

Designing an advanced macro can be difficult, but the mechanics of adding actions and their arguments are simple.

ADDING AN ACTION USING DRAG AND DROP

If you want the macro to include an action that opens an object (OpenTable, OpenQuery, OpenForm, or OpenReport) or to use the RunMacro action to run some other macro, you can add the object to the Action list using drag and drop.

Simply display the Database window and the Macro window so you can see both, and drag an object from the Database window to one of the cells in the

Macro window's Action list. The appropriate action for that object will be added in that cell, and the object's name will be automatically used as the first argument.

ADDING AN ACTION USING THE DROP-DOWN LIST

You can also add actions by using the drop-down lists in the Actions cells, shown in Figure 11.5, which let you choose among all the actions that are available in queries.

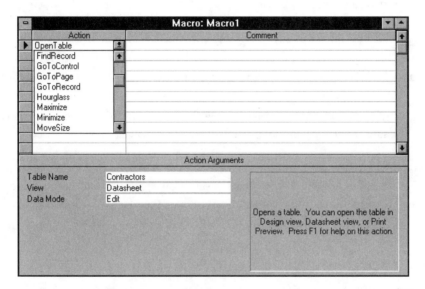

FIGURE 11.5   USE THE DROP-DOWN LIST TO CHOOSE AN ACTIONS.

If you know the name of the action you want to use, you can type it in the Action cell. Access displays the first option on the list that begins with the letters you type. For example, if you type **M**, it displays Maximize, and if you go on to type **MI**, it displays Minimize.

SPECIFYING THE ARGUMENTS OF AN ACTION

When you add actions using the drop-down list, you often must specify its arguments, as some arguments have no default. For example, if you select **OpenTable** as the action, the Table Name argument remains blank until you fill it in.

Many Action Argument cells have drop-downs lists that let you choose among the available arguments. For others, you must type in the argument.

EDITING MACROS

After you have begun creating a macro, you can also edit it in the same way that you do tables and other Access objects. Simply use the mouse to place an insertion point in a cell, and use the usual Windows editing methods, or use cursor movement keys to move among cells in the way they are always used in Access.

In addition, you can click the selection box at the left edge of a row to select the row, and then so the following:

❑ Click or drag the row to change the order in which actions are executed.

❑ Press **Del** or choose **Delete Row** from the Edit menu to delete the row and eliminate that action.

❑ Choose **Copy** or **Cut** from the Edit menu to copy or cut the row. Choose **Paste** from the Edit menu later, to place the row somewhere else.

SHORTCUT

To insert an additional action within a macro, click anywhere in a row to highlight it. Choose **Insert Row** from the Edit menu to add a new blank row above that row where you can enter the new action. Alternatively, place the focus in a row and press **Ins** to add a blank row above it.

USING A MACRO TO COMBINE A QUERY WITH A REPORT OR FORM

One very useful feature of macros is that they let you combine a query with a form or report.

If you use the OpenForm or OpenReport action, you see that one of its arguments is Filter Name. You can enter the name of a query here to specify which records are included in the form or report and the order they are sorted in.

This is easiest to do if the query includes all the fields that are included in the form or report. If it does not, however, you can set its Output All Fields property to **Yes**. To get to this property, display the query in Design View, select the **Properties** tool, and click somewhere in the query that is not in a field list or in the QBE grid. This displays the Query Properties sheet.

You can also limit the number of records included in a form or report by using the Where Condition argument of the OpenForm or OpenReport action to add a SQL WHERE clause or an Access expression that determines which records are displayed. SQL is not covered in this book, but simple expressions such as **[State]** = **"NY"** are all you need to filter forms or reports in most cases.

This argument has the **...** button to its right, which you can use to display the Expression Builder.

Running Macros

You have already seen how to run a macro from the Database window simply by double-clicking it or by selecting it and selecting **Run**. Most users only need to run macros in this way, but there are other methods of running macros that you may sometimes find convenient.

FROM THE MENU

To run a macro from the menu, select **Run Macro** from the File menu. Access displays the Run Macro dialog box, shown in Figure 11.6. Select any macro from the drop-down list and select **OK** to run it.

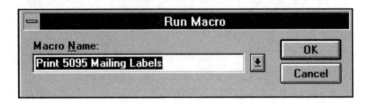

FIGURE 11.6   THE RUN MACRO DIALOG BOX.

FROM THE MACRO WINDOW

When you are designing a macro in the Macro window, a Run tool is added to the toolbar. Click this tool or choose **Run** from the Macro menu to run the macro you are designing. This is meant to be a quick way of testing the macro.

FROM A FORM OR REPORT

You can run a macro as an Event property of an object in a report or form. You learned in Chapter 9 that you can display the properties of an object in a form or report by selecting it and selecting the **Properties** tool, and you can use the drop-down list in the Properties window to display only Event Properties. You can use the drop-down list for an Event property to select any macro, and that macro will be executed when that event occurs.

Reports have only a few Event properties because you cannot edit their data. Figure 11.7 shows the Event properties for a report as a whole. For example, you can select a macro as the On Open or On Close property, and that macro will be executed whenever the report is opened or closed. Report bands also have Event properties.

FIGURE 11.7   EVENT PROPERTIES FOR AN REPORT.

Many controls on forms also have Event properties because they are meant to be manipulated by the user. For example, Figure 11.8 shows the Event properties for a text box that is used to enter or edit data in a field. You can select a macro as the On Enter or On Exit property—for example, to have it executed whenever the user moves the highlight into or out of the field.

You can select the **...** button on the right side of the Event Properties cells to display the Macro window and create or edit the macro associated with that property.

To display complete information on using any of these properties, put the cursor in the property's cell and press **F1**.

FROM A PUSH BUTTON

In Chapter 7, you learned to add a push button to a form, and you saw that the Command Button Wizard lets you assign a large number of predefined actions to it.

You can also assign a macro to a push button by using its On Click property.

FIGURE 11.8   EVENT PROPERTIES FOR A FIELD ON A FORM.

In general, only programmers would assign Event properties to controls in forms, but this is the one exception. Users often find it convenient to add push buttons to forms and have them execute macros in this way.

A Sample Macro

Though they have many other features, these simple techniques will be enough to create most of the macros that are needed by the typical user who is not a programmer. Before going on to look at some of the more advanced features of macros, you should do an exercise to practice the basic techniques that you will find most useful.

You generally use macros to automate sequences of commands that you use frequently. The macro is simply a list of actions that you find you are going through over and over again in your work.

Let's say that you print mailing labels on a different printer than you use for most purposes, and you find that you are repeatedly selecting the mailing label object, choosing **Print Setup** from the File menu to select the printer, **Print** to actually print the labels, and **Print Setup** again to return to the default printer.

It is easy to automate this process. Try opening and closing the labels also so you can see what is being done while the macro is being executed:

1. Click the **Macro** button of the Database window and then select the **New** button.

2. When Access displays the Macro window, click and drag its title bar to move it right so you can see the Database window to its left. Then select the **Report** button of the Database window, and click and drag **5095 Mailing Labels** to the first cell in the Action list of the macro. Access adds the OpenReport action to the macro, with 5095 Mailing Labels as the Report Name argument, as shown in Figure 11.9.

FIGURE 11.9   CLICKING AND DRAGGING TO ADD AN ACTION TO THE MACRO.

3. Click and drag its title bar to move the Macro window back to its original position. As the Comment for the first action, enter **Open the Mailing Label Report**.

4. Click the second action cell in the Macro window, and click its drop-down button to display its drop-down list, and select **DoMenuItem**. Click the cell for the Menu Name property; click its drop-down button, and select **File** from the drop-down list. Then click the cell for the Command property, click its drop-down button, and select **Print Setup** from the drop-down list. As the Comment for this action, enter **Display the Print Setup Dialog Box to choose the printer used for labels**.

5. Use the drop-down list for the third action cell in the Macro window to select **DoMenu Item** also. As the Menu Name property, select **File** again, and as the Command property, select **Print**. As the Comment for this action, enter **Display the Print Dialog Box**.

6. The fourth action is the same as the second. You must display the Print Setup dialog box again to use the default printer. Click the selection box to the left of the second action, and choose **Copy** from the Edit menu. Click anywhere in the fourth row, and choose **Paste** from the Edit menu. Finally, edit the Comment so it reads **Display the Print Setup Dialog Box to return to the default printer**.

7. As the fifth action, use the drop-down list to select **Close**. As the Object Type argument, select Report, and as the Object Name argument, select **5095 Mailing Labels**. As the Comment, type **Close the Mailing Label Report**.

8. Choose **Save** from the File menu. In the Save As dialog box, enter the macro name **Print 5095 Mailing Labels**, and select **OK**. The final design of the macro is shown in Figure 11.10.

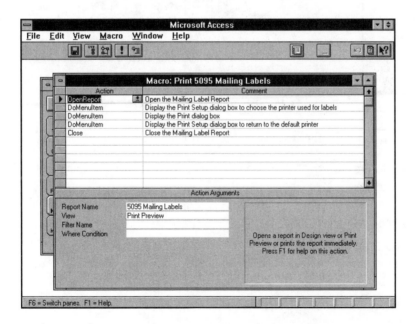

FIGURE 11.10   THE FINAL DESIGN OF THE MACRO.

9. Close the Macro window. Select the **Macro** button in the Database window—the new macro should be selected. To test it, select the **Run** button.

This is a very simple macro, but using it saves time and effort. Most macros that you have occasion to use will be just this sort of simple, time-saving list of actions.

Using More Advanced Macro Techniques

Macros have many advanced features. Here, we look at a few that are available by using the toolbar of the Macro window, shown in Figure 11.11.

FIGURE 11.11   THE TOOLBAR OF THE MACRO WINDOW.

This toolbar has three tools that you have not learned about yet:

❏   *Macro Names* tool is used to name macros that are included in macro groups.

❏   *Conditions* tool is used to add conditional actions to macros.

❏   *Step Into* tool is used for debugging.

The uses of these tools are described below.

Creating Macro Groups

If you select the **Macro Names** tool or choose **Macro Names** from the View menu, Access adds a Macro Name column to the Macro window, as shown in Figure 11.12. You can hide this column by selecting the tool or menu option again.

Macro Name	Action	Comment
▶ Print 5095 Mailing L	OpenReport	Open the Mailing Label Report
	DoMenuItem	Display the Print Setup dialog box to choose the printer use
	DoMenuItem	Display the Print dialog box
	DoMenuItem	Display the Print Setup dialog box to return to the default pr
	Close	Close the Mailing Label Report
Open Data Entry Fc	OpenForm	Open the Contractors Data Entry Form

Action Arguments

Report Name	5095 Mailing Labels
View	Print Preview
Filter Name	
Where Condition	

Enter a macro name in this column.

Macro: Sample Macro Group

FIGURE 11.12 **THE MACRO NAME COLUMN OF THE MACRO WINDOW.**

Macro names are needed only if you create a macro group, which can be convenient if you are creating a number of macros that you do not plan to run from the Database window for example, if you create a number of macros that will be attached to push buttons and are not intended to be run from the Database window.

If you create a large number of macros of this sort, the Macros list of the Database window can become so cluttered that it is inconvenient to scroll through it to find the macros there that you actually do want. To avoid this clutter, Access lets you create groups of macros in a single Macro window, so that only the group name is added to the list, rather than creating each macro individually and having them all added to the list.

To create a group of macros, simply put the name of each in the Macro Name column to the left of its first action. Each name applies to the action to its right and all the actions that follow until the next macro name. In Figure 11.12, for example, the first macro, named Print 5095 Mailing Labels, has the same steps as the macro you created in the last exercise. All the steps above the line with the next macro name are part of this macro.

When you create a macro group, you save and name the Macro window as usual, and its name is used as the group name. Only this name is displayed in the Database window.

If you select this name in the Database window and run it, only the first macro in the group will be run. Other macros in the group must be run in other ways, which are discussed later in this chapter—for example, by attaching them to push buttons. As you can see, grouped macros are useful primarily for application developers, who might use them to hold groups of macros associated with different forms.

To run it in these other ways, you refer to a macro in a group by using the group name, followed by the dot operator, followed by the macro name. In Figure 11.12, for example, you can see in the title bar that the group is named Sample Macro Group, so that the first macro in it would be called **[Sample Macro Group].[Print 5095 Mailing Labels]**.

 If you are developing macros in a group and you do not want anyone to run the first one from the Database window by mistake, you can create a dummy macro in the first row, which has nothing in the Action column, and you can begin the first macro that you really need in the second row.

Using Conditional Actions in Macros

If you select the **Conditions** tool or choose **Conditions** from the View menu, Access adds a Conditions column to the Macro window. You can hide this column by selecting the tool or menu option again.

Enter an expression in this column, and the action to its right will run only if the expression evaluates to true.

When you place the insertion point in a Condition cell, the **...** button is activated, and you can select it to use the Expression Builder to generate the expression to be entered in the cell.

If you want a series of actions to run only if a condition is true, enter the expression in the Condition column for the first of these, and enter an ellipsis (**...**) in the Condition columns for the actions that follow.

Figure 11.13 shows a simple example of a conditional macro, which is equivalent to using a validation rule to check if an entry is valid. The example requires the user to make an entry in the Last Name field. It is selected as the On Exit property of the text box where the Last Name field is entered, so that the macro is executed whenever the user is done making an entry in the field and leaves it.

FIGURE 11.13   A CONDITIONAL MACRO.

The condition on the first row is **[Last Name] Is Null**, which evaluates as true if there is no entry in the Last Name field. The action on the first row is MsgBox, which displays a message in a dialog box. The Message argument determines what this message is—in this case **Please Enter a Last Name,** as shown in Figure 11.14. Because of the condition, this message is displayed only if there is no entry in the Last Name field.

FIGURE 11.14   THE ERROR MESSAGE DISPLAYED BY THIS MACRO.

The second row has an ellipsis in the Condition column, so its action also is executed only if the condition is true. The action is CancelEvent, which undoes the event that called this macro. Since this macro is used as the On Exit property of a field, CancelEvent places the cursor back in the field. Thus, the macro not only displays an error message if there is no entry in the field, it also refuses to let the user leave the field until there is an entry in it.

This illustration is a simple one, and you could do the same thing using a validation rule and validation text when you design the table. Programmers sometimes use much more complex macros then the On Exit Property in order to validate data.

Debugging Macros

Sometimes there are errors when you run a macro, and Access displays a dialog box like the one shown in Figure 11.15.

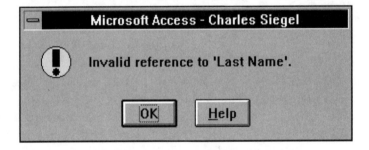

FIGURE 11.15   AN ERROR IN A MACRO.

One common reason for this sort of error is that a macro is run from the wrong place in Access. The error message in Figure 11.15, for example, was produced by the macro that validates data entry in the Last Name field. When it is run, as an Action property of the Last Name field, as it is supposed to be, there is no error message. If you run it from the Database window by mistake, though, Access does not know what *Last Name* refers to in the macro so it displays this error message.

Often, you can diagnose the problem in the macro simply by noting the error message that is displayed and looking through the macro carefully to see where it applies.

When you are debugging a longer macro, however, it is often helpful to run the macro one step at a time to make it easier to find the error.
To do this, simply select the **Step Into** tool on the Macro window toolbar or choose **Single Step** from the Macro menu. As long as this option remains
selected, Access runs the macro one row at a time and displays the Macro Single
Step dialog box, shown in Figure 11.16, when you run a macro.

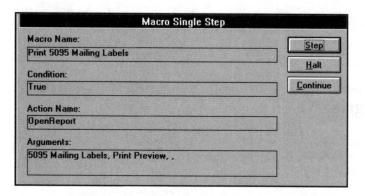

FIGURE 11.16   THE MACRO SINGLE STEP DIALOG BOX.

This dialog box is very easy to understand and contains the following:

❑   *Macro Name* contains the name of the macro you are running.

❑   *Condition* informs you whether the condition in the current row is true
    or false. (If there is no condition, this is displayed as true, meaning that
    the action will be performed.)

❑   *Action Name* is the action in the current row

❑   *Arguments* contains the arguments of the action.

❑   *Step* performs the action of the macro that is listed in the Action Name
    box and then displays this dialog box again before performing the next
    action.

❑   *Halt* cancels the macro. No further actions are performed after using this
    button, but all the actions that had been performed by the macro to that
    point will remain in force.

❑   *Continue* performs the rest of the macro in the usual way rather than
    one step at a time. Selecting this button deselects the Step Into tool of
    the toolbar so future macros also are not performed one step at a time,
    unless you select this tool or menu option again.

If you have trouble understanding the error message of a macro, run it one step at a time until you find out which action it applies to, and try to correct the error in that action.

Creating Self-Executing Macros

Access lets you automate your work even further by creating macros that execute automatically when you open a database or when you start Access.

THE AUTOEXEC MACRO

If you create any macro and save it with the name AutoExec, then that macro runs automatically when you open the database it is in.

You can bypass the AutoExec macro by holding down the **Shift** key when you open the database.

N O T E

OPENING A DATABASE AUTOMATICALLY

You can open a database automatically whenever you start Access by adding its name at the end of the command you use to run Access.

The usual command used to start Access is **C:\ACCESS\MSACCESS.EXE**, though it might differ a bit depending on the setup of your system. If you add the name of a database, such as **TEACHSLF** at the end of this command, Access automatically opens that database when it starts up.

You can add this option to the command that is used to start Access. Click the **Access** icon in the Windows Program Manager and choose **Properties** from the File menu or press **Alt-Enter** to display the Program Item Properties dialog box shown in Figure 11.17. Edit the command line by adding this option to it.

THE SENDKEYS ACTION

The SendKeys action lets you include keystrokes in a macro, which are treated exactly as if you typed them in while the macro was running. For example, you can use this action to fill in a dialog box automatically, rather than typing text into it.

This action includes two arguments:

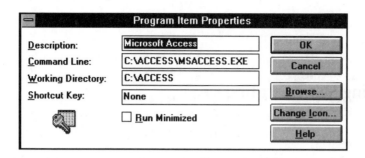

FIGURE 11.17 THE **PROGRAM ITEM PROPERTIES** DIALOG BOX

OF THE **WINDOWS PROGRAM MANAGER.**

❏ *Keystrokes* specifies up to 255 keystrokes that are sent to the application. This argument may also include symbols that represent keystrokes other than letter keys. Most users will need only **[Enter]** or ~, either of which can represent the Enter key. Occasionally, you may also need to use + for the Shift key, ∧ for the Ctrl key, and **%** for the Alt key. For example, you can use %F to represent Alt-F.

❏ *Wait* specifies whether the macro pauses until the keystrokes are processed.

N O T E

If you want to use this action to fill in a dialog box, you must place the SendKeys action before the action that opens the dialog box, and select **No** for the Wait argument. When a dialog box is opened, a macro's execution is suspended until the user finishes with the dialog box. The macro would never get up to the SendKeys action if it was after the action that displays the dialog box. By using SendKeys first, you put the keystrokes in the buffer, where they are waiting to be used in the dialog box once it is opened.

MAKING ACCESS DO YOUR WORK FOR YOU

Lets say that, like many people, you look up and enter data in the same table frequently. Every day, first thing in the morning, you start Access, open the same database, and display the same form. This can all be done automatically for you when you turn on your computer.

In this exercise, you automatically open the Teachslf database, and display the Contractors Data Entry form. You can use the same simple technique for the database, table, or form that you use in your own work.

1. Click the **Macro** button of the Database window, and select **New** to display the Macro window.

2. Choose **Save** from the File menu. In the Save As dialog box, enter the name **AutoExec**.

3. Drag the Macro window right. Click the **Form** button of the Database window. Click and drag the form named **Contractors Data Entry** to the first Action Cell, as shown in Figure 11.18.

FIGURE 11.18   THE AUTOEXEC MACRO.

4. Close the Macro window, saving the changes. Then choose **Exit** from the File menu to exit from Access.

5. You must display the Windows Program Manager. If necessary, choose **Switch To** from the Control menu of the Windows application that is displayed when you close Access, select **Program Manager** from the Task List, and select the **Switch To** button.

6. In the Program Manager, click the **Access** icon to select it, and then choose **Properties** from the File menu. In the Program Item Properties dialog box, add the word **TEACHSLF** at the end of the Command Line box, as shown in Figure 11.19, and select **OK**.

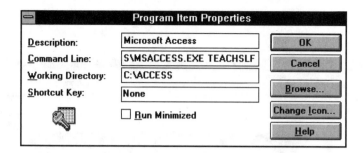

FIGURE 11.19   CHANGING THE COMMAND LINE.

7. Now, double-click the **Access** icon to start the application again. The Teachslf database is opened and the Contractors Data Entry form is displayed automatically. Close this form.

8. Since you do not really want this to happen every time you start Access, select **AutoExec** in the Macros list of the Database window, and choose **Delete** from the Edit menu. Select **OK** to delete the macro.

9. Press **Alt-Tab** to display the Program Manager. Repeat the instructions in step 6, but this time, delete the word **TEACHSLF** from the end of the Command Line box, so that the command line reverts to what it was before this exercise.

To avoid even more work, you could drag the Access icon into the StartUp window of the Windows Program Manager to open Access automatically whenever you start Windows.

Creating Applications

At this point, you have already learned enough that you can begin to set up applications for beginners who know nothing about Access.

A common way to do this is by using a *switchboard*, a group of push buttons used to perform common tasks, like the one in the sample application distributed with Access, which is shown in Figure 11.20.

Before creating a switchboard, you must design all the tables, forms, reports, and other objects needed in an application.

Then, to create the switchboard, create a form with no fields in it. Add a push button to the form for each of the tasks that the user must perform. Some tasks are built into the push button wizard. You must create macros to perform other tasks, and you must use the On Click properties of push buttons to attach the macros to the buttons.

FIGURE 11.20   A SWITCHBOARD DESIGNED FOR A BEGINNING USER.

For example, you could design a form with the mailing labels you need, create a macro to print them, and attach it to a button with the label *Print Mailing Labels*. You could create a data entry form, and use the **Search** option from the Push Button wizard to let the user perform searches. You could use built-in options to perform many routine tasks after you have designed the necessary objects.

For a complex application, you could create a main switchboard, with buttons that open other, more specialized switchboards. The Access Switchboard illustrated in Figure 11.20 has one button that opens a switchboard that lets you use all the application's forms, and another that opens a switchboard that lets you print all the application's reports.

Finally, you could change the command line to open this database automatically when the user starts Access, and you could create an AutoExec macro in the database to open the Main Switchboard form automatically whenever the database is opened.

When you started Access, the switchboard would be displayed just as your Contractors Data Entry form was displayed in the exercise above. Even a user who knew nothing about Access could use the database simply by clicking buttons on the switchboard.

If you want to learn more about developing applications, you can begin by opening the **NWIND** database in the subdirectory **SAMPLEAPPS**, and then opening the form named **Main Switchboard**. After clicking the push buttons to use this application, try looking at its Switchboard forms in Design View.

Access makes it easier to develop applications without programming than other database development environments. Professional developers use its programming language, Access BASIC, for special tasks, but you can set up simple applications for beginners simply by creating the necessary objects, macros, and switchboards with buttons to run them. Bear in mind, though, that designing the application to make it easy for a beginning user to understand can be harder than creating the objects needed to implement it.

This book is meant to teach you to use Access on your own. Designing and developing applications is a study in itself. However, you have reached the point where you know enough about using Access that you can create simple applications.

To Sum Up

In this chapter, you learned to create macros that can save time for Access users, and you glanced quickly at the way that developers use macros.

You learned how to add actions and their arguments to the Macro window, both by using drag and drop for actions that involve objects, and by using the drop-down lists in the window. After creating some simple macros that use these features, you looked at some of the more advanced features of the Macro Window, such as macro groups, conditional actions in macros, and how to debug macros by running them a single step at a time. You also learned to create macros that run automatically, and looked at how developers would use these to create a switchboard to set up an application for a novice.

Now you have learned about all the objects that you need to understand as a user of Access. In the next chapter, you look at a few additional special techniques.

Utilities and
Special Techniques

Y ou have learned all the basic features that you need to work with Access, but in order to get you up and running more quickly, the earlier chapters skipped some Access utilities and special techniques. The first part of this book was designed to help you create and work with simple tables, queries, forms, and reports as easily as possible. In order to do this, it skipped over the numerous utilities that Access provides to make it easier to manage Access objects and to give you more power to work with other applications. You will learn about them in this chapter, which covers the following topics:

❑ using database utilities that let you compact a database, convert earlier versions of Access databases to 2.0 format, encrypt and decrypt a database, and repair a corrupted database

❑ using object utilities that let you rename, delete, cut, copy, and paste objects in Access databases

❑ importing and exporting data to share with other applications

❑ attaching a table from another database application so it can be used by Access and the other application simultaneously

❑ directing the output of a table, query, form, or report to a file type that can be used by word processing, spreadsheet, and other applications.

❑ working with both embedded and linked OLE objects in Access tables and queries

❑ working with bound and unbound OLE objects in forms and reports

Utilities for Access Databases

Access has a number of utilities on the File menu that are displayed when no database is open. Most of these use two dialog boxes, the first to select the source file and the second to select the target file for the operation.

For example, when you compact a database, as described below, Access begins by displaying the Database to Compact From dialog box, shown in Figure 12.1. Once you have selected a file and selected **OK**, Access displays the Database to Compact Into dialog box, shown in Figure 12.2.

FIGURE 12.1   DATABASE TO COMPACT FROM DIALOG BOX.

As you can see, you use both of these dialog boxes to select or name a file in the same way you use the Open Database dialog box. Use the Drives drop-down list and Directories list to select the drive and directory where the file is located. Select the name of the file from the File Name list or type it in the File Name box.

FIGURE 12.2 **DATABASE TO COMPACT INTO DIALOG BOX.**

When you are creating a new file, you must enter a name that follows the usual DOS naming conventions. File names may be up to eight characters long and may not contain spaces. Database files may not use any extension except the default MDB.

As you will see, you use a From and Into dialog box in many of the following utilities. In some cases, you can use the same name in both to perform the operation on the file without changing its name. In others, you must use different file names or locations in the two dialog boxes, so that the result of the operation is kept in a different file from the original. Of course, you can use the Windows File Manager or the DOS prompt later to delete the original.

Compacting a Database

When you delete records from a table or delete queries, forms, reports, or other objects from a database, Access generally does not reduce the size of the MDB file that they are in.

Reducing the size of the MDB file generally requires recopying all the objects in the file. If the file is large, this can take a considerable amount of time, and it would slow performance if Access did it every time you deleted an object. Instead, you must explicitly compact the database to eliminate this wasted space.

Before you can compact a database, you (and any other users on a network) must close it. Then choose **Compact Database** from the File menu to display the Database to Compact From dialog box. Once you have selected a file and selected **OK**, Access displays the Database to Compact Into dialog box, which you use to enter the name and path of the file that will hold the database in compacted form. You can type in the original name of the database to compact it without changing its name.

Converting a Database

Access version 2.0 databases use a different file format from versions 1.0 and 1.1. You can use version 2.0 to open and work with data in databases that were created with earlier versions, but you will not be able to save changes that you make to the definitions of objects unless you convert their format.

To convert earlier versions of Access databases to Access 2.0 format, all users must close the database file. Choose **Convert Database** from the File menu. Select the version 1.0 or 1.1 database in the Database to Convert From dialog box, and specify the name and location of the new version 2.0 database in the Database to Convert Into dialog box.

You must use a new file name or location for the new database in the Into dialog box so that you have two databases after you finish this operation. After you are sure that the operation is successful, you should delete the earlier version of the database. If you retain two versions of the same database, you are likely to enter new data or create new objects in the wrong one occasionally.

After you have converted a database to version 2.0 format, it cannot be used by older versions of Access and cannot be converted back to version 1.0 or 1.1 format. If you are working on a network, all users should update to version 2.0 before you convert databases.

Encrypting and Decrypting a Database

Ordinarily, it is possible to open Access files using any text editor. Much of the file will be codes that only Access can read, but the actual data entered in the table will also be available in text form. Figure 12.3 shows your sample Access database opened as a text file in Microsoft Word, and you can see some of the names and addresses you entered in the table.

FIGURE 12.3   AN ACCESS FILE THAT HAS NOT BEEN ENCRYPTED.

If you encrypt a database, it can only be viewed using Access. People cannot view the text in it by using other applications. If you decrypt a database that had been encrypted earlier, it is returned to its ordinary form.

To use this utility, choose **Encrypt/Decrypt Database** from the File menu. Access displays the Encrypt/Decrypt Database dialog box, which you use to select the source file. Then, if the source file is an ordinary file, Access displays the Encrypt Database As dialog box, or if the source file is already encrypted, Access displays the Decrypt Database As dialog box. Use these dialog boxes to specify the name and location of the new file.

You can use the same name as the original file. Access warns you before overwriting it with a new file that the file has its data in encrypted or decrypted form.

WARNING

Remember that encryption only protects data from being viewed by other applications, and does not protect it from anyone who has a copy of Access. If you want more security than this, you should use a different encryption utility, rather than the one that comes with Access.

Repairing a Corrupted Database

A database may be corrupted if a user turns off the computer without exiting from Access, or if there is a power shortage or other system failure that prevents you from exiting normally from Access.

To repair a corrupted database, choose **Repair Database** from the File menu, and select the name of the database in the Repair Database dialog box. Access repairs the database and keeps the same file name.

Access can usually detect a corrupted database and will automatically ask you if you want to repair it when you open it. The Repair Database command is useful if Access does not detect that a database is corrupted. Use this command if the database behaves erratically.

Utilities for Managing Access Objects

In addition to the database utilities described earlier, which are displayed on the File menu when no database is open, Access includes a number of utilities for working with the objects within a database—tables, queries, forms, reports, macros, and code modules—which are displayed only when a database is open. The utilities for sharing data with other applications are covered in the next section. This section covers utilities for managing objects.

Renaming an Object

To rename an object in an Access database, first select it in the Database window, and choose **Rename** from the File menu. Access displays the Rename dialog box, as shown in Figure 12.4, where you enter the new name for the object using the standard Access naming conventions, described in Chapter 2.

You can choose **Undo Rename** from the Edit menu immediately after renaming an object to restore its original name.

Deleting an Object

To delete an object in an Access database, first select it in the Database window, and choose **Delete** from the File menu or press the **Del** key. You can select **Undo Delete** from the Edit menu immediately after deleting an object to restore it to the database.

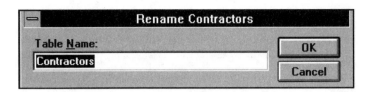

FIGURE 12.4   THE RENAME DIALOG BOX.

Cutting, Copying, and Pasting Objects

You can use the Edit menu to cut, copy, and paste objects in Access databases. Simply select an object and choose **Cut** from the Edit menu to remove the object from the database and place it in the clipboard, or choose **Copy** to leave the object in the database and place a copy in the clipboard.

Select **Paste** to paste the object in a new location. Access displays a dialog box that lets you rename the object. If you are pasting an object, you must enter a name for it using the usual Access naming conventions covered in Chapter 2.

As always, you can use the key combinations **Ctrl-X** (cut), **Ctrl-C** (copy), and **Ctrl-V** (paste) rather than using the Edit menu.

SHORTCUT

If you are pasting a table, the Paste Table dialog box, shown in Figure 12.5, also lets you choose these options:

❏ *Structure Only:* The table you specify will have only the structure of the table you are pasting, and no data

❏ *Structure and Data:* The table you specify will have both the structure and the data of the table you are pasting

❏ *Append Data to Existing Table:* You must specify the name of an existing table, and the data in the table you are pasting will be added to it.

You can cut or copy and paste either within a database or between databases.

Within a database, copy and paste is an easy way of making a backup copy of an object that has a different name before you make changes in the design of the object.

SHORTCUT

FIGURE 12.5   THE PASTE TABLE DIALOG BOX.

You can cut or copy and paste between databases to save time creating new objects that are similar to objects in an existing database. Sometimes the easiest way to create a new table, for example, is to copy and paste a table with a similar structure from another database.

Sharing Data with Other Applications

This book has taught you how to create and work with tables in Access, but there may also be times when you want to use data in other Access database applications or when you want to let people who work with other applications use data from Access. This may be either because you want to exchange data with someone or because you are working on a network where people use a number of database applications.

Access gives you two different ways of sharing data with other applications:

❑ *Importing and Exporting Data*: Importing converts a table from another application into an Access table, and exporting converts an Access table into a type of table used by other applications.

❑ *Attaching a Table*: Attaching a table from another application lets you use its data in Access without changing the original table, so it can still be used in the application where it was created. You can edit the data in the table, create queries, reports, forms, and the like. However, you cannot modify the structure of an attached table.

To show that a table is attached, Access uses a special icon for it. The arrow indicates that the database is linked to an external table, and the rest of the icon indicates the table type. Figure 12.6 shows a database with attached Paradox, dBASE, and FoxPro tables. Access uses the usual icon for imported tables since they are converted to ordinary Access tables.

FIGURE 12.6   ICONS FOR ATTACHED TABLES.

Importing and Exporting versus Attaching

When you import a table, Access leaves the original table as is and makes a copy of it, which it converts to Access format. Likewise, when you export a table, you create a copy of it in another format. In either case, you end up with two copies of the table, and changes you make in one do not affect the original table.

When you attach a table, Access does not make a copy of it. It links the currently open Access database with the table, without changing its format or location, making it easy to share the data with other applications.

The ability to attach a table is one of the features that gave Access its name, since it gives you seamless access to data from other applications. You can use the data just as if it were in an Access table. Although you can change the data in the table, you do not have to change its file format. Other people on a network who use different database management programs can use the same tables simultaneously without even knowing that they are also being used by Access.

However, Access can generally work more quickly with its own tables than with attached tables. For this reason, it is best to import a table if it no longer has to be shared with other applications. Attach tables only if they will continue to be used by the other application in the future.

When you import or export a table, in order to use it in another format on your own system, you should archive the original table and delete it from your hard disk. When there are two copies of the same data available, someone is likely update the wrong one by mistake, so that neither table is current.

NOTE

Importing, Exporting, and Attaching Different File Types

Access can attach tables from a wide variety of database applications. It also can import data from and export data to spreadsheet and text files as well as from these database applications. First, you should look at the general process of attaching tables and of importing or exporting data, and then you can look at some special details for individual applications.

ATTACHING A TABLE

To attach a table, first open a database, and choose **Attach Table** from the File menu to display the Attach Table dialog box, shown in Figure 12.7.

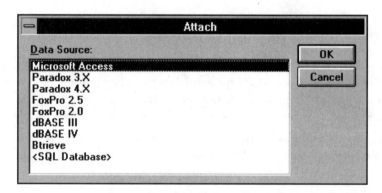

FIGURE 12.7 THE ATTACH TABLE DIALOG BOX.

After specifying the type of table that you are attaching, select **OK**. Access displays the Select File dialog box, shown in Figure 12.8, which you use to select the file to attach.

FIGURE 12.8   THE SELECT FILE DIALOG BOX.

Access adds the file you selected to the Tables list of the database, with the appropriate icon to its left. That is usually all there is to attaching a table.

UNLINKING A TABLE

After you attach a table, you can remove it from an Access database in the same way you delete a table. First select it in the Database window, and choose the File menu then **Delete** or press the **Del** key. This removes the table from the database but does not delete it from the disk. You can choose **Undo Unlink** from the Edit menu immediately after deleting an object to restore it to the database.

IMPORTING AND EXPORTING DATA

To import data, open a database and choose **Import** from the File menu to display the Import dialog box shown in Figure 12.9.

After you use this dialog box to specify the application that you are importing data from, Access displays the Select File dialog box, shown in Figure 12.8, which you use to select the file whose data you want to import, and adds the file you select to the Tables list of the database.

Since files from other applications usually have names that use the DOS naming convention, the imported file will probably have an eight letter name, made up of all capital letters. You can choose **Rename** from the File menu to give it a name based on Access naming conventions.

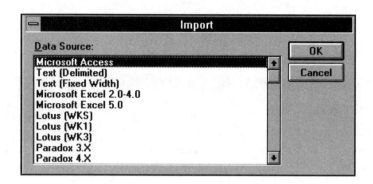

FIGURE 12.9 THE IMPORT DIALOG BOX.

Exporting data is similar to importing data or attaching a table, but with one additional step. First select the type of file to export to, as you do when you import data or attach a table. Access then displays the Select Object dialog box, which lets you select which of the tables or queries of the open database you want to export. Finally, it displays the Export to File dialog box, which lets you specify the name and location of the new file you are creating.

After you are done, use this file in the application that you exported it to.

PARADOX TABLES

Access can attach, import from, or export to Paradox 3.x and 4.x tables, all of which have the extension DB.

If the Paradox table that you are importing from or attaching to is encrypted, you must enter the correct password before Access can open it for the first time. If you attach the table, Access stores the password for future use. You can open the table in the future as you do any other table in your database, without having to reenter the password.

An attached Paradox table must have a primary key file (with a PX extension) for you to be able to update it in Access. If it does not, you will only be able to view it.

DBASE AND FOXPRO FILES

Access can attach, import from, or export to dBASE III, dBASE IV, FoxPro 2.0, or FoxPro 2.5 tables, all of which store their data in compatible files, with the extension DBF.

If you are attaching a dBASE or FoxPro file, after you select the file, Access displays a Select Index Files dialog box, which you can use to specify indexes created in the original application. Access uses the indexes you specify to improve performance.

Index files with the following extensions are used by dBASE and FoxPro:

- ❑ *NDX* is a dBASE file that holds a single index.
- ❑ *MDX* is a dBASE file that holds multiple indexes.
- ❑ *IDX* is a FoxPro file that holds a single index.
- ❑ *CDX* is a FoxPro file that holds multiple indexes.

WARNING

If you do specify indexes, Access cannot use the attached table unless the indexes are current. dBASE and FoxPro indexes are not necessarily updated automatically when data is entered, and you must be sure that indexes used by Access are opened and updated whenever the data in the table is modified in dBASE or FoxPro.

BTRIEVE TABLES

When you attach or import a Btrieve table, you must specify the location of the Xtrieve dictionary file (FILE.DDF). After you specify the file type, Access displays an extra dialog box where you must specify the location of the dictionary file before it lets you select a Btrieve table. Access cannot use a Btrieve table unless the dictionary file is available.

SQL TABLES

Access uses Open Database Connectivity (ODBC) drivers to open SQL tables. Before you can use an SQL table, you must use the ODBC disk included with Access to install the driver for your SQL database.

When you import or attach a file, after you specify SQL as the data source, Access displays a list of SQL sources on your network, and you must select one. Then Access displays the SQL Login dialog box, where you must enter your login ID, password, and other information. Finally, Access lets you select the table to import or attach.

ACCESS TABLES

Though it is not common, there may be times when you want the same Access table included in two databases simultaneously. You can attach a table from another Access database just as you attach tables from other applications. You can also import or export objects from or to other Access databases.

Attaching an Access Table

Unlike other database programs that you share data with, Access has multiple tables in a single MDB file. After you choose **Attach Table** from the File menu, you select a file as the data source, just as you do with other database programs, but then Access displays the Attach Tables dialog box, shown in Figure 12.10. Here you specify which table from the database you want to attach.

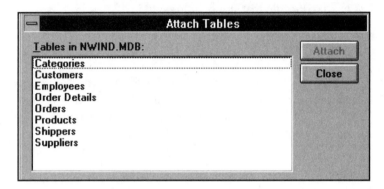

FIGURE 12.10   THE ATTACH TABLES DIALOG BOX.

Importing or Exporting Access Objects

If you import or export objects from an Access database, you select the MDB file as you do with other database applications. Access then displays the Import Objects dialog box, shown in Figure 12.11, or the Export Objects dialog box, which is similar.

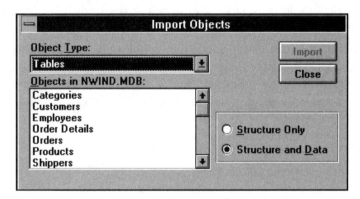

FIGURE 12.11   THE IMPORT OBJECTS DIALOG BOX.

Use the drop-down list to specify the type of object you want to import. Select objects from the list and click the **Import** button to import them into the current database. If the object is a table, you can use the radio buttons to import either its structure with no data or its structure with data. When you have imported all the objects you want, select **Close**.

SHORTCUT

If you want to import just one object, it is easier to copy and paste, as previously described. If you want to import a number of objects from another Access database, this method is faster.

If you are exporting objects, you must select only one object and click the **Export** button. Access then displays a dialog box that lets you choose the Access database it will be exported to.

Importing and Exporting Nondatabase Files

Access can also import data from and export data to Microsoft Excel and Lotus 1-2-3 spreadsheet files. Columns and rows in the spreadsheet are equivalent to columns and rows in an Access table.

Access can also exchange data with two different types of text files:

❑ **Delimited text files** have a carriage return after each record and a separator, such as a comma, between the fields of each record.

❑ **Fixed width text files** have the same size fields in every record. Extra blank spaces are used to pad fields that are shorter. Of course, with all fields fixed in size, each record must also be a fixed size.

One of these two formats must be used in order to make it clear where new records and new fields begin in the text file.

Figure 12.12 shows the data in the Contractors table exported to a comma-delimited text file.

In some cases, you must specify how data is translated between these types of files and Access database tables.

Importing from a Spreadsheet File

When you import from a spreadsheet file, Access automatically considers its rows to be records and its columns to be fields.

To let you specify other options, in addition to the dialog box that lets you select the file you are importing from, Access displays the Import Spreadsheet

Options dialog box, shown in Figure 12.13. You use this dialog box to specify the range of cells within the spreadsheet that the data should be imported from, whether the first row in this range contains field names, and whether to create a new table for the data or append it to an existing table.

FIGURE 12.12   ACCESS DATA EXPORTED TO A TEXT FILE.

FIGURE 12.13   THE IMPORT SPREADSHEET OPTIONS DIALOG BOX.

There is no equivalent dialog box displayed when you export to a spreadsheet. Access automatically creates a new file with the name you specify and includes field names in the first row.

Importing and Exporting a Delimited Text File

When you select **Text** (delimited) as the type to import from, Access displays the Import Text Options dialog box.

FIGURE 12.14   THE IMPORT TEXT OPTIONS DIALOG BOX.

As it is initially displayed, this dialog box lets you specify whether the first row contains field names and whether the data should be imported into a new table or appended to an existing table—features that you also specify when you import a spreadsheet. It is easy to use these features, and they are all you need to import most text files. However, if a text file has some features other than the defaults shown in Figure 12.14 and described below you must specify them so Access knows how to interpret the file it is importing.

To specify other features, select the **Options** button to display the dialog box in its expanded form, as shown in Figure 12.14, which also includes the following controls:

❏ *Specification Name* lets you use the Save As drop-down list that you used previously with the Save As button to name a specification. All the other controls are set accordingly.

❏ *Save As* displays the Save Specification As dialog box, which simply lets you enter a name for the current specification so that you can reuse all of its features.

❑ *File Type* lets you specify the type of text file to use. Windows interprets characters with codes higher than 128 differently from DOS and OS/2.

❑ *Text Delimiter* lets you specify the character to use around text fields. The default is a double quotation mark, but you may also choose a single quotation mark or {none} if there is no delimiter around text fields.

❑ *Field Separator* lets you specify which character to use between fields. The default is a comma, but you may also choose a tab or space.

❑ *Date, Time, and Numbers* lets you specify a different date order than the standard month, day, year; a different date delimiter than the standard / (slash), and whether there are leading zeros and four-digit years in dates; a different time delimiter than the standard : (colon); and a different decimal separator than the standard . (decimal point). All these are standard in the United States, and you generally will have to change them if you are importing a text file from another country.

When you export the contents of a table to a delimited text file, the Export Text Options dialog box gives you the same options as the Import Text Options dialog box, which you may use to specify features of the new text file you are creating. The only feature of the Export Text Options dialog box that it lacks is the choice of whether the data should be imported into a new table or appended to an existing table, since you automatically create a new text file when you export.

Importing or Exporting a Fixed Width Text File

If you import a fixed width text file, Access displays the Import Text Options dialog box shown in Figure 12.15, which is similar to the one used to import a delimited text file. It also lets you create a new table append the data to an existing table, and it lets you select the name of a specification.

FIGURE 12.15   IMPORT TEXT OPTIONS DIALOG BOX.

When you are importing a fixed width table, however, you must define the specification that tells Access how to translate the text file into fields. If you have created and named it previously, you can select it from the Specification Name drop-down list. If you have not, you must select the **Edit Specs** button to display the Import/Export Setup dialog box, shown in Figure 12.16, which you use to describe the specification.

FIGURE 12.16   THE IMPORT/EXPORT SETUP DIALOG BOX.

As you can see, this dialog box has all the features that you use to import or export a delimited text file, but it also has the Field Information grid which applies only to fixed width text files. You must use this table to specify the following:

❏ *Field Name*: the name of each field in the Access table.

❏ *Data Type*: the data type of each field in the Access table.

❏ *Start*: the field's starting position in the text file, which is equal to the widths of all the fields before it plus one.

❏ *Width*: the field's width in the text file, which is the maximum size needed to hold the data in the field in text form.

You can fill this in automatically with the specifications of an existing Access table by selecting the **Fill Specification Grid from Table** button. Access displays the Fill Specification Grid from Table dialog box, which simply contains a drop-down list that lets you select one of the tables in the current database.

If you export a table to a fixed width file, Access displays the Export Text Options dialog box shown in Figure 12.17. Use the drop-down list to select a specification that you named previously or select the **Edit Specs** button to display the Import/Export Setup dialog box and fill it in as described above.

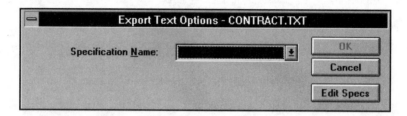

FIGURE 12.17   THE EXPORT TEXT OPTIONS DIALOG BOX.

SHORTCUT

When you are exporting a table, it is easy to fill in the Import/Export Setup dialog box to export a file. Simply select the **Fill Specification Grid from Table** button, and select the name of the table you are exporting from the Fill Specification Grid from Table dialog box. Figure 12.17 shows the grid filled in with the specifications of the Contractors table from your sample database.

Outputting to Another File Type

You can direct the output of an Access table, query, form, report, or programming module to a Rich Text Format (RTF), Microsoft Excel (XLS) or plain ASCII text (TXT) file. The RTF file can be used by Microsoft Word and by other word processing programs. The XLS file can be used by Excel or imported by most other spreadsheet applications. Virtually any spreadsheet, word processing, or database application can import TXT files.

Unlike exporting, which only shares data with other applications, redirecting output shares the entire stream of output from the object with other applications. For example you can share the entire contents of a report, including the header and any other text you added, with another application.

Then if you output a report to an RTF file, you can import the entire contents of the report, with its formatting preserved, into Microsoft Word or another word processor, and edit it there.

To direct the output of object data to one of these file types, select an object in the Database window and choose **Output To** from the File menu to display the Output To dialog box shown in Figure 12.18. Use the dialog box to select one of the file formats. If you selected some of the data in the object before choosing this option, the **Output** radio buttons are enabled, and you can use them to output all or the selected data to the application you select.

FIGURE 12.18 THE OUTPUT TO DIALOG BOX.

When you select **OK**, Access displays a dialog box that lets you specify the name and location of the file you want the output to be stored in. In addition to letting you name the file, this dialog box has an AutoStart checkbox, which you can select to start Excel (for an XLS file), Microsoft Word (for an RTF file), or Windows Notepad (for a TXT file) with this file open in it.

The Output to Excel tool on the toolbar bypasses these dialog boxes and immediately opens Excel with the selected file open in it.

If you use any of these options with a table, the data is output to a table with the records as its rows and the fields as its columns. For example, Figure 12.19 shows the Contractors table output to an RTF file which is opened in Word.

Using OLE Objects

Object Linking and Embedding (OLE) is a feature of many Windows applications which allows objects from one application to be used in another. For example, if you create a logo using a draw program that supports OLE, you can include it in Access forms as an OLE object.

FIGURE 12.19   THE CONTRACTORS TABLE OPENED IN WORD.

OLE objects have many uses in databases. The most common is to hold pictures. For example, you can scan photographs of all the contractors in your table (or of the people in any other list), include the picture in an OLE field in each record, and create a form that displays it when you display the person's name and address.

OLE objects can also be used to hold sounds. For example, a music store could have a computer with a table of all the recordings it has in stock. Along with the data on each, the table could have an OLE field which you could double-click to play a sample of music. A video store could have a database table with a field that you double-click to play a sample of each video in stock.

Working with more mundane applications, you could create a database to keep track of all the letters you write. Include a few fields with the description, addressee, and date of the letter, and store the letter itself in an OLE object field.

In another application, you could use a spreadsheet application to record the hours that each of your contractors worked, and you could include either an entire spreadsheet file or certain cells from the spreadsheet in each record as an OLE object. You could also use the spreadsheet application to graph the hours worked, and then you could create a form that displays the graph of the hours each contractor worked whenever it displays that contractor's name and address.

In any case, you must have another Windows application that supports OLE to create the picture, sound, graph, or other OLE object. Then you can use it in Access tables, forms, or reports.

Linking versus Embedding

As the name implies, OLE objects can be included in other applications in two ways:

❑ *Linking*: If the object is linked, it retains its connection with the application where it was created. Access displays the object, but it is still stored in its original file. Any changes that are made in it in the original application will also be incorporated in the application where it is included as a linked OLE object. You can also open the application from within Access and change the object.

❑ *Embedding*: If the object is embedded, a copy of the original object is made and is actually stored in your database. If you use the application where it was created and change the object, the changes are not reflected in the embedded OLE object. You must change the OLE object from within Access. You can double-click the embedded OLE object to invoke the original application to make changes in the OLE object.

Use linked objects if you want the object to change when the original changes. For example, if you have a file to keep track of letters that someone else might edit in Word for Windows, you must use them as linked objects so that changes made to them in Word are incorporated in the database.

Use embedded objects if you want to protect the object from changes or if you want the database to be portable. Because linked objects are stored in separate files, they will not be included if you copy a database to a floppy disk and give it to someone else. Embedded objects are included with the database. Of course, this also means that they require more disk space.

OLE Objects in Tables and Queries

After you have created a field of the OLE object type, you can add objects to it in the three ways described in the following sections.

CREATING AND EMBEDDING A NEW OBJECT

You can open another application from within an Access table or query and use it to create an embedded OLE Object.

Simply put the cursor in the OLE object field where you want the object to be embedded, and choose **Insert Object** from the Edit menu to display the Insert Object dialog box shown in Figure 12.20. The options in the Object Type list depend on the applications you have available that support OLE.

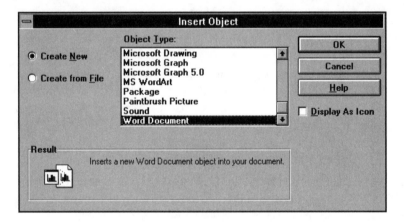

FIGURE 12.20   EMBEDDING A NEW OBJECT.

The **Create New** radio button is selected by default. Simply select the type of object you want to embed and select **OK** to open the source application, which you can use to create the object. When you are done, choose **Exit** from the File menu of the source application.

EMBEDDING EXISTING FILES

You can use **Insert Object** from the Edit menu if you have already created the files that you want to have embedded in a table or query—for example, if you have already scanned a number of photographs and have them stored in graphics files.

Put the cursor in the OLE object field where you want the object to be embedded, and choose **Insert Object** to display the Insert Object dialog box. Then select the **Create from File** radio button to change the dialog box to the form shown in Figure 12.21

FIGURE 12.21   EMBEDDING AN OBJECT FROM A FILE.

You can either enter the file's name in the File text box, or click the **Browse** button to display the Browse dialog box, which you use to select a file exactly like you do with the Open dialog box.

COPYING AND PASTING EMBEDDED OBJECTS

You can also use copy and paste commands from most source applications to embed an object in an OLE field.

Create the object in the source application, select it, and choose **Copy** or **Cut** from the Edit menu of the source application. Then select an OLE object field in an Access table or query and choose **Paste** from the Edit menu to embed the object in the field.

If the source application does not support copy and paste, the Paste option will not be enabled on the Edit menu when you return to Access.

N O T E

You can use Copy and Paste to add objects from Windows applications to Access databases, even if the application does not support OLE. However, you will not be able to open the source application from Access, and the object in Access will not reflect changes in the object made in the source application. The only way to change the object is to change it in the source application, and use Copy and Paste once again to add the new version of it to Access.

ADDING A LINKED OBJECT

To add a linked object to a table or query, create the object in the source application, select it, and choose **Copy** or **Cut** from the Edit menu of the source application.

Then select an OLE object field in an Access table or query and choose **Paste Special** from the Edit menu to display the Paste Special dialog box shown in Figure 12.22.

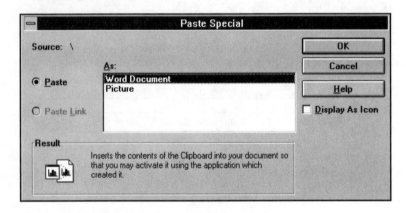

FIGURE 12.22   THE PASTE SPECIAL DIALOG BOX.

Select the **Paste Link** radio button and select **OK** to add a linked OLE object to the table or query. The name of the source file that it is linked to is displayed at the top of the dialog box, and any changes made in that file will also be made in the OLE object.

CHANGING AN OBJECT'S FORMAT

To embed an object in a different format, create it in another application, select it, and choose **Copy** from the Edit menu. In Access, select the OLE object field where you want it added and choose **Paste Special** from the Edit menu to display the Paste Special dialog box shown in Figure 12.22.

Select the **Paste** radio button and Access displays the formats that you can use for the object in the As list of this dialog box. In addition to the initial format, this list may include Picture or Bitmap formats. These formats may reduce the amount of space that the object occupies in the database, and they let you change its size in forms and reports. However, you can no longer use the original application to edit the object after converting it to Picture or Bitmap format.

EDITING AN OLE OBJECT

To edit an OLE object from within Access, double-click it or choose **...Object** and then **Edit** from the Edit menu. Access opens the application with the object displayed in it. The ellipsis is included before the word Object, because the name of this option changes depending on the type of source application and type of object that is selected.

As you know, you can also edit linked but not embedded OLE objects from the source application.

DELETING AN OLE OBJECT

To delete an OLE object from a table or query, simply select its field and choose **Delete** from the Edit menu or press the **Del** key. This does not affect the object in the source application.

OLE Objects in Forms and Reports

So far, you have looked at OLE objects in tables and queries, where they can be added only in fields. In forms and reports, there are two categories of OLE object controls, as there are of other controls:

❑ *Bound OLE object controls* display the OLE objects in a field. The content of the control changes when you change records. For example, you would use a bound OLE object control to display people's photographs that are stored in a table with their names and addresses.

❑ *Unbound OLE object controls* display OLE objects that are not stored in the table and that are used purely to enhance the design of the form or report. For example, you would use an unbound OLE object control to display a company logo in a form's header. The logo remains the same as the records change.

The toolbox contains a Bound Object Frame tool and an Object Frame tool, shown in Figure 12.23, which you can use to add these objects.

FIGURE 12.23 TOOLS FOR ADDING UNBOUND AND BOUND OLE OBJECTS TO FORMS AND REPORTS.

BOUND OLE OBJECTS

You can add a bound OLE object as you do other fields. The easiest way is to display the field list and click and drag the name of an OLE object field to the form or report design.

You can also use the Bound Object Frame tool of the toolbox and click and drag to the form or report design to display the frame. Then use its Control Source property to indicate the field it is bound to.

You work with bound OLE objects in forms and reports using all the methods previously described for working with OLE objects in tables and queries.

For example, to add an OLE object to a table, select the **Bound Object Frame** tool in a form, and use any of the methods for adding objects described above, just as you would after selecting the OLE object field it is bound to in the table or query.

UNBOUND OLE OBJECTS

To add an unbound OLE object to a form or report, click the **Object Frame** tool on the toolbox and click and drag to place the frame. When you release the mouse button, Access displays the Insert Object dialog box.

This dialog box was described earlier in the chapter in "Creating and Embedding a New Object" and "Embedding Existing Files." When you are adding an unbound object, you can use this dialog box in the same ways to open an application, create and embed an object, or to specify an existing file to hold the object.

To embed part of an existing object or to embed an object from an application that does not support OLE, use the Copy and Paste options, as described previously.

You can always run an unbound OLE object from Design View of a form or report, but you usually do not want people to run the object from Form View. For example, you do not want the people who are using a form to enter data to be able to redesign the logo that is displayed in an unbound object frame at the top of the form. For this reason, the Enabled property of an unbound OLE object is set at **No** by default. To run the object from Form view, set this property to **Yes**.

MOVING AND RESIZING OLE OBJECTS

You can select, move, and resize bound or unbound OLE objects as you do other objects in Form and Report designs.

Click the object frame to select it. Then click and drag the object frame or its Move handle to move it, or click and drag its Resize handles to resize it.

Scaling an OLE Object

A bound or unbound OLE object may not be the same shape or size as the frame you create for it. Of course, the way the object fits into the frame changes when you resize it.

You can use the object frame's Size Mode property to specify how Access deals with objects that do not fit in their frames properly. This property has these settings to choose from:

❑ *Clip* displays only a part of the object that can fit into the frame without changing its size or shape if the object is too large. Clip is the default setting.

❑ *Scale* makes the object larger or smaller to fill the frame, even if this means distorting its shape. For example, if the frame is square and the object is taller than it is wide, this property compresses the height of the object more than it compresses its width, so that it fills the frame completely.

❏ *Zoom* makes the object larger or smaller to fill the frame without distorting its shape. For example, if the frame is square and the object is taller than it is wide, the zoom property compresses the height of the object to fit into the frame, and compresses the width of the object proportionately. The shape of the object is not distorted, but there is empty space beside it in the frame.

Rather than changing the size of the object to fit the frame, you can choose **Size to Fit** from the Layout menu to expand or shrink the frame to fit the object, as you can with other controls.

To Sum Up

This chapter covered utilities and special techniques that let you use Access more easily and more powerfully. It began with database utilities that let you compact, convert, encrypt, and repair databases, and object utilities that let you rename, delete, cut copy, and paste. Then it covered the different ways that Access shares data with other applications, importing and exporting data, attaching tables, and redirecting the output of a table, query, form or report. Finally, it covered embedding and linking OLE objects in tables, and using both bound and unbound OLE objects in forms and reports.

Installation

Installing Access is very easy. Once you get started, the Setup program tells you what to do, and you simply follow its instructions.

This appendix includes instructions for installing Access on a stand-alone personal computer. If you want to set up Access so it can be shared on a network, see Chapter 1 of the user's guide that came with Access.

System Requirements

To run Access, you must have a computer with:

❏ An 80386SX or higher processor. A 386/20 or higher is recommended for best performance..

❏ A hard disk with at least 19 megabytes of free space for standard installation or at least 5 megabytes of free space for minimum installation

❏ At least 4 megabytes of RAM. 6 megabytes or more is recommended for best performance.

❏ MS-DOS version 3.1 or later.

❏ Windows version 3.1 or later.

❏ A mouse.

❏ An EGA, VGA, or compatible display.

If your computer meets these requirements, follow the instructions in the next section to install Access.

Running the Setup Program

You install Access using the Setup Program on disk 1 of the Access distribution disks.

The following instructions assume that you are using disk drive **A:** for installation. If you are using a different drive, substitute its letter for **A** as you read the instructions.

1. Begin with Windows running on your computer, with the Program Manager open. It is best to close all other Windows applications except for the Program Manager before installing Access.

2. Insert distribution disk 1 in drive **A:**.

3. From the Windows Program Manager menu, choose **Run** from the File menu to display the Run dialog box.

4. In the Command Line text box, type **A:SETUP**. Then press **Enter** or select the **OK** button.

5. Follow the instructions on the screen to install Access. The Setup program will guide you through the installation procedure.

WARNING

If you already have Access installed on your computer, the Setup program will ask you if you want to keep it or replace it with the new version you are installing. You should be aware that you must convert databases created in Access 1.0 or 1.1 before you can use them with Access 2.0. Once they are converted, they can no longer be used by version 1.0 or 1.1.

You should not replace the earlier version of Access unless you are willing to convert any existing databases and use them only with Access 2.0 in the future. If you are familiar with an earlier version, the transition to Access 2.0 is not difficult, but some users prefer to continue using the earlier version to work with existing databases until they are comfortable with the new version.

For more details on converting files created in earlier versions of Access, see the section on "Converting a Database" in Chapter 12.

Windows Basics

The body of this book assumes that you understand the basic features of Windows that you would know if you have ever used other Windows application. This appendix goes over the basics for people who have little or no experience with other Windows applications. It covers:

- ❏ using the mouse
- ❏ making menu choices with the mouse or the keyboard
- ❏ the types of dialog box controls that are commonly used in window applications and how to use them
- ❏ resizing and moving windows
- ❏ using the application and document control menus

❑ using the scroll bars

❑ searching for a topic in the Windows Help system

❑ searching alphabetically in the Windows Help system

❑ using the menus of the Windows Help system

❑ using cue cards

Using the Mouse

Access requires a mouse, and you use it constantly when you are working with Access, as you do when you are using other Windows applications. There are four different actions you can perform with the mouse:

❑ *Click:* move the pointer to the right location, and then press and release the left mouse button quickly.

❑ *Double-click:* move the pointer to the right location, and then click twice in rapid succession.

❑ *Click and Drag:* move the pointer to the location where the action begins, and then press and hold down the left mouse button. Move the pointer to the location where the action ends. Then release the mouse button.

❑ *Right Click:* move the pointer to the right location and then click the right mouse button.

You use the left mouse button for most actions. The right button is used as a quick way of displaying shortcut menus.

Using Menus

Windows applications all have a menu bar with the main menu options displayed at the top of the application. When you select one of the items on the menu bar, a menu "drops down" and you can make selections from it.

Figure B.1 shows the initial Access screen after you have selected **File** from the menu bar to display the File menu.

Some items on the drop-down menus have an arrowhead to their right to indicate that, if you select them, an additional submenu will drop down up to present you with more options.

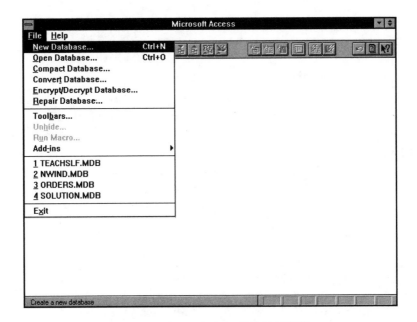

FIGURE B.1   **DISPLAYING THE FILE MENU.**

Making Menu Choices with the Mouse

To select an option from the menu using the mouse, simply click the item on the main menu bar to display the drop-down menu. Then click the option that you want to select on the drop-down menu.

You can also click the item on the main menu bar to display a drop-down menu. Hold down the mouse button white dragging downward or upward to highlight the menu option you want. Release the mouse button to select the highlighted option.

Making Selections Using the Keyboard

It is often easier to make menu selections using the keyboard than using the mouse.

Hold down the **Alt** key and press the underlined letter of a main menu option to display its drop-down menu. Then press the underlined letter of the menu option you want. For example:

1. Press **Alt-F** to display the File menu.
2. Then press **O** to choose Open Database.

Unless you are already using the mouse, this is the easiest way to use the menu.

After displaying a pop-up submenu, you can also use the Up and Down arrow keys to move among its options. As you move the highlight, a help line is displayed in the status bar describing what each option does. Press **Enter** to choose an option.

Press the **Esc** key to back out of the menu without selecting an option. If you press Esc once, the pop-up menu will disappear, but an option of the menu bar will still be highlighted. You must press **Esc** a second time to leave the menu system entirely.

SHORTCUT

Many menu options also have Control-key shortcuts, which are the quickest and easiest way of selecting them. The shortcut key is displayed to the right of the option on the pop-up menu. For example, pressing **Ctrl-O** is equivalent to selecting **Open Database** from the File menu. Look at the Control key shortcuts as you make menu selections. After a while, you will learn the key combinations for commands you use frequently.

Dialog Box Controls

Many menu options end with an ellipsis (...) to show that a dialog box with more choices is displayed after you select them. These dialog boxes and many Access Windows use the following controls, as shown in Figure B.2:

❏ *Text Box* lets you type text in a text box, after clicking it to move the insertion point to it. Many Access text boxes also let you enter data by making a selection from a list.

❏ *Lists* let you choose among a large number of options. If there are too many options to fit in the list box, the scroll bar to its right is activated. You can use this scroll bar or the PgUp and PgDn keys or the arrow keys to scroll through the list.

❏ *Drop-down Lists* save space by not displaying the full list. Instead, you must click the arrow at the right of a drop-down list to display all the options, and then select one as you would from a pop-up menu.

Instead of using the list in this way, you can simply type one of its options in the control box. In many Access dialog boxes, the arrow that lets you display the list appears only when you activate the control box. Before you click it or move the cursor to it, it looks like a text box.

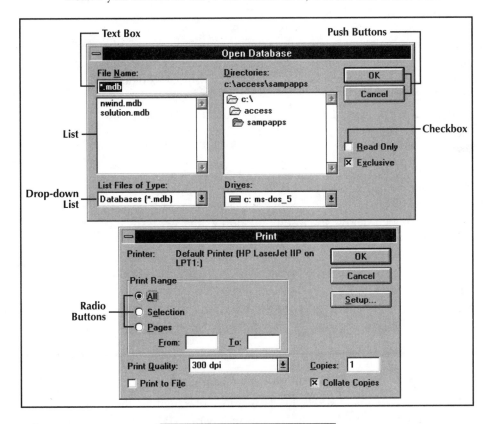

FIGURE B.2 **DIALOG BOX CONTROLS.**

❏ *Check Boxes* are used when only two choices exist. If the box has an X in it, the option is turned on; if it has no X, the option is turned off. Click the checkbox to add an X or to remove it if it is already there. Using the keyboard, tab to the check box and press the **space bar** to add or remove the X.

❏ *Radio Buttons* (also called Option Buttons) are used when only one of a number of choices can be selected. A set of radio buttons is a series of circles with a dot in the center of one. Click any one of them to move the dot to it and remove it from the one that was selected previously.

❏ *Buttons* (also called Push Buttons or Command Buttons) are used to take some action. For example, you use a push button to move an item from one list to another or to display another dialog box. To select a push button, simply click it. Using the keyboard, tab to it and press the **space bar**, or use its shortcut key.

In dialog boxes, after you have used these controls to specify the choices you want, select the **OK** button to close the dialog box and use these settings or select the **Cancel** button to close the dialog box without using these settings.

You can press **Enter** instead of selecting the **OK** button, or press Esc instead of selecting the **Cancel** push button of a dialog box.

If these controls are in a window rather than a dialog box, choose **Save** from the File menu to save the settings. You can also choose **Close** from the Control menu, as described below, to close the window, and Access will prompt you to save or discard the settings.

Working with Windows

There are two different types of windows that you work with when you are using Windows applications.

❏ the *application window* holds the program itself.
❏ the *document windows* holds features used within the program—for example, a letter you are typing in a word processing program, or a worksheet in a spreadsheet program.

These windows are illustrated in Figure B.3.

The application window holds Access itself. Document windows are used to work with Access databases, tables, forms, reports, and so on.

Resizing and Moving Windows

You can resize and rearrange windows to make them more convenient to work with.

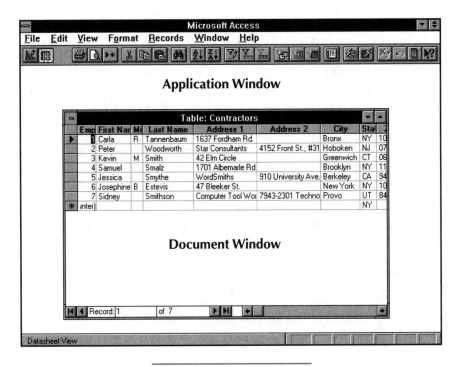

FIGURE B.3   TYPES OF WINDOWS.

To move a window, click and drag its title bar.

To resize a window, click and drag its bottom or right border, or click and drag the lower right corner to change both its height and width simultaneously. When you move the mouse pointer to one of these borders, it becomes a double-headed arrow at the time when you can click and drag the window border.

The Maximize, Minimize, and Restore buttons are arrows in the upper right corner of the window that let you change the size of the window instantly.

❑ Click the **Maximize** button to make the application window fill the entire screen or to make a document window fill its entire application window.

❑ Click the **Restore** button to return the window to the size it was before you maximized it.

❑ Click the **Minimize** button to reduce the window to an icon.

Control Menus

Both the application and document windows have control menus, which you display by clicking the box in the upper-left corner of the window. You can also display the control menu of the application window by pressing **Alt-space bar** and the Control menu of the current document window by pressing **Alt-hyphen**.

As you can see in Figures B.4 and B.5, both the Application and the document Control menus have options that are equivalent to the methods of resizing and moving windows that were described previously.

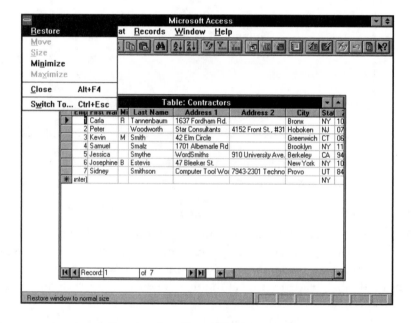

FIGURE B.4   THE APPLICATION CONTROL MENU.

The following options are on both types of control menu:

❏ After choosing **Size**, you can use the arrow keys to move the lower and right borders of the window to resize it. Use the Left or Right arrow key to move the right edge of the window and make it smaller or larger, and use the Up and Down arrow keys to move the bottom edge of the window and make it smaller or larger.

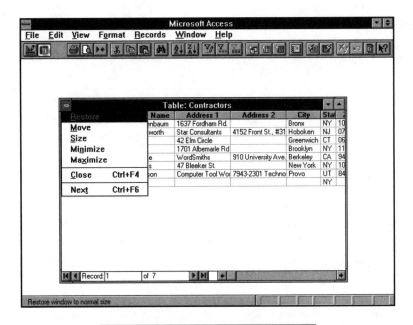

FIGURE B.5 **THE DOCUMENT CONTROL MENU.**

❑ After choosing **Move**, you can use the arrow keys to move the window. Use the four arrow keys to move the entire window up, down, left, and right.

❑ Choose **Restore**, **Minimize**, and **Maximize** instead of using the equivalent buttons.

❑ Choose **Close** to close a window. If you select this from the application Control menu, it is the same as exiting from the application. As a shortcut, you can double-click the Control menu box to close the window.

The document Control menu also has a Next option that lets you cycle among all the document windows that are open within the application. Keep selecting **Next** from the Control menu until the window you want is displayed.

The application Control menu also has a Switch To option that lets you cycle among all the Windows applications you are using. Choose **Switch To** from the Control menu to display the Task List, a list of all applications that are currently open. Select one and then select the **Switch** button to switch to it. The current application also remains open and you can switch back to it in the same way. (You can also display the Task List by pressing **Ctrl-Esc**).

You can also switch among Windows applications quickly by pressing **Alt-Tab**. Windows displays the names of all open applications in sequence, and you can switch to any one by releasing the **Alt** key.

After you have minimized a window, you can use it again by clicking the icon that represents it to display its Control menu and then choosing **Restore** or **Maximize**. You can also restore the window by double-clicking the icon.

The Scroll Bars

If a document in a window is too large to be displayed fully, you can use the scroll bars at the right and bottom of the window to see it all. (These scroll bars are displayed only when a document is too large for the window to hold.)

To use the right scroll bar to scroll up and down through the application, do one of the following:

❑ Click the arrow at the top or bottom of the scroll bar at the right of the window to scroll one line up or down in the document.

❑ Click anywhere between the scroll box and the up or down arrow to scroll one window up or down in the document.

❑ Click and drag the scroll box to scroll quickly through the window. The location of the scroll box in the bar indicates which part of the document is currently displayed. For example, it is at the top of the bar when the beginning of the document is being displayed. Simply click and drag it to a different location in the scroll bar to move to the equivalent location in the document.

The Help System

Access's Help system, shown in Figure B.6 is generally similar to the help systems of other Windows applications.

The Help system is a separate application, not a document window within Access. You can close it by choosing **Exit** from its File menu or by choosing **Close** from its Control menu, or you can switch between it and Access just as you switch between other Windows applications.

You can use the Access Help system in several ways:

FIGURE B.6   **THE HELP WINDOW.**

❏ Choose **Contents** from the Help menu to display the Help system and search through it by topic.

❏ Choose **Search** from the Help menu to display the help system and search alphabetically for keywords.

❏ Choose **Cue Cards** from the Help menu to use the Help system's cue cards to teach you about Access.

❏ Press **F1** to display the Help system with context-sensitive help on the feature of Access that you are currently using.

❏ Click the **Interface Help** tool or press **Shift-F1** to display the mouse pointer with a question mark next to it. Then click any feature of the Access interface to display the context-sensitive help on it. Press **Shift-F1** or click the **Interface Help** tool again—or simply press **Esc**—to return the pointer to its usual form without using the Help system.

Once you have displayed the Help system in any of these ways, you may search it by topic or alphabetically, using the methods described next.

Searching by Topic

The Table of Contents that is displayed when you select **Contents** from the Help menu, shown in Figure B-6, includes a list of topics, each underlined and, if you have a color monitor, displayed in green. When you move the pointer to any of these, it is displayed as a hand with the index finger extended. Simply click to jump to a window of text on the topic.

This help window itself will have words underlined in the same way to show that there are cross-references on them. You can click any underlined word to jump to the help window describing it.

Using the keyboard, you can press **Tab** to move from topic to topic, and press **Enter** to jump to the highlighted topic.

Other topics are underlined with dotted lines. You can click these to display temporary help in a small box. Click again or press any key to remove this box. These are often used for *glossary* entries—definitions that you just want to display temporarily as you read through help screens. In Access, they are also used for cross-references.

It can become confusing to navigate through the Help system after you have jumped from one topic to another in this way, so the push buttons at the top of the help window let you move among screens that you have seen previously. Use them as follows:

❑ *Contents* displays the initial table of contents of Help Topics.

❑ *Back* displays the last topic viewed.

❑ *History* displays a window with a list of the last forty help topics viewed. Select any topic from this list to view it again.

❑ << and >> move to the previous or the next topic in a series of related topics that you are viewing.

❑ *Glossary* displays an alphabetical listing of glossary entries.

You can select any of these either by clicking it or by pressing its underlined shortcut key.

Alphabetical Searches

Choose **Search** from the Help menu of the Access menu system or use the **Search** button of the Help window to search for help alphabetically by keyword.

Access displays the Search dialog box shown in Figure B.7.

FIGURE B.7 **THE SEARCH DIALOG BOX.**

You can scroll through the list of key words in the top half of this dialog box and select a word from it, or you can type a word in the text box above this list. The list automatically scrolls to the nearest word as you type.

When you have found the keyword you want in the list, select the **Show Topics** button. In the bottom half of the dialog box, the Help System displays all the topics that include help on that key word. Select a topic from this list and select the **GoTo** push button to display help on that topic.

The Help System Menus

The Help system's menus are not necessary to search for help, but they do give you extra power or convenience in using the Help system.

THE FILE MENU

The Help system's File menu has features that are similar to the File menu of many Windows applications. It lets you open another Help file, print the topic that is currently displayed, display the Print Setup dialog box that lets you control your printer, or choose **Exit** to close the Help window.

THE EDIT MENU

The Help system's Edit menu has only two options:

❑   *Copy* displays the Copy dialog box, which includes all the text in the current topic. You can select text in this dialog box and then select the **Copy** button to copy it to the clipboard.

❑   *Annotate* displays a dialog box where you can you add your own notes (also called annotations) to the current help topic. When you add a note, a paper-clip icon is displayed to the left of the topic's title. You can view the annotation at any time by clicking this icon or by tabbing to it and pressing **Enter**.

THE BOOKMARK MENU

The Bookmark menu let you add bookmarks to save your place in the Help system:

❑   *Define* displays a dialog box that lets you add a bookmark. It suggests a name for the bookmark based on the name of the current topic, but you can edit it and give it any name you want.

❑   *Bookmark names* are added to the Bookmark menu after you have defined bookmarks. You can go to any one immediately by selecting it from this menu. If more than nine bookmarks have been defined, a **More** option is added, which you can select to display all the bookmark names.

THE HELP MENU

Finally, the Help system itself includes a Help menu. Use the Help menu to display the "How to Use Help" Help system, which works like the Access Help system.

Cue Cards

Choose **Cue Cards** from the Access Help menu or click Access' **Cue Cards** tool to display cue cards that give you step-by-step help on specific tasks. Their main menu is shown in Figure B.8.

Simply click a > button or a **Next** button on a cue card to go to an option that is available as a next step in the task. Click the **Back** button at the top of the Cue Cards window to back through steps you already have looked at, or press the **Menu** button to return to the main menu.

Because it is meant to be looked at while you are working the task it is describing, the Cue Cards window always remains on top of all other windows, even when it is not active. If you select its **Minimize** button, its icon also remains on top. To close the Cue Card window, choose **Close** from its Control menu.

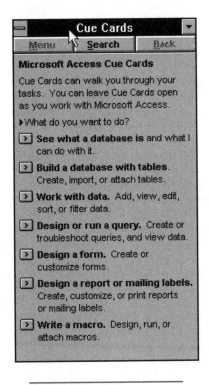

FIGURE B.8   USING CUE CARDS.

specifying automatic display
for forms, 139
Cue Cards tool, 25, 26
currency data type, 34
currency fields, 103
currency properties, 37, 38-39
current record, 57
CurrentUser() function, 275, 280
cursor
changing tab (accessibility)
order for controls, 222-223
moving, 57, 60
customizing keyboard behavior,
61-62
Cut/Copy/Paste commands (Edit
menu), 66, 409, 427-428
cutting, copying and pasting
objects, 409

D

Database Container command
(Window menu), 145
database containers, 5, 145
databases
advantages of multiple tables,
16-18
compacting, 404, 405-406
converting from version 1,
406, 435
creating, 22-26
described, 2
encrypting/decrypting, 406-
407
opening, 4-5
opening automatically with
macro, 396, 397-399
relational, 17
repairing corrupted, 408
sample, 24
single-table, 164-165
structure of, 164-174
See also datasheets; relational
databases; tables
database window, 5-6
data entry
adding and modifying records,
62-67
adding sample data, 69-74
deleting records, 64
selecting records to add to or
modify, 56-58
undoing or canceling changes,
63, 67
See also navigating
Data Entry command (Records
menu), 62
data normalization, 164, 174-175
data sharing. *See* attaching
tables; importing and exporting files
Datasheet command (View

menu), 209-210
datasheets
as Datasheet Views of tables,
8
printing, 86-90
saving settings, 85
See also databases; tables
Datasheet View
advantages, 55
for forms, 11, 143
for tables, 8
Datasheet View tool, 11, 30, 51
data types
caution on possible data loss
when changing, 53
of foreign keys, 184-184
selecting for table fields, 29,
30
for table field definitions, 33-
34
data validation with expressions,
281-283
DateDiff() function, 278
date field queries, 104
Date() function, 115-116, 275,
280
date literals, 109
date/time
calculations, 271
data type, 33
functions, 115-116, 278
grouping by range on reports,
313
inserting, 65
properties, 38
DAvg() function, 279
dBASE file imports, 414-415
DCount() function, 279
DDB() function, 277
debugging macros, 394-396
Decimal Places property, 34, 38,
39
default properties, 246-247
defaults
expressions for entering, 283-
285
inserting as values, 66
for printer, 323
default value property, 41-42
Delete Column command (Edit
menu), 102
Delete command (Edit menu),
64
Delete command (File menu),
408
Delete command (Query menu),
349-350
Delete key, 59, 64
Delete Query tool, 334, 335,
349-350
Delete Row command (Edit

menu), 30
Delete Row tool, 31
deleting
bands (sections) of forms or
reports, 214-215
controls, 217, 296
fields (rows) from tables, 30
objects, 408
OLE objects, 429
records in tables, 64
tables or fields from queries,
98-99, 101-102
delimited text files, 417, 419-420
depreciation functions, 277
descending indexes, 129
descending sorts, 102-103, 126
descriptions for table fields, 29
design considerations for tables,
18, 21
Design tool, 6
Design View
for forms, 11, 143
for tables, 8
Design View tool, 8, 11, 30, 51
detail bands on forms, 213
dialog box use in Microsoft
Windows, 440-442
directories for new files, 23-24
displaying
blank spaces in input masks,
41
columns in tables, 82-83
data types available, 30
Expression Builder, 264
functions, 276
gridlines in datasheets, 85
grids in Design windows, 210
headers and footers, 295, 312
lists of fields, 210
lists of objects, 6
lists of reports, 15
lists of tables, 6, 27-28
properties, 210
queries, 9-10
query results in dynasets, 92
records with macros, 381
reports, 14
rulers, 210
table names in QBE grid, 339
toolboxes, 210
wizard dialog boxes, 136
See also datasheets; forms;
reports
display (monitor) requirements
for Access, 434
division operator, 115, 270
domain aggregate functions, 279
DoMenuItem (macro action),
380
DOS version requirements for
Access, 434

459